A FORTUNE
in your ATTIC

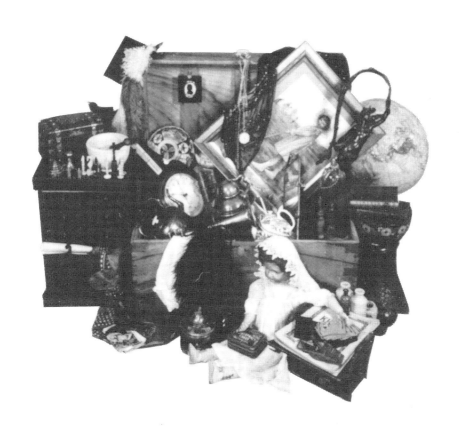

The publishers wish to express their sincere thanks to the following for their kind help and assistance in the production of this volume:

ANNETTE CURTIS
DOREEN RILEY
TANYA FAIRBAIRN
EELIN McIVOR
TRACEY BLACK
LESLEY MARTIN
FRANK BURRELL
JONN DUNLOP
LOUISE SIMPSON
KERRY McCONNELL
ROBERT NISBET
EILEEN BURRELL

Text by Liz Taylor, Eelin McIvor, Annette Curtis, Tony Curtis, Paul Shepherd

ISBN 0-86248-115-5

Printed and bound by
Butler & Tanner Ltd., Frome, Somerset.

Introduction

Hold on! Don't throw that away! So maybe it's just an old jug, an oil can, or an elderly pair of spectacles that you are about to 'bin', but, unlikely as it sounds, that seemingly insignificant piece of 'rubbish' could be the source of a useful sum of money or the beginning of a lifelong passion for you.

Nowadays, with antiques in general and the new collectables in particular rising in value, there can be no doubt that one man's rubbish is certainly another man's treasure and, strangely enough, once something starts to be collected, it acquires a new value.

There is no limit to the sort of things that hold some special fascination or unexpected value for someone. Enthusiasts do not only seek out bisque headed dolls, vintage cars, Old Master prints or Chelsea china. Not all of them go to the big London sale rooms and bid in telephone number sums; they also dig in rubbish tips, haunt jumble sales and street markets, turn out their attics and use their eyes to appreciate the attractive quality of hitherto little regarded everyday items.

Anyone who wants to make a profit out of buying and selling unusual items should cast aside prejudices against 'junk' and develop an eye for the potential value of what can seem to be the most improbable pieces. They should be prepared to search out their quarry wherever they go, and they should, above all else, take the trouble to find out as much about their subject as possible.

The really nice thing is that, in most cases, the actual objects are only part of the story. As interest grows, so does knowledge, greater discrimination and the ability to spot a true rarity. There is a profit to be made in such assorted things as railway porters' badges, soup can labels, light bulbs, beer mats, bicycles or pictures of film stars, just as much as in Chinese porcelain or fine French furniture — *but, you must be able to recognise it when you see it.* Every day, hundreds and thousands of pounds worth of saleable items are unwittingly thrown away for lack of basic information on the myriad of common or garden objects that have only in recent years become sought after, marketable goods.

The purpose of 'A Fortune in Your Attic' is to take a detailed look at just the type of article that has been pushed under the stairs, stuck in the garage, or stashed away in the loft, for, with a little research and a bit of good luck, you really could have *A FORTUNE IN YOUR ATTIC.*

TONY CURTIS

Acknowledgements

Abridge Auction Rooms, Market Place, Abridge, Essex RM4 1UA
Aviation Antiques, 369 Croyden Road, Caterham, Surrey
Ball & Percival, 132 Lord Street, Southport, Merseyside PR9 0AE
Bearnes, Rainbow, Avenue Road, Torquay, TQ2 5TG, Devon
Bermondsey Antique Market, Tower Bridge Road, London
Christopher Binns (Matchbox Toys)
J. J. Binns (Vanity Fair, Door Knockers)
Border Bygones, The Vallets, Forge Crossing, Lyonshall, Kington, HR5 3JQ
British Antique Exporters, 206 London Road, Burgess Hill, West Sussex RH15 9RX
R. Brocklesby, 8 Whites Road, Bitterne, Southampton SO2 7NQ (Cigarette Packets)
Bill Brooker, Record Printers (Printing Blocks)
Brown & Merry, 41 High Street, Tring, Herts HP23 5AB
Alan Cadwallender, 47 Athol Street, Gorton, Manchester M18 7JP (Bubble Gum Wrappers & Bubble Gum Cards)
Capes Dunn & Co., The Auction Galleries, 38 Charles Street, Manchester, Lancs M1 7DB
Chancellors Hollingsworth, 31 High Street, Ascot, Berkshire SL5 7HG
The Chicago Sound Company, Northmoor House, Colesbrook, Gillingham, Dorset (Jukeboxes)
Christie's, 8 King Street, St James, London SW1Y 6QT
Christie's South Kensington Ltd., 85 Old Brompton Road, London SW7 3LD
Robert C. Coley, Droitwich, Worcestershire (Fishing Tackle)
Nic Costa & Brian Bates, 10 Madeley Street, Tunstall, Stoke on Trent ST6 5AT (Amusement Machines)
Courts Miscellany, (George Court), 48 Bridge Street, Leominster
Alan Cunningham, 10 Forth Street, Edinburgh EH1 3LD (Football Programmes)
Dacre, Son & Hartley, 1-5 The Grove, Ilkley, West Yorkshire LS29 8HS
Sandra Dobbinson (Teapots)
Paul, Joyce & Ron Drew (Miscellaneous)
Dreweatt Neate, Donnington Priory, Donnington, Newbury, Berks RG13 2JE
Du Mouchelles Art Galleries Co., 409E Jefferson Avenue, Detroit, Michigan 48226
Gwen Edwards, Lyonshall, Herefordshire
Eddie Ganderson, 1 Stirrup Close, Ainsty Park, York YO2 3LU (Automobilia)
Mr & Mrs Gardner, The Children's Bookshop, Hay on Wye (Cuckoo Clocks)
Gorringes, Auction Galleries, 15 North Street, Lewes, East Sussex
Goss & Crested China Ltd, 62 Murray Road, Horndean, Hants PO8 9JL
W. R. J. Greenslade & Co., 13 Hammet Street, Taunton, Somerset TA1 1RN
Mark Harrison, Middlesex (Telephones)
Giles Haywood, The Auction House, St John's Road, Stourbridge DY8 1EW, West Midlands
Heathcote Ball & Co., 47 New Walk, Leicester
Hobbs & Chambers, 'At the Sign of the Bell', Market Place, Cirencester, Gloucestershire
Mark Hudson, 95 James Turner Street, Winson Green, Birmingham B18 4ND (Milk Bottles)
Edelweiss James, 5 Blunts Hall Drive, Witham, Essex CM8 1LZ (Nurses Badges)
Michael Jones, 5 Blunts Hall Drive, Witham, Essex CM8 1LZ (Beer Bottle Labels)
G. A. Key, Aylsham Salerooms, Palmers Lane, Aylsham, Norfolk NR11 6EH
Kingsland Auction Services, Kingsland, Leominster
Bob Krasey, 134 Lansdowne Avenue, Winnipeg, Canada R2W 0GY (Coca Cola)
Lalonde Fine Art, 71 Oakfield Road, Clifton, Bristol, Avon BS8 2BE
Lawrence Fine Art, South Street, Crewkerne TA18 8AB, Somerset
David Lay, The Penzance Auction House, Alverton, Penzance, Cornwall TR18 4RE
Tim Lewis, Woonton, Herefordshire
Locke & England, Walton House, 11 The Parade, Leamington Spa
Lots Road Chelsea Auction Galleries, 71 Lots Road, Chelsea, London SW10 0RN
R. K. Lucas & Son, 9 Victoria Place, Haverfordwest, SA61 2JX
Lynn Private Collection, Tyne & Wear (Children's Books)
Duncan McAlpine, Flat 4, 55 Lordship Road, Stoke Newington, London N16 0QJ (American Comics)
Miller & Co., Lemon Quay Auction Rooms, Truro, Cornwall TR1 2LW
Mortimers Cross Inn, Herefordshire
Onslow's Auctioneers, 14-16 Carroun Road, London SW8 1JT
Osmond Tricks, Regent Street, Auction Rooms, Clifton, Bristol, Avon BS8 4HG
Andree Oughton, Hill Top Farm, Deerfold, Shropshire (Horse Books)
Hobbs Parker, Romney House, Ashford Market, Ashford, Kent TN23 1PG
Phillips, Blenstock House, 7 Blenheim Street, New Bond Street, London W1Y0AS
Fred Price (Gnomes)
Geoff & Linda Price, 37 Camberford Drive, Tiffany Green, Wednesbury WS10 0UA (Model Buses)
Prudential Fine Art Auctioneers, 5 Woodcote Close, Kingston upon Thames, Surrey KT2 5LZ
Reeds Rains Prudential, Trinity House, 114 Northenden Road, Manchester M33 3HD
Alex Pryde, Rustics, Airnlie Cottage, Cannonbie (Farm Equipment)
Record Collector, 45 StMarys Road, Ealing, London W5 5RQ
Brenda W. Riley (Ladies Underwear)
Russell, Baldwin & Bright, The Fine Art Saleroom, Rylands Road, Leominster HR6 8JG
The Peter Savage Antique Bottle Museum, Cambrook House, Nr Warwick CV35 9HP
Lacy Scott (Fine Art Dept) 10 Risbygate Street, Bury St Edmunds, Suffolk IP33 3AA
Robt. W. Skinner Inc., Bolton Gallery, Route 117, Bolton, Massachusetts
Mike Smith's Motoring Past, Chiltern House, Ashendon, Aylesbury HP18 0HB (Oiliana)
Ricky Smith (Records)
David Stanley Auctions, Stordan Grange, Osgathorpe, Leicester LE12 9SR
Tim J. Stannard, Lombard House, 145 Great Charles Street, Birmingham B3 3LP (Beer Mats)
Vincent Stocks, Moston, Manchester
Street Jewellery Society, 16 Eastcliffe Avenue, Newcastle on Tyne NE3 4SN
Brian Swan, 19 Lavendar Avenue, Conndon, Coventry CV6 1DA (Car Club Badges)
Louis Taylor & Sons, Percy Street, Hanley, Stoke on Trent, Staffordshire ST1 1NF
Trench Enterprizes, Kevin Holmes, Three Cow Green, Bacton, Stowmarket, Suffolk (Jigsaw Puzzles)
M. Veissid & Co., Hobsley House, Trodesley, Shrewsbury SY5 7ND (Bonds, Share Certificates & Cheques)
Wallis & Wallis, West Street Auction Galleries, West Street, Lewes, East Sussex BN7 2NJ
Tim & Shirley Ward (Post Cards etc.)
Keith Wilkinson, 18 Hinton Street, Fairfield, Liverpool L6 3AR, Merseyside (Football Badges)
John Wilson, 50 Acre End Street, Eynsham, Oxford OX8 1PD (Autographed Letters)
Peter Wilson Fine Art Auctioneers, Victoria Gallery, Market Street, Nantwich, Cheshire
Woolley & Wallis, The Castle Auction Mart, Salisbury, Wiltshire SP1 3SU
Worsfolds Auction Galleries, 40 Station Road West, Canterbury, Kent
Yesterday's News, 43 Dundonald Road, Colwyn Bay, Clwyd LL29 7RD
Yesterday's Paper, 40 Southview, Holcombe Rogus, Wellington, Somerset TA21 0PP

Contents

CONTENTS

ADVERTISING POSTCARDS

The collecting of postcards — deltiology is the proper word for it, deriving from the Greek word 'deltion' for a small card — covers an immense spectrum because after 1902 when postal regulations were relaxed to allow the address side of the card to be divided in two to allow for a message, advertisers recognised the possibility of proclaiming their wares by postcard. At one stage before the First World War, so many cards were being produced that it was predicted Europe would be submerged in them within ten years. Everything from baby food to tonic wine was advertised on cards. One was even issued to mark the inauguration of a monument commemorating the foundation of the Universal Postal Union in 1909. Sometimes cards were miniature reproductions of posters, particularly those of Mucha or Elizabeth Sourel who worked in Mucha's style in the 1920's. Highest prices are paid for Art Deco and Art Nouveau cards.

'One of the sights of London (Fleet Street). For the People', Hudson's Soap. $45 £25

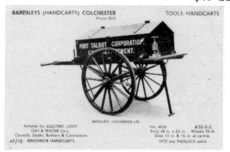

Milkmaid Brand Milk, 'The milk of 40,000 cows is condensed daily at our eleven factories'. $45 £25

Fry's Cocoa, the celebrated 'Famous Advertisement' Series. $25 £14

Bardsleys Handcarts, Colchester, 'suitable for Electric Light, Gas and Water Companies'. $9 £5

C.W.S. Pelaw Polish, 'The old lady who lived in a shoe'. $30 £16

'He shells the 'Shell' on the sea shore. Saved'. Shell Motor Spirit. $50 £30

(Border Bygones)

ADVERTISING POSTCARDS

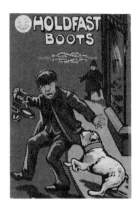

Nixey's Blue, 'The purest I have ever used'. $45 £25

Holdfast Boots, printed by James Walker, Dublin. $30 £18

The Foden Steam Wagon, 'Up-to-date road transport'. $38 £22

Bird's Custard, 'Delicious with Stewed Prunes'. $38 £22

Crawford's Ginger Nuts, 'The character and quality are outstanding. $30 £16

Oxo, 'And so to bed. It's Meat and Drink to you'. $45 £25

Silvox, 'Fluid Beef with Vegetable Extract', C.W.S. Ltd. $27 £15

Burrough's Beefeater, 'Purest and Best Gin', $27 £15

"Groaten, the 8 minute porridge", by Chamberlain, Pole and Co. Ltd. $27 £15

ADVERTISING SIGNS

From the Victorian age till the mid 20th century, mass market advertising had to catch the passing public's eye. Large metal or card signs in shop windows or stuck on walls were a favourite way. They were designed to make an immediate impact and so most were at least one metre square, brightly coloured and bearing a trade emblem or figure. The most valuable signs today are enamel on metal from the Art Nouveau or Art Deco periods though cardboard ones in good condition are also popular. Famous artists like McKnight Kauffer, Nerman and Harry Rountree designed signs for brand name firms like Oxo, Fry's, Nestle's, Rowntree's, petrol and oil companies. Car manufacturers' signs are very collectable — especially those for Lagonda, Bentley, Rolls Royce and Bugatti.

Fry's Pure Breakfast Cocoa. (Street Jewellery) $160 £85

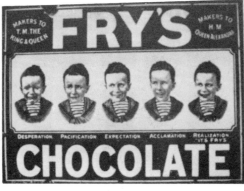

Fry's Chocolate. (Street Jewellery) $187 £150

Player's 'Drumhead' cigarettes. (Street Jewellery) $185 £100

Belga Vander Elst. (Street Jewellery) $120 £65

Sunlight 'Guarantee of Purity. (Street Jewellery) $700 £375

Singer Sewing Machines, 11 x 7½in. (Street Jewellery) $127 £85

Coleman's Mustard Cabinet, a printed tin facsimile packet, 46cm. high. (Onslow's)
$363   £210

Lazenby's Specialities, showcard, 74 x 92cm., in original frame. (Onslow's)
$830   £480

A jeweller's shop sign, America, late 19th century, wood and metal in the form of a pocket watch with a gilt painted frame, 20in. high. (Robt. W. Skinner Inc) $550   £312

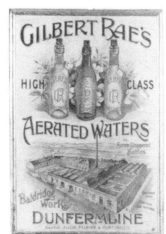

Gilbert Rae's High Class Aerated Waters Dunfermline, printed tin sign, embossed, 71 x 51cm. (Onslow's)
$743   £430

Brasso The New Metal Polish, enamel advertising sign, pictorial, 61 x 38cm. (Onslow's)
$190   £110

C.W.S. Crumpsall A Lucky Dip Crumpsall Cream Crackers, printed tin sign, 61 x 46cm. (Onslow's) $1,522   £880

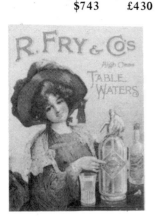

R. Fry & Co's High Class Table Waters, showcard, 51 x 38cm. (Onslow's) $709   £410

A polychrome zinc trade sign, America, early 20th century, in form of a hip-roofed house with projecting porch, 32in. high. (Robt. W. Skinner Inc.)
$800   £454

Olympic Ale, showcard, published Brussels 1937, 46 x 31cm. (Onslow's) $27   £16

This Is The Union Label of The Felt Hatters and Trimmers Unions of Gt. Britain, showcard, laminated, 23 x 31cm. (Onslow's) $34   £20

A polychromed cast zinc cigar store Indian Princess, attributed to W. Demuth & Co., New York, circa 1870, 54½in. high. (Robt. W. Skinner Inc.) $16,000   £9,090

Bluebell Metal Polish, showcard, 38 x 53cm. (Onslow's) $20   £12

Brasso Metal Polish, showcard, 51 x 33cm. (Onslow's) $311   £180

Jones Sewing Machines, enamel advertising sign, pictorial, 81 x 87cm. (Onslow's) $346   £200

Cherry Blossom Boot Polish Is The Best, enamel advertising sign, shaped pictorial, 175cm. high. (Onslow's) $4,152   £2,400

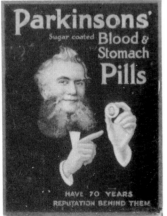

Parkinson's Sugar Coated Blood and Stomach Pills, showcard, 48 x 38cm. (Onslow's) $112   £65

Bassett's Liquorice Allsorts shop dispenser, tin. (Onslow's) $86   £50

Robin Starch, showcard, 38 x 26cm. (Onslow's) $553   £320

ADVERTISING TAPES

Advertising tapes seem poised to become one of the hottest of 20th century collectables of the future.

They are usually issued as part of a company's promotional campaign and are obtained by collecting and sending tokens or taking part in a competition. Their outer covers usually advertise the product in question, and the compilations of music they contain are mostly unique to that cassette.

Look out for early examples where popular artistes recorded music for early TV ads. How pictorial the advertising is, whether or not it is a limited edition, and the inclusion of early advertising theme music are all likely to be further criteria for establishing value. Start collecting now!

BP Lifestyle, Classic Love Songs, BP3. $2 £1

Martini, Motown Classics, SMMC174. $7 £4

Tango, Soul Sounds, Stiletto, 7M5012. $9 £5

Kellogg's Start Chart Collection, Volume 2, 'Club Classics', CSP980029. $5 £3

Pepsi, 'Feed the World' Band Aid Hits, PBC0079. $3.50 £2

Ski, 25 years of No. 1 Hits. $3.50 £2

(Border Bygones)

14

ADVERTISING WARES

Something for nothing has always been a favourite way for manufacturers to tempt customers. Advertising give-aways are sought after by collectors. It is possible to concentrate on gifts from a certain firm like Bovril or Globe Polish or seek out specific items — fans, needle cases, toy cars, bottle openers, ashtrays or needle threaders. Visitors to trade and industry exhibitions like the 1924-25 British Empire Exhibition at Wembley came home loaded with free gifts or miniature special offers like tiny tins of boot polish and these make good items for collecting. Plastic flowers were given away with soap powder in the 1960's and they would form the basis of a modern collection but the most desirable giveaways are Victorian and Edwardian children's books and card cut-outs which are not difficult to find and only cost a few pounds.

A replica decanter made for Fortnum & Mason, as held in their crypt dated 1700 A.D., 7in. high, c.m.l. & c. $50 £28

An earthenware presentation beaker, 'Victoria R.I. Diamond Jubilee', made for Lewis & Hyland, Ashford, circa 1897. $80 £45

Royal Doulton wireless loud-speaker made for Artandia Ltd. in the form of a feathered cockatoo perched on a rock, 15½in. high. $260 £150

Display sign of a Beefeater for Illustrated London News, 8in. high. $1,500 £850

A Royal Doulton advertising jug, William Grant, Specially Commissioned for Wm. Grant & Sons Ltd., limited edition of 500, 1986. $700 £400

Counter display sign for Grossmith's perfume, 'Tsang Ihang' the perfume of Tibet, circa 1923. $800 £450

A stoneware jug made for Style & Winch Ltd., 4¼in. high, circa 1910. $80 £45

Blondeay & Cie, Premier Vinolia Shaving Cream for Sensitive Skins, circa 1920. $45 £25

A small cream jug made for The Waldorf Hotel, 2½in. high, circa 1920. $18 £10

Display sign for 'Army Club Cigarettes' depicting the bust of a soldier. $140 £80

Set of four Robertson's Golly Musicians, 3in. high. $25 £15

'The McCallum' a large Kingsware character jug made for D. & J. McCallum Whisky Distillers, circa 1930. $2,500 £1,450

Carlton advertising piece for Pear's soap, 110mm. high. (Goss & Crested China Ltd.) $122 £80

Staffordshire Pottery teapot, inscribed 'Nectar Tea', complete with milk jug. (Border Bygones) $70 £40

A water jug made for William Younger & Co., circa 1920. $60 £35

AMUSEMENT MACHINES

The delights of Victorian seaside holidays always included a stroll along the pier and several attempts at the amusement machines lined up there. They ranged from the naughty "What the Butler Saw" — nothing very much it turned out — to fortune telling machines, weighing machines that announced your weight in a loud voice and Test-Your-Strength punch balls. Now that amusement machines have been herded together in arcades and powered by electronics, Victorian pieces look out of date and old fashioned — except to collectors of course. They seek out pin-ball machines like the Genco ones that were popular in the 1930's and grip-test machines that used to stand on railway platforms or seaside boulevards around the turn of the century. Some machines had miniature grabs inside and when pennies were put in the slot they would reach down for a packet of sweets. Others showed two football teams valiantly kicking balls at each other. Today the price for some of these machines can be in excess of £600.

The Clown by Jentsch & Meerz, Leipzig, circa 1915. (Brian Bates) $480 £275

The Misers Dream, working model by Bolland, circa 1950. (Brian Bates) $1,300 £750

Conveyor, manufactured by Stevenson & Lovett, 1947. (Nic Costa) $260 £150

Try Your Grip, by the Mechanical Trading Company, circa 1895. (Brian Bates) $1,750 £1,000

1930's Aeroplane Allwin. (Nic Costa) $300 £175

1930's Mills Century One Arm Bandit, U.S.A. origin. (Nic Costa) $480 £275

AMUSEMENT MACHINES

1950's All Sport two-player
game by Bryans. (Nic Costa)
$300 £175

Sapphire, Allwin type 'reserve'
machine of French manufacture, 1920's. (Brian Bates)
$300 £175

Gipsy Fortune by Bolland,
1950's. (Nic Costa) $260 £150

Personality 'Love Test Meter'
manufactured by Oliver Whales,
Redcar, circa 1950. (Brian
Bates) $245 £140

1930's, Allwin nine cup. (Nic
Costa) $300 £175

Mid 1930's, Mutoscope 'Adam
& Eve', manufactured in the
U.S.A. (Nic Costa) $875 £500

Fruit Bowl by Bryans, circa
1963. (Nic Costa) $200 £150

Reel 21 gaming machine by
Groetchen, U.S.A., 1930's.
(Brian Bates) $350 £200

Matrimonial Bureau, 'Correct
photo of your future husband,
wife or baby,' by Bolland,
1930's. (Brian Bates) $435 £250

ANIMAL FIGURES

Animals have figured in decorative arts from the earliest cave paintings, and man has always found their depiction irresistible. Even the Moorish sculptor of the Plaza de los Leones in the Alhambra defied the edicts of his religion to carve stone lions round the fountain. (By not giving them eyes he probably kept his!) This fascination has found a ready outlet in china and pottery — examples exist from every age and culture, from priceless Chinese tigers to the two-a-penny cats and dogs found in any seaside souvenir shop. The Victorians had a passion for introducing 'wild life' into their ordered homes, as the stuffed figures of their favourite pets or wild animals bear witness, and just about every pottery of the time had its range of animal figures.

Collectors can concentrate on one animal type, one pottery or even one designer. They form a superb range of collectables to suit all pockets.

A large Royal Doulton Flambe model of a fox, glazed in black and red, 23.6cm. high, c.m.l. & c., signed Noke. (Phillips)

$171 £120

A Ralph Wood figure of a recumbent ram, on an oval green rockwork base moulded with foliage, circa 1770, 18.5cm. wide. (Christie's)

$3,801 £2,640

A 19th century painted chalkware cat, America, 10¾in. high. (Robt. W. Skinner Inc.)

$850 £505

A Staffordshire saltglaze agateware cat, with irregular blue markings and brown striations, circa 1750, 13.5cm. high. (Christie's)

$2,692 £1,870

Pair of Kakiemon cockerels standing on rockwork bases, circa 1680, 28cm. high. (Christie's)

$35,200 £22,000

'Dog Begging with Lump of Sugar on nose', produced 1929, probably a prototype, 8in. high. (Louis Taylor)

$759 £460

An Art Deco Wedgwood animal figure, modelled as a fallow deer, designed by J. Skeaping, 21.5cm. high. (Phillips) $230 £160

A Portobello cow creamer, with milkmaid on a stool, 16cm. wide. (Phillips) $734 £440

A late Wemyss small model of a pig, 15.5cm. high, painted mark Wemyss, printed mark Made in England. (Phillips) $1,337 £700

Late 19th century German figure of a monkey, decorated in grey and yellow glazes, 46cm. high. (Christie's) $638 £440

A Doulton mouse group moulded with three minstrels on a green mound, by George Tinworth, circa 1885, 3¾in. high.(Abridge Auctions) $1,275 £850

An attractive small Derby model of a Pug, modelled and coloured with a gold studded collar around its neck, 6cm. high. (Phillips) $699 £380

A Staffordshire figure of an Alcibiades hound, on a black marbled base edged in green and turquoise, circa 1810, 42cm. high. (Christie's) $2,059 £1,430

Late 17th century model of a Kakiemon seated tiger, 18.5cm. high. (Christie's) $35,530 £20,900

Late 19th century painted chalkware horse, 10in. high. (Christie's) $286 £161

ANIMAL FIGURES

One of a pair of 17th century Arita standing puppies, 24cm. long. (Christie's) $37,400 £22,000

A Staffordshire seated dog, circa 1790, 3½in. high. (Christie's) $240 £143

A Zsolnay Pecs lustre group, modelled as two polar bears on a large rock in a green and blue golden lustre, 4½in. high. (Christie's) $400 £250

A Minton 'majolica' garden seat modelled as a crouching monkey, circa 1870, 47cm. high. (Christie's) $12,512 £7,150

Seated Bulldog with Union Jack, hat and cigar, 7.5in. high. (Louis Taylor) $858 £520

A 19th century Arita model of a tiger climbing on rocks among dwarf bamboo, 71cm. high. (Christie's) $5,610 £3,300

A 19th century Coalport porcelain peacock in gold and white on a rococo base, 6in. high. (G. A. Key) $222 £135

'The Bull', a Poole pottery stoneware figure, designed by Harold and Phoebe Stabler, 33.5cm. high. (Christie's) $252 £165

Royal Doulton china model of a Siamese cat, 5½in. high, HN1655. (Prudential Fine Art) $33 £20

ASHTRAYS

In the days when almost every adult smoked, ashtrays were found in every room of the home. They were a favourite present and were also used as an advertising medium by astute manufacturers. Ashtrays come in every possible shape, on stands, on legs, looking like aeroplanes or horses' hooves. They were made in a wide variety of materials ranging from bronze, china, horn, silver and pewter to bakelite. Collections can be built up of ashtrays bearing the names of clubs, hotels, ocean liners, railway companies, manufacturers, brewers and distillers. Some are very elegant, especially those from hotels and sea-going liners in the 1920's and 1930's. Souvenir ashtrays for holiday makers bearing names and pictures of seaside resorts are avidly collected. Among the most expensive are those produced by Goss which fetch around £20 each.

Empire Nut Brown Tobacco ashtray. $35 £20

Doulton Dick Turpin ashtray, issued 1936-70. $85 £50

Castrol Oil glass ashtray. $9 £5

1930's wooden barrel type ashtray. $9 £5

Doulton stoneware ashtray, circa 1900. $50 £30

Pip Squeak and Wilfred ashtray made for the Daily Mirror, circa 1930. $425 £250

Guinness is Good for You, by Ashstead Potteries. $45 £25

Burns ashtray by W. H. Goss. $45 £25

Doulton Lambeth stoneware ashtray and match holder. $50 £30

AUTOGRAPH LETTERS & DOCUMENTS

Libraries and museums all over the world avidly collect the letters and holograph writings of famous people which are prized not only because they are the raw material of history but for the insights they give into notable lives and events. There is a peculiar thrill at seeing at the signature of Queen Elizabeth the First written by her own hand or reading a note penned by Charles Dickens. The identity of the writer is of paramount importance when collecting autograph manuscripts and so is rarity because some people were more generous in signing their name than others. It is the rare ones that are most valuable.

Some artists like Edward Lear, Picasso and Chagall were often generous when signing their names or writing letters because they would frequently add a little drawing as well. These make the value soar.

The content of a note or letter is very significant. If something of interest is being recounted, the value of the manuscript is higher than if the writer was only refusing an invitation to dinner. Condition of autograph letters is also important and so is provenance because if authenticity can be proved that is a bonus. Some famous people did not sign their own letters but had a secretary copy their signatures and there is a brisk trade in forged Churchill letters for example.

Official documents concerning the lives of famous people can be valuable. Thomas Chippendale's 1748 marriage certificate was sold for £620 and a 1940 cheque from Bernard Shaw changed hands at £160. Even documents relating to the lives of lesser people are eagerly collected – records of Victorian hospitals or lunatic asylums; boxes of old legal deeds or wills are all the stuff of history.

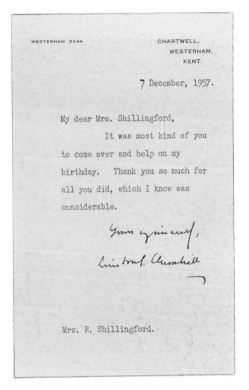

Sir Winston Churchill, Typewritten Letter signed, 1957. $775 £450

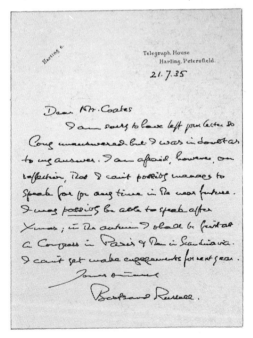

Bertrand Russell, Autograph Letter signed, 1935. $260 £150

(John Wilson)

46, Gordon Square,
Bloomsbury.

14th June 1932

Edward A. Filene Esq.,
Messrs. Wm. Filene's Sons Co.,
Washington Street,
Boston.

Dear Mr. Filene,

It is very good of you to have
asked your publishers to send
me a copy of your new book. It
reached me safely and I shall read
it with very great interest.

Yours very truly,

J. M. Keynes, Typewritten Letter signed, 1932.
$260 £150

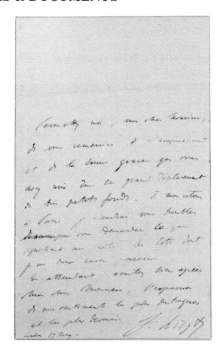

Franz Liszt, Autograph Letter signed in French,
17th May, no year. $850 £485

Augustus John, Autograph Letter signed, 1933.
$115 £65

Robert Browning, Autograph Letter signed
accepting an invitation, undated. $650 £375

(John Wilson)

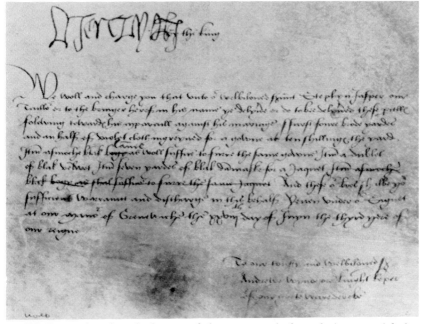

Henry VIII, Letter signed to the keeper of the great wardrobe ordering materials for the wedding apparel of Stephen Jasper, 6 x 7½in. on vellum, 1512. $15,000 £8,500

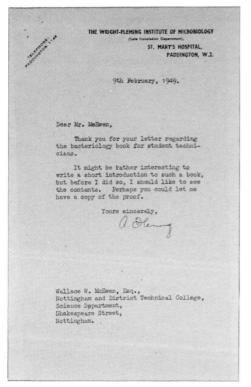

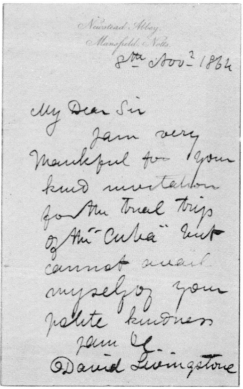

Sir Alexander Fleming, Typewritten Letter signed, 1949. $775 £450

David Livingstone, Autograph Letter signed, 1864. $575 £325

(John Wilson)

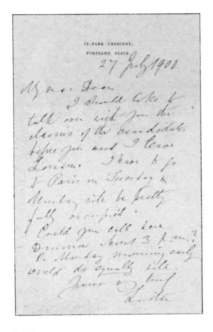

Joseph Lister, Autograph Letter signed, 1900.
$425 £250

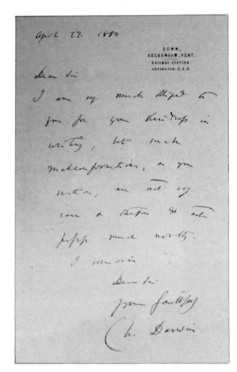

Charles Darwin, Autograph Letter signed, 1880.
$2,200 £1,250

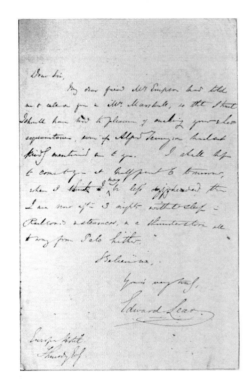

Edward Lear, Autograph Letter signed,
'Thursday evening'. $600 £350

Florence Nightingale, Autograph Letter to Dr
Ord, 1893. $600 £350

(John Wilson)

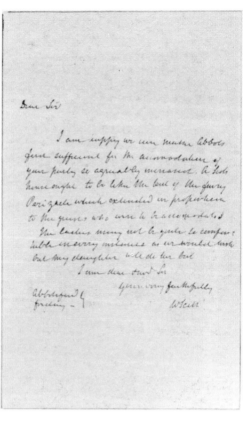

Sir Arthur Conan Doyle, Autograph Letter
signed mentioning Holmes, undated. $675 £385

Sir Walter Scott, Autograph Letter signed,
undated. $850 £485

Charles Dickens, Cheque completed and signed,
1866. $600 £350

William Ewart Gladstone, Autograph Letter   Alfred, Lord Tennyson, Cheque signed, 1871.
signed to John Murray, 1863. $100 £55 $130 £75

(John Wilson)

AUTOMOBILIA

In less than a century the automobile has transformed life. Anything connected with it can be collected from old log books to hub caps. In car design there was a great attention to style and detail and even the smallest artefact had to conform with the general look of the automobile. "Streamlining" influenced artistic trends in the 1920's and artists like Lalique designed magnificent bonnet mascots in the flowing style of the day. Hub caps, petrol cans, radiator caps, steering wheels, even the massive headlights that adorned fast cars like Lagondas and Alvis roadsters are collected. So are books, postcards and magazines connected with cars and motoring. They range from copies of 'Autocar' and 'Motor Sport' to Laurence Pomeroy's comprehensive book on Grand Prix cars which changes hands at over £100 a copy.

'Old Bill' car mascot in brass, after the cartoon character by Bruce Bairnsfather. $175 £100

A large A. A. poster, 'Ways & Communications Bill', circa 1919. $70 £40

'Bullnose' Morris Service sign, 1926. $525 £300

Monsieur Bibendum, Michelin Man, bronze paper weight.

USA manufactured nickel and stove enamel rear light. $80 £45

Motorine enamel sign, circa 1925. $100 £60

$100 £60

Lucas 'King of the Road', holophote, motor cycle front light. $35 £20

Double sided enamel sign, 'Guaranteed Shell from this Pump', with right angle fixing.
$175 £100

Millers all brass Celolite motor cycle front light. $60 £35

Cut out enamel sign for Crown Spark Plug, 'fully guaranteed, why pay more?', 1933. $130 £75

'The Winner' racing car enamel sign for B.P., 'The British Petrol'. $700 £400

Licence to drive a motor car, July 1914. $18 £10

The first A.A. badge, circa 1906, for a motor cycle, very rare. $700 £400

Double sided enamel sign for 'Coventry Eagle' motor cycles, circa 1915. $190 £110

Ford pre electric rear light for a Model T, circa 1909. $80 £45

Peugeot Automobiles and
Cycles brass ashtray, circa
1915. $45 £25

Barometer advertising
'Goodyear Tyres'. $35 £20

Glass petrol globe 'Power'.
                    $95 £55

R.A.C. Badge, circa 1907, with
'sculptured out' arms on
mercury. $875 £500

Single sided enamel sign for
the New Hudson Cycle Co.
Ltd., early 20th century.
                $950 £550

Shell Oil ½ gallon measuring
can. $18 £10

Cardboard counter display for
Belling-Lee Distributors, circa
1935. $35 £20

Shell oil bottle, 1 quart
measure. $4 £3

A. A. Membership card for
1929, complete with its
leather wallet. $14 £8

BABY PLATES

With the increasing use of plastic in infant feeding, any baby plate made of china or pottery is a potential collectable – including such modern ones as Beatrix Potter, Walt Disney and even Kermit the Frog. Look out for German plates brought over between 1880-1900, which were sold as baby plates but had illustrations aimed firmly at the adult market – an interesting piece of subtle marketing policy.

Staffordshire baby plate decorated with a country scene, 7in. diam. $13 £8

Royal Doulton bone china 'Bunnykins'. $14 £8

Royal Doulton baby plate. $10 £6

Doulton 'Bunnykins' bowl. $10 £6

Rockwood pottery dish, Cincinnati, Ohio, 1882, signed by Nathaniel J. Hirschfield, diam. 6½in. (Robt. W. Skinner Inc.) $125 £66

'Painted Feelings' rack plate, Behind the Painted Masque Series, 9in. diam., 1982. $18 £12

Saturday Evening Girls pottery motto plate, Mass., 1914, signed S.G. for Sara Galner, 7½in. diam. (Robt. W. Skinner Inc.) $3,700 £2,569

Wedgwood Beatrix Potter's 'Peter Rabbit'. $9 £5

Royal Doulton bone china 'Bunnykins'. $14 £8

Carrigatine Pottery, 'Winnie the Pooh'. $5 £3

BADGES

The British have always been a nation of badge-wearers. They sported them because of their jobs, their hobbies or their political affiliations and recently they've taken them up to show the things they protest against. There is a vast range of badges that can be collected ranging from Golly badges that used to be given away with jars of marmalade to Trade Union badges or motor cycle club badges. Other subjects include military badges. To be collectible a badge must be in good condition and these are hard to come by because constant wearing tended to dull their original glory. Some are made of metal, chrome or silver and are occasionally enamelled. Others are made of cloth and there is a growing body of interest in tin, pin back badges. A large amount of reproduction badges are around, so take care.

Queen Elizabeth II
Silver Jubilee, 1977.
$1 50p

Royal Masonic Institution
for Girls by G. Hennings &
Son, London. $18 £10

Mr Bradford and
Mr Bingley. 50c 25p

An officer's gilt and silvered
1878 pattern helmet plate
of The 88th (Connaught
Rangers) Regt. (Wallis &
Wallis) $222 £135

A U.S.A. gilt and enamelled
sterling silver badge of The
Joint Chiefs of Staff, by H.
S. Meyer Inc., New York.
(Wallis & Wallis) $46 £35

An officer's silver (not HM)
Maltese Cross shako plate
of The 6th Lancashire Rifle
Vols. (Wallis & Wallis)
$112 £68

British is Best, Volvo.
$2 £1

Land Rover.
$2.50 £1.50

Darth Vadar Lives.
$1 50p

BADGES

Hey and Humphries badge, a bottling firm in Leeds now ceased trading. $18 £10

Rare badge depicting Father William, footballer. $18 £10

Dennis the Menace Fan Club. $2 £1

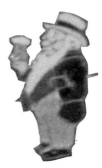

Pre War 'Golden Shred' pale yellow waistcoated Golly. $5 £3

Very rare Guinness Toucan bowling club badge. $25 £15

William Youngers 'little old man holding a pint' $9 £5

A chromium plated and enamelled Brooklands Aero-Club badge inscribed 21, 3¾in. high. (Christie's) $520 £420

A George IV fireman's arm badge, by R. Emes and E. Barnard, 1823, 6in. high, 9oz.5dwt. (Christie's) $2,479 £1,540

An Indian brass puggaree badge worn by gun lascars of the Artillery Train. (Wallis & Wallis) $57 £40

Russells Winner Ales, a rare badge. $18 £10

Post War fruit badge without Golly heads. $5 £3

Midland Railway Service badge by Thos. Fattorini, Bolton, crescent back. $14 £8

BAKELITE

Hailed as a miracle medium when it was invented in 1909 by L. H. Baekeland, bakelite was put to a million different uses before it was superseded by plastics in the 1960's. Baekeland's material was a synthetic resin which could be moulded into any shape and its only drawback was a tendency to crack which is where plastic proved superior. Because it would not melt or burn, bakelite was originally devised for use in the ignition systems of aeroplanes but it was quickly realised that it could be used for many other things as well. Manufacturers began turning out cheap and cheerful ashtrays, dishes, ornaments and toys and bakelite was used for everything from the cases of radio sets or heavy domestic equipment to jewellery or small decorative objects. Artists, realising the possibility of creating fluid-looking figures with bakelite seized on it and made some very sophisticated Art Deco pieces with the material which are quite valuable today.

An Allcocks Aerialite Cadet reel made out of bakelite in its makers box, circa 1950.
$18 £10

A Lalique red bakelite box and cover, of square section, the cover moulded and carved, with carved signature R. Lalique, 7.5cm. x 7.5cm. (Christie's)
$1,394   £825

Black bakelite stand, made in Hong Kong. $3.50 £2

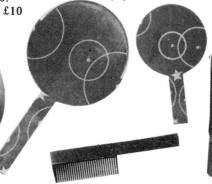

'Ekco' AC Mains model A22 round, bakelite, 1938.
$175 £100

An Art Deco bakelite comb, brush and mirror set, by R. Amerith, France, 1920's. (Robt. W. Skinner Inc.)
$444 £300

'Ekco' Mains AC Radio model 830A bakelite 1932.
$150 £85

1930's bakelite cigarette case. $3.50 £2

1940's bakelite pen tray. $7 £4

Bakelite dolls house settee, 3in. long. $9 £5

BARREL TAPS

Among the most attractive artefacts of the old time pub were barrel taps, often made of brass and proudly polished. The advent of keg beer made them unnecessary and if they are now found in pubs today, they have been kept for decorative reasons only. They were fitted to beer kegs, wine and cider barrels and collectors seek them out in rubbish dumps and old stores. The ones that are most highly prized are stamped with a brewer's and a maker's name and among the most attractive specimens are those of porcelain though the most common material was wood, closely followed by brass, silver plate, chrome or nickel plate. Some barrel taps were fitted with locks to prevent pilfering and later versions had a thumbturn tap on top that featured a locking lever and padlock.

Victorian brass barrel tap with integral key and hammering pin. $18 £10

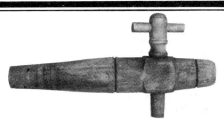

Early 20th century wooden barrel tap. $9 £5

Early 19th century barrel tap, 9in. long. $18 £10

A large Victorian brass barrel tap. $14 £8

Brass tap with swivel lever and locking plate, late 19th century. $14 £8

Late Victorian brass tap, 3in. high. $9 £5

Small early 19th century brass barrel tap, 5in. long. $10 £6

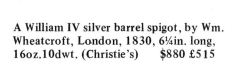

A William IV silver barrel spigot, by Wm. Wheatcroft, London, 1830, 6¼in. long, 16oz.10dwt. (Christie's) $880 £515

BARRELS

Barrels have been used for storing everything from biscuits to beer, from gunpowder to gin, and the shape is so pleasing that it has been reproduced for decorative purposes where it has no practical application, eg. tiny silver sewing cases made to hang on a chatelaine.

While beer barrels and so on are strong wooden constructions, more decorative and infinitely more expensive examples are the beautiful spirit barrels made of china or glass.

A Westerwald grey stoneware spirit barrel, 33.5cm. high. (Christie's) $1,093 £810

A brass bound oak rum barrel inscribed 'HMS Victory No. 3', 16½in. high. (Christie's) $3,162 £2,592

A German porcelain wine barrel supported on a wood stand, circa 1880, the barrel 30cm. wide. (Christie's) $1,512 £1,045

One of a pair of blue and white late 18th century hexagonal barrel-shaped garden seats, 49cm. high. (Christie's) $4,847 £3,672

Saltglaze water barrel, circa 1880. (British Antique Exporters) $130 £75

Pair of Staffordshire pottery spirit barrels with metal taps, 12in. high. (G. A. Key) $272 £165

Royal Doulton 'Ginger Wine' barrel made for Rawlings, complete with tap, 10in. high. (Abridge Auctions) $180 £120

BASKETS

Perhaps the best documented basket is the one in which Moses found himself in the bulrushes. They have been around for a long time and have served a multitude of purposes in the everyday life of the ages. 19th century baskets were an indispensible part of a genteel lady's equipment, whether of the lidded variety to carry jellies and cordials to ailing cottagers, or the flat, wooden slatted Sussex trugs in which she could carry her cut flowers. Attractive in themselves, they are eminently collectable today.

California coiled basketry bowl, Pomo, diam. 12in., 5¾in. high. (Robt. W. Skinner Inc.) $500 £280

A Cascade/Plateau imbricated coiled basket, Klikitat, 19th century, 10¼in. high. (Robt. W. Skinner Inc.) $700 £400

An Indian-style covered woven basket, 1916, 8¼in. high, 10½in. diam. (Robt. W. Skinner Inc.)$450 £267

A mahogany octagonal waste paper basket with tapering fretwork sides and bracket feet, 11½in. wide. (Christie's) $4,329 £2,640

A Gustav Stickley slat sided wastebasket, circa 1905, no. 94, signed, 11¾in. diam. (Robt. W. Skinner Inc.)
$2,500   £1,428

A 19th century American large polychrome woven splint market basket, 19in. wide. (Christie's) $286 £161

One of a pair of Edwardian giltwood baskets, on rope moulded bases, lined interiors, 41cm. and 36cm. (Phillips)
Two $748   £400

BATHROOM ACCESSORIES

Today's decorating trends mean that older bathroom fittings are much in demand by designers seeking to create a 'period' feel to their bathrooms. Brass taps, enamelled toilet roll holders, ceramic chain pulls, even toilet seats in mahogany, beech and pine are greatly in demand, while larger items, such as marble washstand surrounds, can fetch hundreds.

The early toilet was designed by W. L. Crapper and has been produced in many decorative designs over the last hundred years. Early decorative examples can fetch in excess of £250. Look out for ceramic chain pulls (£10 – £50), splash backs (£20 – £100) and good quality early fittings.

A finely decorated floral bowl and pitcher, circa 1860.
$130 £75

Victorian mahogany shaving stand, 1880.
$435 £250

A Qianlong blue and white violin-shaped bidet, 60cm. wide.
$1,750 £1,000

1940's Elsan model 44 bakelite lavatory seat. $18 £10

English saltglazed stoneware water closet.
$350 £200

Blue and white lavatory pan, 'Niagara'.
$350 £200

BEER BOTTLE LABELS

Printed paper labels were first stuck on beer bottles to identify the brewer and the type of beer in the 1850's. In the early days, the labels were always oval shaped. When the Trade Marks Registration Act came into operation on January 1st, 1876, the brewing company Bass took the opportunity of registering their trade marks. These were for Bass Pale Ale, Burton Ale and Extra Stout. On January 16th, 1876, they registered their distinctive Bass triangle trade mark, the first brewer to do so. Since then more than a thousand brewers' trademarks have been registered including such famous names as McEwans, Tennents and Ind Coope.

Oval labels on beer bottles were the rule until the introduction of high speed bottling machines in the late 1950's which made it possible to use a larger number of shapes and over the years hundreds of thousands of different beer bottle labels have been produced worldwide. There is a thriving body of collectors all over the world as well. The hobby is particularly popular in Eastern Europe but there are Beer Bottle Label Societies in Britain, Germany, America, New Zealand and Australia as well. The king of the collectors must be the man in East Germany who has over 300,000 labels but some British enthusiasts have managed to amass as many as 25,000.

Collections can be built up across the board, for particular brands or of labels relating to special occasions like Royal Weddings or Coronations and Victory celebrations to mark the end of both World Wars. Some collectors only keep labels though others collect the bottles as well — either full or empty.

Crown Crystal Ale, an attractive label in yellow, red and black on white.
$2 £1

Walsall & District Clubs' Brewery Ltd., Bitters, featuring athleticism combined with alcohol.
$7 £4

Dunmow Brewery Ltd., Flitch Stout, in brown and black on white. $1 50p

Old Noll, East Anglian Breweries Ltd., Ely, multicoloured label on white, featuring Oliver Cromwell, a local man.
$3.50 £2

Robert Younger Ltd., Edinburgh, Pale Ale, 1940's label in green, black and red on white.
$1.50 75p

Octagon Brewery Ltd., Plymouth, Two in One Ale, an oddly named beer from a small local brewery. $5 £3

Brickwoods Light Bitter Ale, a 1940's label in blue, yellow and red on white. $3 £1.50

Coronation Year, '53 Ale, Drybrough & Co. Ltd., Edinburgh, multicoloured label on white, a popular event for brewers. $5 £3

Bent's Coronation Ale, Liverpool and Stone, in the patriotic colours of red, white and blue on a cream ground. $2.50 £1.50

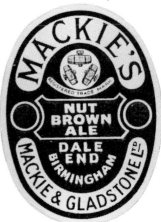

Thwaites Big Ben Strong Ale, named after Ben, the Brewery's founder, in red, blue and black on white. $2 £1

Dog's Head, British Lager Beer, Export Bottlers Ltd., in blue, orange and black on white. $1 50p

Mackie's Nut Brown Ale, an attractive 1950's bottlers label, in brown and red on white. $2 £1

Festivale Gold Medal Ales by Eagle Brewery, Leicester, produced for the Festival of Britain in 1951, in green and black on white. $7 £4

Jenner's Double Nut Brown Ale, an attractive 1930's label in green, brown and black on buff. $9 £5

Salt & Co's East India Pale Ale, an attractive label from 1894, in black and yellow on white. $45 £25

Magpie Pale Ale, W. B. Reid & Co. Ltd., Newcastle on Tyne, named after the local football team in red and black on white. $7 £4

Coronation Ale, David Roberts and Sons Ltd., Aberystwyth, red, white and blue on cream. $7 £4

Young & Co's Pale Ale, an attractive label from a company which still keeps rams, in red and black on white. $7 £4

Nicholsons' Double Nick Strong Ale, in red, black, gold and yellow on white. $7 £4

Paine & Co's Old English Ale, an attractive 1930's label in red, yellow and black on pink. $3.50 £2

Hambridge Brewery Ltd., Home Brewed Ale, a 1930's label showing the trademark in red, with blue and black lettering on white. $5 £3

Gilmour Sheffield Shield Extra Stout, an attractive 1950's label in brown, buff and green on white. $7 £4

Isleworth Stout, The Brewery, Isleworth, a 1940's label on a buff ground. $3.50 £2

King & Barnes Ltd., Festive Ale, a 1960's label in red, yellow and black on white. $1 50p

BEER MATS

From the Latin teges, meaning 'small rug', collectors of beer mats or drip mats, have taken the term Tegestology to describe the subject— a collector being known as a Tegestologist.

The first wood pulp drip mat was patented in 1892 by Robert Sputh in Dresden, Germany but, although used in the rest of Europe from that time, it was not until 1920 that they came into common use in the United Kingdom. It was from these somewhat primitive examples that the beautifully coloured and highly attractive beer mats of today have developed.

With over 100,000 beer mats, Leo Pisker of Austria is thought to hold the largest collection in the world.

Buckingham Palace, British Brewery Export, 1950's. $5 £3

British Overseas Airways Corporation.   35c 20p

Stella Artois, Belgian, 1980's. 5c 3p

Dale's Cambridge Ales, 1935. $20 £12

Holden's Black Country Bitter, 1980's.   10c 5p

Bullard's Ales, 'Strength and Quality', 1930's. $14 £8

Doris & Alf Rushton, The Shoulder of Mutton, 1950's.   25c 15p

The Rewarding Experience, Aston Manor Brewery Co. Ltd., 1970's.   35c 20p

Guinness, 'No beer comes near', 1980's.   10c 5p

BEER MATS

Moor's & Robson's Brilliant Beers, late 1940's. $10 £6

Aitchison's Export Ale, British Brewery, 1960-64. $1 50p

Germania Munster, Westfalen, 1960's.   5c 3p

Baksor, East European, 1930's. $2 £1

Hanson's Special Stout, 1960's.   50c 30p

The West Auckland Brewery Co. Ltd., 1934. $35 £20

M & B, Woodbine — the great little cigarette, 1950's 20c 10p

J. Wray & Nephew Ltd., Rum, Appleton, 1950's.   20c 10p

Whiteways Cider, Pure Devon, 1930's. $3.50 £2

Richard Clarke & Co. Ltd., Mild Ale, Stockport, 1936. $25 £15

The Swan, The Romance of Inn Signs, 1960.   50c 30p

Ogden's Juggler Tobacco, 1930's. $5 £3

43

BILL HEADS

The introduction of the penny post in 1840 ushered in a boom in communication. People who rarely wrote letters started putting pen to paper. As with all booms, it sparked off subsidiary industries like printing because enterprising merchants and manufacturers wanted to put across their firms by eye-catching letter heads. Engravers produced designs for butchers, bakers, candlestick makers, mill owners and hotels to name only a few.

Some of the designs, especially the early black and white ones before the introduction of colour printing, are a delight to the eye. Mill chimneys belch smoke; inn yards are full of bustling ostlers and coaches; butchers' billheads show woolly sheep or ferocious looking bulls. As cheaper printing became available the vogue even passed to private householders who commissioned letter heads with elegant script and pretty flourishes.

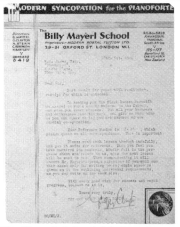

The Billy Mayerl School, Modern Syncopation for the Pianoforte, 1939. $5 £3

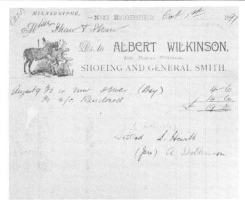

Albert Wilkinson, Shoeing and General Smith, 1897. $3.50 £2

Dr. to William Shaw & Sons, Grove Mills, 1893. $7 £4

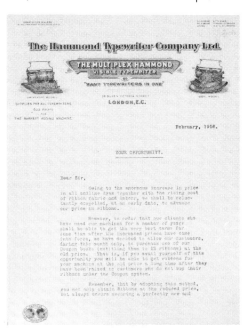

The Hammond Typewriter Company Ltd., 1916. $3.50 £2

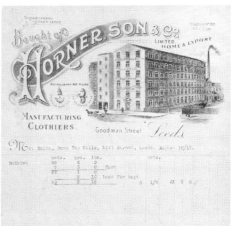

Horner, Son & Co., Manufacturing
Clothiers, 1917. $9 £5

Tom Norton, the Automobile Palace, 1910.
$12 £7

R. A. Harding, Manufacturer of Invalid
Carriages & Motors. $2 £1

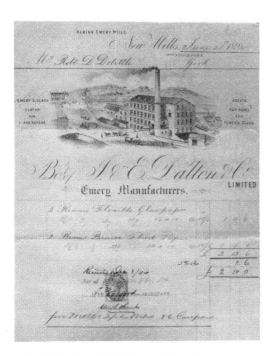

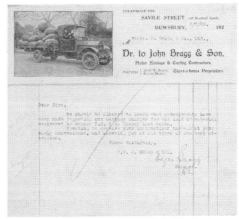

J. & E. Dalton Ltd., Emery Manufacturer,
1894. $9 £5

Dr. to John Bragg & Son, Motor Haulage and
Carting Contractors, 1922. $3.50 £2

BIRDCAGES

The keeping of a caged bird as a toy and a diversion has been common in every country since very early times. Indian Rajput paintings and Roman friezes show birds in cages, caged birds are referred to in poetry and their popularity has persisted to the present day. In the Middle Ages people kept jays and magpies – which often talked – in cages as pets while larks and goldfinches were popular because of their song, especially in Italy.

The cage was often as prized as its inhabitant and these to be found by collectors can range from a 1930's Art Deco type of cage in chrome on a tall stand for the family budgie to tiny jewelled cages of gold which were made for the finches of the rich in Renaissance Italy. Sometimes these exotic cages were inhabited by stuffed birds because they were less trouble to keep.

Cages can vary enormously in size, shape and in the materials used for their manufacture. The earliest ones, of which few survive, were made of basket work with turf on the floor. In the 18th and early 19th centuries bird cages were made in wood and designed like houses. Parrots and cockatoos became popular during this period because they were brought home by travellers to distant countries, and they were housed in miniature mansions with make-believe doors and dome shaped roofs. Later brass cages for parrots became more popular though these were always expensive and cheaper versions in metal could be bought. Some of the most interesting bird cages are miniature aviaries modelled on the Crystal Palace which was built in 1851.

Mid 19th century red-painted birdcage of Gothic design with sloping roof, 14½in. wide. $875 £500

An architectural wire birdcage with a mahogany base, circa 1900, 2ft.9in. wide. $1,750 £1,000

A wooden framed wire birdcage. (Worsfolds) $268 £160

19th century ormolu birdcage with ogee top, 24in. high. $3,500 £2,000

A late Georgian birdcage, complete with its contemporary glass feeder. $700 £400

A Dutch mahogany birdcage, the stepped front with four compartments, late 18th century, 41in. wide. (Christie's) $30,525 £16,500

46

BISCUIT BARRELS

Biscuit barrels are popular with collectors perhaps because of the infinite variety of decorative designs, makers, and the many different materials from which they can be made, such as wood, pottery, metal, fine china, or cut glass. The most highly esteemed potteries, such as Wedgwood, included them in their production lines, and set their best designers, such as Hannah Barlow to work on their conception.

The rim mounts and handles, too, were subjects for endless imaginative variations, and these could range from simple cane to the most intricately crafted and engraved precious metalwork.

A conception perhaps of a more gracious and elegant age, biscuit barrels are above all practical as well as ornamental, and even today make a most attractive addition to a dinner party table.

Victorian oak biscuit barrel with plated mounts, 1870. (British Antique Exporters) $45 £25

A Clarice Cliff Bizarre biscuit barrel with wicker handle, 16cm. (Osmond Tricks) $252 £135

1950's hand painted wooden biscuit barrel. $9 £5

A Doulton Lambeth stoneware biscuit barrel, by Florence and Lucy Barlow, 20cm. high, r.m. 1883. (Phillips) $686 £480

An English cameo glass biscuit barrel with plated mount, swing handle and cover, 17cm. diam. (Phillips) $1,337 £700

Victorian biscuit barrel with plated top. (British Antique Exporters) $85 £50

BISCUIT TINS

Towards the end of the 18th century a technique was devised for printing onto metal sheets. Because metal could not absorb ink as paper does, the development of lithography made printing on metal a possibility but it was not till 1837 that a system of chromolithography was developed by Godefroye Engelmann in Paris and some beautiful results were obtained. In the 1860's mass production started because Benjamin George worked out the earliest form of off-set printing in Britain using rubber cylinders to effect the transfer of the design directly onto metal. From that date the manufacture of colourful tins, especially for the Christmas market, became a booming industry. They were made in every shape and form — some in simple shapes with pretty designs on the lids and others in the shape of houses, jewel caskets, treasure chests, trains or motor cars. Biscuit manufacturers, in particular Huntley & Palmer, made the design of their tins a speciality and produced a catalogue listing the dozens of types available.

Huntley & Palmers 'Mirror' circa 1914, with detachable lid and handle which becomes a hand held mirror. (Phillips)$109   £65

W.R. Jacob & Co. 'Houseboat' circa 1923, fair to good condition. (Phillips) $169   £100

1953 Coronation Queen Elizabeth souvenir biscuit tin. (Border Bygones) $14 £8

Huntly & Palmers Assorted Cocktail Biscuits tin. (Border Bygones) $3.50 £2

A pair of Huntley & Palmer 'Statuary' tins, circa 1910, with hinged lids. (Phillips) $210 £120

Huntley & Palmers 'Literature' circa 1901, very good condition. (Phillips) $321   £190

McVitie & Price 'Bluebird' tin, circa 1911. (Phillips)$175 £100

A Mettoy 'OK Biscuits' spring drive tin delivery van, brightly coloured in yellow and red, 10cm. x 24cm. (Phillips) $118   £70

Huntley & Palmers 'Bookstand' circa 1905, very good condition. (Phillips) $143   £85

Peek Frean & Co. book tin with a portrait of a woman on the front, 20.5 x 16cm. (Phillips) $85 £50

W. & R. Jacob & Co. 'Coronation Coach' circa 1936, lacking box, very good condition. (Phillips) $304 £180

Victoria Biscuit Co. book tin of Dordrecht — Holland 'Gourmets Delight', 24.5x17cm. (Phillips) $85 £50

Huntley & Palmers 'Oval Basket' circa 1905, basket work and tin in good condition, lacking basket lid. (Phillips) $84 £50

1950's Tally Ho biscuit tin by Scribbens Bakeries. $9 £5

Huntley & Palmers 'Scallop' shell shaped tin with a hinged lid, 8.5cm. high. (Phillips) $175 £100

John Buchanan & Bros. Ltd., two dark blue urn shaped confectionery tins decorated in the Art Nouveau style, 31cm. x 13cm. (Phillips) $338 £200

Crawfords Biscuits Bus OK 3852, with original box, 25.5cm. (Phillips) $4,488 £2,400

The Queen's Silver Jubilee, 1952-1977 biscuit tin. (Border Bygones) $2 £1

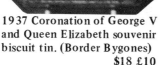

Huntley & Palmers 'Books' circa 1909, very good condition. (Phillips) $270 £160

1937 Coronation of George V and Queen Elizabeth souvenir biscuit tin. (Border Bygones) $18 £10

Huntley & Palmers 'Arcadian' circa 1902, very good condition. (Phillips) $270 £160

BONDS & SHARE CERTIFICATES

"Busted bonds" are stock or share certificates which have no longer any value — though there are sometimes surprises. The collecting of them is called scripophily and it was almost unknown until the 1970's. There has been a strong American interest since the 1980's however and more people are becoming attracted to it because of the decorative appearance of the certificates which are often highly coloured and beautifully designed. Bonds and shares have been issued since the 17th century. Early examples were printed on vellum but printers like Waterlow, Bradbury Wilkinson and the American Banknote Co produced some very attractive certificates. Often they were signed by famous people who were associated with the companies.

The fall of kings and the rise of revolutions has always caused an avalanche of busted bonds and some of the most common relate to Russian and Chinese companies. A couple of years ago the Russian government suggested that some recompense would be made to the holders of stocks and shares in Tsarist companies and families who retained their certificates did indeed reap some return from those old holdings. Some of the most interesting certificates relate to American railway companies and banks which often had an ephemeral existence and other collectors pick a theme — like steamship companies or Egyptian cotton mills and stick to that. In the United Kingdom, a share or bond certificate is legally the property of the person named on it but in Canada and America shares were often made out "to the bearer" so if the company is still in existence, the certificate could be worth serious money.

Mexico, El Buen Tono, Cia Manufacturera del Cigarro Sin Pegamento, $50 share, 1912, good vignette of cigar making machine, ornate border.
$35 £20

Germany, Kingdom of Westphalia, 1808 Loan, 100 frank bond, dated 1809, ornate border, black, with numerous coupons. $435 £250

(M. Veissid & Co.)

Russia, Riazan-Uralsk Railway Co., 4½% loan, 1893, bond for 5000 roubles, mauve (D/H 1107d), lacks coupons. $210 £120

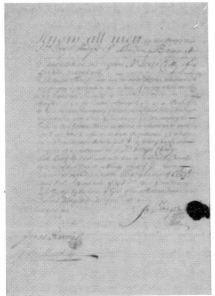

South Sea Company, printed form of power of attorney, 1714, empowering Joseph Chitty, a London Merchant, to deal with stock belonging to Sir Joseph Hodges, Baronet, signed and sealed by Hodges and witnessed by two others, 3 embossed revenue stamps. $1,000 £600

East Kent Light Railways Co., £1 shares, 1921, 2 vignettes of a steaming train and colliery buildings at Tilmanstone, blue. $100 £60

Tuolumne County Water Company, $250 share, Columbia 1862 over 185-, lovely vignette of miners sluicing for gold in the mountains, black. $50 £30

Snowdown Colliery Ltd., group of 3 certificates for founders' shares, 1908; ordinary shares, 1913 and preferred shares, 1908, all with good vignette of mine at top. $70 £40

(M. Veissid & Co.)

Brooklyn & Brighton Beach Railroad Co.,
5% consolidated mortgage bond, $1,000, 1896,
steam train at top, ornate border. $60 £35

Roumania, Monopolies Institute, Stabilisation
and Development Loan, 1929, £100 bond,
vignette of castle, ornate border. $45 £25

Andover National Bank, Massachusetts, $100
shares, 1896, lovely vignette of Government
building at top, gentleman at lower left, ornate
border. $30 £16

Ilex Mill Co. Ltd., £5 share, 1876, vignette of
mill at left, printed in Rochdale, black. $60 £35

Exchequer receipt, 1707, printed with
manuscript insertions, for 3 months interest
on £300, subscribed in 1693 under the Act
of that year, signed by John, Lord
Colepepper. $175 £100

(M. Veissid & Co.)

Victor Gold Mining Co. Ltd., Cripple Creek, Colorado, 5 shares of $5, 1895, vignette of miners, ornate border, red and black. $40 £22

Columbus Gold Mining Company of the Black Hills, $10 shares, 1880, 2 vignettes of miners, black. $45 £25

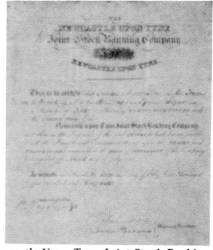

Canterbury Navigation & Sandwich Harbour Co., £25 share, 1826, large vignette of coats of arms, cathedral and proposed canal, black on thick paper. $435 £250

Newcastle Upon Tyne Joint Stock Banking Company, £25 shares, 1836, black, on vellum. The Company was formed during the boom period of 1836. $300 £175

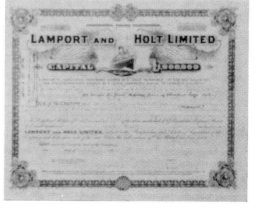

Farmers & General Fire & Life Insurance & Loan & Annuity Co., £10 shares, 1848, vignette of wheatsheaf at top and plough at bottom. $60 £35

Lamport & Holt Limited, 6% preference shares of £1, 1913, vignette of steam ship, ornate border, black, pink underprint.
$25 £15

(M. Veissid & Co.)

Spain, Sociedad General de Automoviles S.A., 500 pesetas share, Barcelona 1911, vignette of early motor car, black, with coupons, only 1,000 issued. $80 £45

Elder Dempster & Co. Ltd., 6% preference shares of £1, 1914, vignette of steam ship, ornate border, green and pink. $25 £15

India, Apollo Mills Ltd., 100 rupee shares, 1920, large vignette of Apollo at left, black and brown. $25 £15

India, Mahalakshmi Woollen & Silk Mills Co. Ltd., 10 rupee shares, 1923, extremely ornate border with vignettes of factory, shepherd, elephants & peacocks, blue and green. $25 £15

Spain, Compania de los Ferrocarriles Economicos de Villena a Alcoy y Yecla, bond for 475 pesetas, Barcelona 1902, lovely Art Nouveau design. $30 £16

New Centaur Cycle Co. Ltd., 10/- ordinary shares, 1906, vignette of Centaurs and other figures, green. $55 £30

(M. Veissid & Co.)

BOOKENDS

Bookends were almost exclusively a 19th century creation, earlier books having been kept in presses or laid flat.

They were made from all sorts of materials, from carved wooden blocks to alabaster arches or cherubs cast in bronze or marble. The 1880's and 90's saw a vogue for embossed leather, ornamented with oriental designs, while in the early 20th century marble, silver and glass were widely used.

A rosewood book tray, the whole outlined with mosaic borders, 1ft.3in. wide.

$700 £400

A pair of bronze bookends by Alexander Kelety. (Christie's)　　$3,500 £2,000

A pair of Nancy pate de verre bookends fashioned as dolphins, signed X Momillon, 6½in. high. (Lots Road Chelsea Auction Galleries)　　$4,550 £2,500

Royal Doulton bookends featuring Mr Micawber, Mr Pickwick, Sairey Gamp and Tony Weller, issued 1934-39. (Abridge Auctions)　　$275 £160 each

A Regency period book trough veneered in pollard oak, 12in. long.　　$1,400 £800

A Regency rosewood bookrack with spindle-filled superstructure and one drawer, 16¼in. wide.　　$3,500 £2,000

BOOKMARKS

Bookmarks are making a come-back today after a long time in the doldrums. They used to be used as a means of advertising and modern bookshops are adopting this method again but in the 19th and early 20th centuries, the bookmark promoted all kinds of goods ranging from chocolate bars to insurance policies. Walter Crane, the illustrator of children's books, designed a lovely bookmark for the Scottish Widows' Fund and there were also attractive shaped marks like the cricket bat which promoted Wisden and a hand advertising Fry's chocolate creams. Bookmarks were also often given as gifts by skilled needlewomen who made them for their friends and these were particularly popular with the Victorians. Bookmarks of woven silk were sold in their thousands, particularly Stevengraphs and others made of embroidered French ribbon.

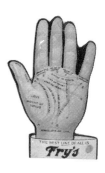

Hoyts German Cologne bookmark, Lowell, Mass. $10 £6

Cherry Blossom, bookmark, Perfume Toilet Powder and Soap, 1890. $20 £12

Wisden's Exceller Bat bookmark, from the 1936 Wisden's. $3.50 £2

Fry's Cocoa and Chocolates, the best line of all is Fry's. $9 £5

Wright's Coal Tar Soap, the seal of health and purity. $3.50 £2

Kleen-eze Brush Co. Ltd., Royal Silver Jubilee souvenir bookmark, 1935. $3.50 £2

Sons of the Empire, with compliments Dr Lovelace's Soap. $7 £4

Singer's bookmark with portrait of Lt. Col. R.S.S. Baden-Powell. $7 £4

Yesterday's Paper

Air France, Fastest to 4 Continents. $1 50p

Lloyd's Weekly News, the Best Family Paper. $13 £7.50

Theatre Royal, Manchester, Little Women with Katharine Hepburn. $5 £3

St Ivel Cheese, the Pride of the West Countrie. $4 £2.50

Allenbury's Foods for Infants, the Milky Way to Health. $4 £2.50

Scottish Widows' Fund, the largest British Mutual Life office. $2 £1

The Studio bookmark for a carol, 'Good King Wenceslas'. $2.50 £1.50

Silk bookmark, 'In loving memory of Private James Brodie', 1918. $7 £4

Fry's Milk Chocolate, Pull up his head. $21 £12

Brown & Polson's Cornflour, nearly 40 years world wide reputation. $5 £3

Yesterday's Paper

BOTTLE OPENERS

Bottle openers were used by brewing companies and soft drinks manufacturers as a way of advertising their wares. The majority were for opening crown topped beer bottles but several were produced by foundries as examples of their work. The best openers are printed with the company's name, as well as a date and a slogan in some cases. If they have a slogan from a popular holiday resort – *Welcome to Blackpool*, for example – they are not so highly regarded by collectors. Bottle openers were cheap to produce and were given away in vast numbers. The earliest ones made of iron are the most valuable. Later examples made out of pressed steel are not so desirable. Collectors especially seek out examples issued by breweries that are now out of business and some date back to before the First World War. Prices range from 10p to around £25 for rare early ones shaped like faces with the mouths as the openers.

Face shaped opener by Allbright, Wooton & Thomson of Ramsgate. $18 £10

Oranjeboom crown cork opener. $9 £5

'Guinness is good for you'. $3.50 £2

Crown cork bottle opener, PT46644. $5 £3

C.H.B. opener with stopper. $9 £5

Guitar shaped opener with can pierce. $3.50 £2

Tuborg, 'The World Famous Beer'. $2 £1

Unusual key-shaped bottle opener. $9 £5

BOTTLES

Four categories of bottles are most popular with collectors – mineral water, beer and beverage bottles; quack medicine bottles; glass and stone ink bottles; poison bottles.

The most popular mineral water bottles are Hiram Codd's marble stoppered lemonade bottles, preferably with the marble intact. Sometimes unfortunately the necks of these bottles were broken off by children wanting to get at the marbles. The best are the coloured ones, some of which fetch over £100 each especially the cobalt blue variety. They are followed in the popularity stakes by transfer printed stone ginger beer bottles which can be found in rubbish dumps over the entire country.

Quack cure bottles often carried fascinating labels or had slogans printed on the glass and one of the most valuable is Warners Safe Cure which is green in colour and can be priced at around £50. The most common ink bottles are made of glass and are octagonal in shape but the ones made of stone and shaped like little cottages with embossed doors and windows have a strong following. Overseas collectors will pay up to £250 for a good specimen.

Poison bottles are also often found by treasure hunters in rubbish dumps. They were usually coloured a bright colour – blue, purple or viridian green – to alert users to the danger of their contents and they were also often made in peculiar shapes for the same reason. There was even one shaped like a coffin and others were marked with embossed skulls and crossbones which could be felt by the fingers if picked up in the dark.

Early stoneware ginger beer bottle with applied seal, circa 1840.　$350 £200

Cobalt blue Prices Patent candle bottle.　$85 £50

Black glass shaft and globe shaped, small size (6in. high) wine bottle with applied glass seal, circa 1650.
$5,250 £3,000

Stoneware Reform flask for gin, circa 1840.
$700 £400

Martin's Patent medicine bottle.　$260 £150

Roman flask with handle, circa 4th century A.D.
$2,600 £1,500

(Peter Savage Antique Bottle Museum)

59

BOTTLES

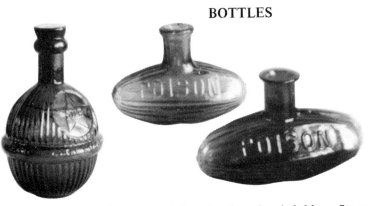

Fire Extinguisher bottle. $70 £40

Submarine shaped, cobalt blue poison bottles. $435 £250

Stoneware ginger beer bottle with picture transfer on body, circa 1890. $45 £25

Black glass soda water bottle with pontilled base, circa 1830. $3,500 £2,000

Black glass wine bottle with applied glass seal, circa 1760. $875 £500

Black glass bear shaped bottle for liqueurs, circa 1880. $105 £60

Cobalt blue marble stoppered pop bottle. $1,800 £1,000

English, black glass, straight sided onion shaped bottle, circa 1720. $600 £350

Stoneware ink bottle in the shape of Mr Punch. $875 £500

(Peter Savage Antique Bottle Museum)

BOTTLES

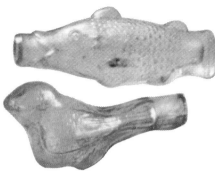

Roman flask with handle, circa 4th century A.D. $2,600 £1,500

Aqua colour glass figural bottles in shape of a bird and a fish, circa 1870. $40 £25

English onion shaped wine bottle, circa 1695. $700 £400

Black glass Dutch embossed gin bottle, circa 1860. $260 £150

Black glass square wine bottle with applied glass seal, circa 1780. $260 £150

Amber bitters bottle dated 1872. $85 £50

Stoneware Reform flask for gin, circa 1840. $700 £400

T-kettle shaped inkwell inside very ornate gilt cage. $875 £500

Black glass shaft and globe shaped wine bottle, circa 1665. $1,750 £1,000

(Peter Savage Antique Bottle Museum)

61

BOTTLES

Patent medicine bottle 'True Daffy's Elixir', dark green glass, circa 1830. $1,400 £800

Stoneware egg ended mineral water bottle, circa 1840.
   $350 £200

Black glass, quarter size, wine bottle with applied glass seal, dated 1791. $600 £350

Very rare shaped pop bottle with glass marble stopper.
   $435 £250

English, black glass, mallet shaped wine bottle, circa 1740.
   $600 £350

Dutch black glass wine bottle with long stretched neck, circa 1760. $175 £100

Early stoneware stout bottle made by Stephen Green's Pottery, circa 1840. $350 £200

English, black glass, onion shaped wine bottle, circa 1700.
   $600 £350

Rare shape pop bottle with one flat side and glass marble stopper. $260 £150

(Peter Savage Antique Bottle Museum)

BOY SCOUT ITEMS

Robert Stephenson Smyth Baden-Powell, famous as the man who defended Mafeking against the Boers in 1900, founded the Boy Scout Movement in 1908 and since then it has gone from strength to strength and spread all over the world. Part of the ethos of the Baden-Powell movement was expressed in the uniform − military-type shorts, peaked hat, neckscarf and badges. All these, and especially the badges, have been collected by enthusiasts for many years.

Northamptonshire was the first county to adopt a distinctive Scouting emblem in 1910 but it was closely followed by Kent which issued a county badge incorporating a white horse in July 1912.

In the early days of scouting, badges were made of metal, though during the war years because of shortages, paper had to be used. From the 1930's onwards however woven cloth badges became universal. Collectors pay high prices for metal badges and especially for those from counties which are no longer in existence like Yorkshire West Riding, Rutlandshire or South Warwickshire. The most sought after badges are those which commemorate the great World Scouting Jamborees of 1937 and 1947 and they can be worth at least £30. Some of the rarest are from the French Province in 1947. Condition is of paramount importance when pricing badges which can be as cheap as 25p or as much as £30.

Other sought-after scouting memorabilia include hats and scarves, books and photographs, particularly of jamborees. King George VI was an enthusiastic supporter of the Boy Scout Movement and during his visits to camps and jamborees during the late 1930's many photographs were taken.

France 1947 Jamboree. $70 £40

South Warwickshire. $45 £25

Dorset (Felt). $18 £10

County of Edinburgh and Leith. $45 £25

Leeds. $45 £25

Suffolk (Felt) $18 £10

Peterborough (Felt). $18 £10

1937 Jamboree, Wereld, Nederland. $70 £40

Yorkshire West Riding. $45 £25

Guernsey (Felt) $18 £10

BREWERIANA

Breweriana, as its name suggests, involves the collecting of all items related to beer and brewing. Beer mats and beer bottles are perhaps the most popular of the related specialist collections and are dealt with as such elsewhere. Other highly collectable items, however include counter displays, pump handles and heads, trays, ashtrays, advertising signs, posters — the list is endless. Some counter displays in the form of china figurines, for example the Guinness Toucan or Younger's 'Father William', can be small works of art in their own right.

Beer badges form another specialist subject. Some of these go back 60 years or more, and used to be worn by workers in various breweries, some of which may be no longer in existence. They can be very colourful and show a wide range of emblems, from the Fremlin elephant to the Guinness Toucan. Rare ones can fetch up to £20.

A brown and stone coloured ½ pint water jug for Watkins Brewers Dublin Stout, by Thos. Watkins of Llandovery, 1927. $50 £30

Advertising figure 'Brewmaster', brewed by Flowers. $85 £50

A white 1 pint mug for Thos. Dutton Brewery, produced for Henry Milner Ltd., Stoke-on-Trent, 1962. $25 £15

A Royal Doulton figural bottle for Sandiman's Port, 10¼in. high, circa 1920.1956. $70 £40

Black & White Scotch Whisky tray. $50 £30

A whisky bottle made for Bell's Old Scotch Whisky, 7¾in. high, circa 1950. $35 £20

Doulton Lambeth stoneware match-holder and striker for John Dewar & Sons. $60 £40

'Schlitz Brewery' tin sign, circa 1915, 24in. diam. (Robt. W. Skinner Inc.) $375 £290

My Goodness, My Guinness statuette, 4in. high. $60 £40

Whisky flask in the form of a crow made for National Distillers of Kentucky, circa 1954. $200 £130

Card advertisement for Coronation 'Cheerio'. $35 £20

A water jug made for William Younger & Co., circa 1920. $52 £35

Younger's Tartan Beer plaster advertising sign, 'Get Younger every day'. $45 £25

1950's printed metal sign for Fremlins Ale, in the form of an elephant, 9in. high. $175 £100

A small Johnnie Walker advertising figure. $52 £35

BRONZE ANIMALS

"Les animaliers" is the name given to sculptors who produced realistic decorative figures of animals, a school of artistic creation which began in France in 1831 when Antoine-Louis Barye exhibited his "Tiger Devouring a Gavial" at the Paris Salon of that year. He started a fashion that was to provide almost every well to do house in Europe with a bronze or metal statuette of an animal – prowling tigers, dozing lions, stalking dogs, prancing horses or snarling wolves. In England people were particularly fond of figures of racehorses, preferably in motion, and one of the most skilled artists in this field was Isidore Bonheur, brother of the painter Rosa. Rich racehorse owners even commissioned statuettes of their favourite horse with their jockey in the saddle. The keynote of the work of "Les animaliers" was realism and the animals were shown as if in life. Some of the best known practitioners of the art apart from Bonheur and Bayre were P. J. Mene, Jules Moigniez and Christophe Fratin.

A 19th century bronze group of a whippet carrying a dead hare in its mouth, inscribed P. J. Mene, 7in. wide. (Woolley & Wallis)
$1,166 £720

A 19th century animalier bronze of a cock pheasant perched on a stump with weasel hiding beneath, the base inscribed J. Moigniez. (Phillips) $1,304 £800

A mid 19th century French bronze figure of the 'Cheval Turc', signed Barye, 38.5 x 29.5cm. (Christie's)
$82,665 £49,500

One of a pair of bronze statues of Abyssinian cats, 32in. tall. (Chancellors Hollingsworths) $972 £600

Late 19th century bronze models of elephants rearing in pain, signed Seiya and Saku, 29cm. and 22cm. long. (Christie's) $2,112 £1,320

An early 20th century bronze model of a seated bloodhound bitch, base signed Paolo Troubetskoy, 22.5cm. high. (Christie's) $1,542 £935

BRONZE ANIMALS

A 19th century French bronze model of a lion crushing a serpent, after Barye, 40cm. high. (Christie's)
$4,776 £2,860

A late 19th century English bronze model of a wild cat crouching on a rocky promontory, cast from a model by J. Macallan Swan, 23.5cm. high. (Christie's) $2,453 £1,728

A late 19th century French bronze model of a grazing sheep, signed Rosa Bonheur, 14 x 21.5cm. (Christie's)
$1,194 £715

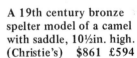

A 19th century French bronze model of a stag, signed on the base Isidore Bonheur, 80 x 56cm. (Christie's)
$11,022 £6,600

A 19th century animalier bronze group of two whippets playing with a ball, inscribed P. J. Mene, 16cm. high. (Phillips) $2,445 £1,500

A 19th century bronze spelter model of a camel with saddle, 10½in. high. (Christie's) $861 £594

A bronze model of a seated rabbit, signed Shosai chu, Meiji period, 17.3cm. long. (Christie's) $1,101 £810

A late 19th century French bronze model of a pointer called Aro, cast from a model by Alfred Barye, 18.5 x 25.5cm. (Christie's)
$1,996 £1,210

A 19th century bronze model of a seated ape, unsigned, 16cm. high. (Christie's) $2,316 £1,620

BUBBLE GUM CARDS & WRAPPERS

American troops in Britain during the war brought bubble gum with them but it was not until the 1950's that a home based industry began when the market leader emerged as A. & B.C. Bubble gum manufacturers gave picture cards away with their packs and also designed colourful wrappers of waxed paper printed with pictures of topical events in film, television, football and pop music. The Beatles, Cliff Richard and The Monkees were all portrayed on these wrappers which proved to be very popular. Other wrappers depicted the Heroes of the Wild West and the 1957 launch of the Sputnik which sparked off a theme of space travel in the wrapper covers. Wrapper collecting has a limited time span in this country for they only appeared between 1953 and 1973 but in America examples dating from the early 1930's are available.

Most sought after is 'Mars Attacks' issued in 1962 and quickly withdrawn because there were complaints that it frightened children — it's now worth £100.

Man from U.N.C.L.E., A. & B.C. Gum, 1965. $1 50p

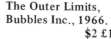

THE RADIO-ACTIVE MAN

The Outer Limits, Bubbles Inc., 1966. $2 £1

Captain Scarlet, Anglo, 1968. $2.50 £1.50

James Bond 007, Somportex, 1965. $2.50 £1.50

DESERTED PLANET

Star Trek, A. & B.C. Gum, 1969. $3.50 £2

Mars Attacks, Bubbles Inc., 1962. $10 £6

EXPLODING GRENADE

Battle, A. & B.C. Gum, 1966. $1 50p

ATTACK

Civil War News, A. & B.C. Gum 1965. $1 50p

20. MISSION CONTINUES

The Champions, A. & B.C. Gum, 1969. $1.50 75p

Cinema, A. & B.C. Gum, 1955. $25 £15   Hocus Pocus, Wow Productions Ltd., 1955.
$45 £25

Star Trek, Topps Chewing Gum, 1979.   Popeye, Klene's Chewing Gum, 1945. $45 £25
$3.50 £2

Outer Limits, Bubble Inc., 1964. $35 £20   Superman, Topps Ireland Ltd., 1978. $2 £1

BUCKETS

Buckets in bygone times could be quite upmarket items designed for very specific purposes. One such was the plate pail, used in 18th and 19th century homes for preheating plates and fetching them to and from the table. These were usually made in pairs, and a pair is worth much more than a single. A voiding pail is another specialised example; its uses include catching table crumbs or even transporting ice for the wine cooler.

A George III mahogany brass bound peat bucket with brass liner, 11¾in. high. (Christie's) $1,730 £1,210

A Georgian mahogany caned plate bucket with brass liner and loop handle, 14in. (Worsfolds) $3,520 £2,200

An 18th century Dutch peat bucket on triple ball supports with metal liner. (Greenslades) $630 £360

1st World War water carrier of kidney section, painted red and bearing crest, rope carrying handles, 21in. high. (Peter Wilson) $70 £40

A fine painted leather ceremonial parade fire bucket, branded by John Fenno, Boston, circa 1790, with enclosed leather swing handle, 13½in. high. (Christie's) $1,980 £1,169

A pair of George III Irish brass mounted mahogany plate buckets of large size, 40cm. high. (Phillips) $7,200 £4,000

A painted leather fire bucket, America, 1822, 12½in. high. (Robt. W. Skinner Inc.) $8,500 £5,059

CABINET PHOTOGRAPHS

Cabinet card photographs were popular between 1866-1914 and were used for both portraiture and publicity photographs. The photo was usually pasted onto specially printed cards bearing the photographer's name and address, and some very ornate printed backs can be found. Collecting cabinet photographs which show the dress of the period is becoming very popular, and with such a variety of fashions in vogue the clothes are often an excellent means of dating them.

King and Company's 'Light and Truth' Studio, Southsea. Study of children at play on a rocking horse, 1897. $26 £15

Cabinet photograph by W. G. Wise, Bulford Camp. Study of Boer War Soldier. $3.50 £2

Cabinet portrait, chromotype photograph by Turner and Drinkwater, Hull. $2 £1

Cabinet portrait of H.R.H. Prince Albert Victor of Wales. $9 £5

Rare cabinet photograph of a Traction Engine and crew. $60 £35

Unusual cabinet photograph by Symonds and Co., Portsmouth, 'Joy, Health and Peace be Yours on Christmas Day'. $14 £8

(Border Bygones)

CADDY SPOONS

Tea was first imported into England in the early 17th century but it was not in general use until the 1650's when it was bought only by the rich for it cost around £10 a pound. Little wonder that tea caddies were provided with a lock and key and the precious leaves were measured out with a special spoon! Caddy spoons can be made of a wide variety of materials ranging through horn, ivory, tortoiseshell, silver, pewter, mother of pearl, treen and porcelain. The most sought after are early and have seal tops. Apostle spoons which have a cast finial joined to the flattened stem with a V joint are also highly prized. Some caddie spoons were called mote spoons for scooping floating leaves off the top of the tea in the cup and others were moustache spoons with a barrier on the leading edge. The most valuable spoons have large ornate bowls and short handles. Those with handles in the shape of eagles can be worth around £1,000.

A Victorian caddy spoon with scalloped bowl, the openwork handle of vine leaf, tendril and grape bunch design, by George Unite, Birmingham, 1869. (Phillips) $193 £110

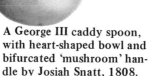

A George III caddy spoon, with heart-shaped bowl and bifurcated 'mushroom' handle by Josiah Snatt, 1808. (Phillips) $211 £120

A rare William IV die-stamped eagle's wing caddy spoon, the bowl chased with overlapping feathers, by Joseph Willmore, Birmingham, 1832. (Phillips) $1,408 £800

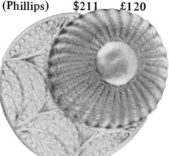

A good and realistic George III caddy spoon with acorn bowl, the bifurcated handle ending in an octagonal 'fiddle' terminal, by Hart & Co., Birmingham, 1806. (Phillips) $774 £440

An unmarked George III filigree jockey cap caddy spoon, the corrugated cap with wide filigree peak, circa 1800. (Phillips) $457 £260

A good George III caddy spoon with acorn bowl engraved with diaperwork, the shaped handle with central oval panel, by Elizabeth Morley, 1809. (Phillips) $457 £260

A George III silver-mounted natural shell caddy spoon, the bifurcated octagonal handle with double-thread edge, by Matthew Linwood, of Birmingham, circa 1800. (Phillips) $616 £350

A George III die-stamped caddy spoon, chased with overlapping stylised feathers enclosing an oval centre, by Wardell & Kempson, Birmingham, 1818. (Phillips) $228 £130

A George IV caddy spoon, with plain scallop-shaped bowl and ovoid handle, by Joseph Willmore, Birmingham, 1822. (Phillips) $193 £110

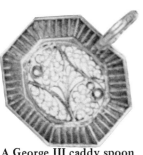

A George III caddy spoon with octagonal bowl, the sides with ribs separated by bands of chevrons, by Samuel Pemberton, Birmingham, 1806. (Phillips) $440 £250

An unusual George III scuttle-shaped caddy spoon, engraved with diaperwork, by Cocks & Bettridge, Birmingham, 1804. (Phillips) $387 £220

A George III caddy spoon with gilt oval fluted bowl and oval filigree central panel, by Samuel Pemberton, Birmingham, 1807. (Phillips) $422 £240

A George III filigree caddy spoon, the bowl of near anthemion shape, each flute terminating in a disc motif, unmarked, circa 1800. (Phillips) $211 £120

A George III right-hand caddy spoon, the flat handle with curved top and incurved sides, by Josiah Snatt, 1805. (Phillips) $616 £350

A George III silver-mounted natural shell caddy spoon, the bifurcated octagonal handle with double-thread edge, by Matthew Linwood, of Birmingham, circa 1800. (Phillips) $598 £340

A George III shovel caddy spoon, engraved with wriggle-work on a hatched background, by William Pugh, Birmingham, 1808. (Phillips) $281 £160

A George III jockey cap caddy spoon, of ribbed design with reeded surfaces, by Joseph Taylor, Birmingham, 1798. (Phillips) $387 £220

A rare George III cast caddy spoon, decorated in relief with a Chinese Mandarin holding a tea plant, by Edward Farrell, 1816. (Phillips) $2,200 £1,250

A George III caddy spoon, the feather-shaped bowl chased with stylised overlapping feathers, by William Pugh, Birmingham, 1808. (Phillips) $739 £420

A Victorian caddy spoon, the thistle or bellshaped bowl parcel gilt and embossed with grapes and vine leaves, by Hilliard & Thomason, Birmingham, 1852. (Phillips) $176 £100

A George III 'frying pan' caddy spoon. the circular, engine-turned bowl with central rosette, by Matthew Linwood, Birmingham, 1807. (Phillips) $352 £200

CALENDARS

For many years it has been a practice for friends to send each other calendars at Christmas. They have always been brightly coloured and though today they usually have a page for each month, earlier ones had a square picture with a little booklet containing a leaf a month hanging beneath them. Favourite calendars were cherished for years and some from the 1930's are very collectable especially those that offer a nostalgic view of the past and the countryside. The same kind of pictures appeared on calendars as on jig-saw puzzles – gardens full of flowers; ladies in crinolines gathering blossoms and, a great favourite, a black dog and a white one surrounded by sprigs of heather and in a Highland background. The firm of Duttons made some of the most popular. Other trade calendars were given away as gifts for customers and they range from superbly engraved calendars gifted by Victorian merchants to the super-photography of the Pirelli calendar which is the most eagerly collected of all.

Varga Calendar, 1948, with verses by Earl Wilson.
$50 £30

The Pirelli Pin-up Calendar, 1973.
$210 £120

Calendar for 1900 by E. P. Dutton & Co., with a moving ship operated with a string. $45 £25

Playboy 'Playmate Calendar', 1978.
$7 £4

74

CAMERAS

Cameras for the common man began being produced in considerable numbers towards the end of the 19th century and late 19th century wood and brass cameras are very popular with today's collectors. The majority of wooden cameras found today were produced after the introduction of dry plates in the 1880's and maker's names to look for include Meagher, Ross, Dallmeyer, Hare and Sands Hunter. British cameras are reckoned to be the best for the early period and in the early 20th century popular makers were Lancaster, Thornton-Pickard, Underwood, Lizars and Sanderson, Sinclair and Newman & Guardia.

In the 1920's however the German Leica camera appeared and dominated the quality market. Even the Japanese are today eager collectors of Leicas. Those made before about 1960 all have screw thread lenses and the ones manufactured afterwards have bayonet fitting lenses. Before 1931, Leica also made cameras with fixed lenses – the Leica 1 (model A) and Compur-Leica. Almost any Leica will sell at auction or to a collector. Other cameras to look out for include the early Kodak camera by George Eastman which appeared in 1888 – one of those will sell for over £1,000 today. A 1915 Kodak box Brownie is a fairly common item still and should not make much more than £5. Other cameras that turn up for sale include Rolleiflex T twin lens reflex cameras which were popular in the 1950's and their successors, the Tele-Rolleiflex twin lens which actually sells for a higher price because it was a special purpose camera and not so many were sold.

An Eastman Kodak Co. rare Cine Kodak Special II camera with a Kodak Cine Ektar 25mm. f 1.4 lens. (Christie's) $935 £495

A Nippon Kogaku, 325 mm. Nikon SP camera, with a Nippon Kogaku Nikkor-S f 1.4 5cm. lens. (Christie's) $1,247 £660

A half plate brass and mahogany studio camera with revolving carte de visite back, Tessar f 4.5 210mm. lens. (Christie's)
$156 £83

A blue Girl Guide Kodak camera with matching blue leather case stamped with the Girl Guide insignia. (Christie's) $249 £132

An E. Lorenz, Berlin, 4½ x 6cm. rigid bodied Clarissa camera, with a Meyer and Co. Plasmat f 2 9cm. lens. (Christie's) $2,702 £1,430

A Houghton-Butcher Mfg. Co. Ltd., tropical model Ensign roll-film reflex camera No. E1053. (Christie's) $500 £264

A Kodak Suprema camera No. 189646K with a Schneider Xenar f 3.5 8cm. lens No. 1182748 in maker's leather case. (Christie's) $374 £198

A Kleinbild-Plasmat Roland camera No. S1137 with a Rudolph 70mm. f 2.7 lens, set into a rim-set Compur shutter. (Christie's) $831 £440

An Arthur S. Newman, London, rare and important prototype 9.5mm. cinematographic hand camera with polished aluminium casing. (Christie's) $2,702 £1,430

A rare Super Kodak Six-20 camera No. 2209 with a Kodak Anastigmat special f 3.5 100mm. lens No. 622. (Christie's) $1,247 £660

An Eastman Kodak Co., No. 1 Brownie camera with winding key in maker's canvas case and an EKC Brownie finder. (Christie's) $52 £28

A green Boy Scout Kodak camera with maker's leather case. (Christie's) $177 £94

A Fabrik Fotografische Apparate, Germany, rare sub-miniature Fotal camera with an E. Rau, Wetzlar lens. (Christie's) $1,143 £605

Eastman Kodak Co., Rochester, NY, 5 x 4 in. No. 4 Folding Kodak camera No. 465 with a Bausch and Lomb pneumatic shutter. (Christie's) $415 £220

A Le Coultre Co., Switzerland, Compass camera, with a CCL3B f 3.5 35mm. anastigmat lens. (Christie's) $935 £495

Kodak, Stuttgart, a very rare new type Retina IIIC camera No. 94058 with a Schneider Retina-Xenon f 2.0 50mm. lens. (Christie's) $540 £286

A good brown Vanity Kodak camera No. 98343 with catch 'Vest Pocket Kodak Series III', a Kodak Anastigmat f 6.3 83mm. lens No. 48988. (Christie's) $228 £121

A Ihagee, Dresden, Original Kine Exakta camera, with a Dallmeyer super-six anastigmat f 19 2in. lens. (Christie's) $1,039 £550

An Adams & Co., London, 5 x 4in. Idento camera No. 3192 with a Ross, London, Homocentric 6in. F 6.3 lens. (Christie's) $124 £66

A Voigtlander, Braunschweig, pre-war Prominant camera, with a Voigtlander Heliar f 4.5 10.5cm. lens. (Christie's) $790 £418

A rare and important Original Kodak camera No. 1127 with winding key, barrel shutter and film holder, stamped 'Pat May 5, 1885'. (Christie's) $3,308 £1,760

CAR CLUB BADGES

The most popular car club badges are those issued by the A.A. and the R.A.C. which motorists used to display proudly on their mudguards. Patrolmen were ordered to salute members of their organisation. The earliest A.A. badges were made of brass or nickel and fifteen different styles have been produced to the present time. Early ones change hands today at around £100 each. R.A.C. badges are more varied because they were made in several different metals and in a large number of designs. They were first issued in 1907 and it is the early ones that demand the highest prices which can go up to £300.

As well as the motoring organisations, clubs like the Caravan Club, sporting clubs, factory clubs and specialist car clubs like the M.G. Club all issued badges for their members. Another great favourite were regimental car badges and collectors can specialise in any of these categories. Particular badges — like those of defunct regiments for example — can cost three figures and badges associated with Brooklands Race Track are perhaps the most desirable of all. For example, a Brooklands Automobile Racing Club badge of the 1930's with a 120 m.p.h., badge is worth at least £700 while an ordinary club badge is worth about £250. If it has a 130 m.p.h. badge the price goes up to £900 however. A 1930's Brooklands Aero Club badge can also cost £900 and a Flying Club one about £700. Prices are rising for those rarities all the time.

A. A. Cycle Badge, 1920's rare. $100 £60

R. A. F. A. Motor Club, 1960's, scarce. $45 £25

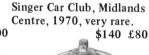

Royal Automobile Club, Junior Car Club, 1920's, rare. $175 £100

Singer Car Club, Midlands Centre, 1970, very rare. $140 £80

British Automobile Racing Club, 1950-60, fairly common. $70 £40

Royal Automobile Club Associate, 1920's, rare. $100 £60

Margate and District Car Club, 1930's, rare. $70 £40

Chiltern Car Club, 1930's, rare. $90 £50

R.A.C. Auto Cycle Union, 1920's, rare. $60 £35

Morris Motors Motor Club, Coventry, 1950's, rare. $50 £30

Hillman Register 1907-1952, 1950's/60's, scarce. $45 £25

A.A. Commercial, 1920's, rare. $140 £80

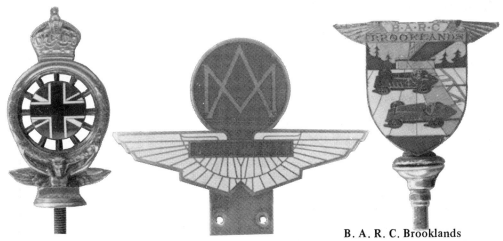

R.A.C. Full Members Badge, 1920's, rare. $140 £80

Aston Martin Owners Club, 1960's, common. $50 £30

B. A. R. C. Brooklands Automobile Racing Club Badge, 1930's, very rare. $875 £500

CARDS

Greeting cards for birthdays, Christmases and especially Valentine's Day really took popular hold in the 19th century with the advent of cheap postal services. Valentine cards had been exchanged by lovers since the end of the 18th century but by 1835 the Post Office reported mailings of 60,000 on February 13th and after the introduction of the penny post in 1840, the number increased even more. At the same time the Victorian popularisation of Christmas started a vogue for Christmas cards. Over the years many famous artists have designed greetings cards and if the artist can be identified, the card's value is enhanced. Rarer greetings cards are those which were produced for Hallowe'en, the Jewish New Year and Krampus, a name little heard today. While Santa Claus rewarded good children at Christmas, Krampus punished naughty ones. Among the more accessible cards for collectors are deckle edged cards dating from between 1918 and 1945 and photographically reproduced cards with hand coloured pictures. Many attractive examples were produced in the Beagle and Rotary series.

46th Infantry Division Christmas greetings, Austria, 1946. $3 £1.50

Pleasant Hours, 'May all the Joys and Mirths of Christmas be Yours'. $5 £3

'From over the sea to greet you, a Happy Christmas'. $1 50p

'Oh lead me, holy dove to rest', by Ernest Nister, printed in Bavaria. $3.50 £2

'Wishing you a joyous Christmas'. $3.50 £2

Valentine's Greetings, 1914-18. $7 £4

Wireless Greetings, received by M.V. Landaura from London. $7 £4

Good Wishes, 'Here's my pug and little kitty'. $5 £3

Happy Tune record Christmas Card, 'Hark the Herald Angels Sing'. $5 £3

Yesterday's Paper

'May nothing floor your happiness this Christmas', Davidson Bros., London. $5 £3

A Birthday Greeting, 'Many Happy Returns'. $7 £4

'To Greet You, with loving Christmas greetings'. $7 £4

'A New Year Greeting with love', Faulkner. $3.50 £2

'Hearty Greetings, A happy New Year to you'. $5 £3

'Hurrah for dear old Christmas Day, May you be happy blithe and gay', $3.50 £2

Conveying Good Wishes, Christmas, 1934. $2 £1

'May your Christmas be Happy'. $9 £5

Happy Birthday, 1957, Emmett artwork. $1 50p

'Christmas Greetings, Come what may', 1940. $2.50 £1.50

The first Christmas card sent to Henry Cole by William Makepeace Thakeray. (Phillips) $4,775 £2,500

'Like merry robin redbreasts, we ring our roundelay'. $2.50 £1.50

CARLTON WARE

The name Carlton Ware was given to pottery produced by Wiltshaw and Robinson of Stoke on Trent from 1890 till 1957. After that date the firm was renamed Carlton Ware Ltd. The firm's usual mark is a circle enclosing a swallow and topped by a crown and some pieces are marked Carlton Ware. The most popular lines were porcelain vases decorated with bright enamelling and gilded decorations in flower or fan motifs often on black backgrounds which were turned out in large numbers in the 1920's. The firm also made pieces in Art Deco styles with designs of lustrous trees in unusual colours or decorated with Kate Greenaway style fairies, mythical birds or chinoiserie designs.

Carlton Ware
Handpainted
MADE IN ENGLAND
"TRADE MARK"

Carlton Ware
ENGLAND

Oviform vase with dark grey ground simulating nightfall, signed by E. F. Paul, with Kate Greenaway style fairies design, 230mm. high. (Goss & Crested China) $950 £550

Carlton Ware lustre jug with gilt loop handle, the body painted and gilded with stylised floral and fan decoration, 5in. high. (Prudential Fine Art) $189 £115

A Carlton Ware ginger jar and cover, the oviform body painted with clusters of stylised flowerheads, 10¾in. high. (Christie's) $801 £495

A Carltonware plaque painted in gilt, orange, blue, green and white with wisteria and exotic plants, 15½in. diam. (Christie's) $308 £200

A Carlton Ware service decorated in polychrome enamels, coffee pot 20.4cm. high. (Christie's) $1,174 £810

Vibrant lustrous red 'Rouge Royale' leaf, one of a series introduced after 1930, 220mm. long. (Goss & Crested China) $18 £10

CARTES DE VISITE

The carte de visite consisted of a small portrait, usually full length but occasionally only head and shoulders, measuring about two and a half by three and a half inches and mounted on a visiting card. It was first mentioned in the French magazine "La Lumiere" in 1854 which said it had been invented by two anonymous Frenchmen but the idea was patented by the photographer Disderi who promoted the cards with the public and sold so many that he is reputed to have earned as much as £50,000 a year. It soon became the fashion to have one's portrait on a carte de visite and society photographers did a roaring trade turning them out. Everyone who was anyone in society wanted a carte de visite and even the Princess of Wales sat for a photographer called W. Downey in 1867. The card with her likeness sold 300,000 copies. Photographers to look out for include Downey and Disderi; C. Silvy who had a sophisticated clientele in London; Saroni and Claudet.

Study of three Welsh ladies taking tea, circa 1880, by Charles Allen Photographic Artist, Tenby and Haverford West.
$7 £4

Envelope containing two cartes de visite posted from David Rees, Clapham Road, London, Certified Artist and Photographer — Prize Medal Awarded, 1872, bearing penny red stamp.
$9 £5

Full length portrait study of a girl by M. Boak, Driffield and Pickering. 'This portrait can be enlarged to life size', on reverse.
$3.50 £2

Portrait study of a bearded gentleman by W. J. Welsted and Son, 'Photographers of the Prince and Princess of Wales'.
$2 £1

Pair of cartes 'Joy' and 'Sorrow', Girl holding Punch puppet, by 'Dicksee', circa 1877.
$7 £4

Portrait study of lady, circa 1880, by J. R. Dowdall, Great Western Studio, Swansea.
$2 £1

CARTES DE VISITE

A fine portrait study of the Duke of Edinburgh. $10 £6

Australian carte de visite portrait study of a man in a bowler hat by A. Lomer and Co., Brisbane. $2 £1

H.R.H. The Prince of Wales, later Edward VII. $12 £7

A fine portrait study of Queen Victoria in the 1890's. $9 £5

Portrait study of a country gentleman, with a typical pictorial reverse back, by M. Boak, Bridlington. $3.50 £2

'Fun' type carte de visite of Matrimony and Courtship by Perry and Co., London. $14 £8

His Grace the Archbishop of Canterbury, Dr Tait, by the London Stereoscopic and Photographic Co. (Prize medal for portraiture Vienna Exhibition 1873.) $10 £6

Twelve views of Shrewsbury, circa 1893. $20 £12

Portrait study of The Duke of Connaught. $9 £5

(Border Bygones)

CARTRIDGES

The eight-track stereo cartridge system reached its popularity peak in the mid 60's. It was especially popular in the States as an in-car entertainment medium, and tapes and equipment were manufactured by most of the major companies.

The system differs from the cassette in that instead of the tape feeding between two spools, the eight-track works on an endless loop system from a single spool. This made it popular in pubs and clubs here for its continuous play capabilities.

Eight-track systems were superseded as the quality of the neater cassette improved. However, they are fast becoming collector's items, especially as much otherwise unobtainable material can be found on them. Players can still be found cheaply, and are easily adaptable to modern hi-fi systems via tape inputs, or, in the case of mobile units, by using a standard CB 12v power supply to run them.

The Beatles, 'Abbey Road', EMI Records. $9 £5

The Rolling Stones, 'Black and Blue', WEA Records. $9 £5

Mike Oldfield, 'Hergest Ridge', Virgin Records. $7 £4

Pink Floyd, 'Dark Side of the Moon', EMI Records. $9 £5

John Lennon, 'Rock 'n' Roll', EMI Records. $18 £10

Deep Purple, 'Come taste the band', EMI Records. $5 £3

(Border Bygones)

CHAMBER POTS

The "po", a name which derived from the French 'pot de chambre' was an essential in bedrooms in the days before modern plumbing. They were usually part of a set consisting of a jug, a basin, slop pail and soap dish and these ranged from coarse pottery to lovely porcelain. Chamber pots have even been made from silver and gold. Every major pottery company made those sets and they can be found by Wemyss Ware, Masons Ironstone, Wedgwood pottery or even from Limoges, decorated with elegant painting and gilding. Some chamber pots were vulgarly crude in their designs, bearing rude inscriptions and pictures inside. Some held a crouching pottery frog within the bowl while others were decorated with the face of Napoleon or a watching eye.

A blue and white chamber pot painted with peony and bamboo issuing from rock-work, circa 1750, 18.5cm. diam. (Christie's)
$2,293 £1,489

A late Victorian chamber pot, with a scroll handle. (Woolley & Wallis) $619 £480

An English china chamber pot by Brown-Westhead, Moore & Co., circa 1870, with polychrome rhododendron decoration on cream ground.
$80 £45

20th century white enamel chamber pot with blue rim.
$9 £5

Sunderland lustre pottery chamber pot with an applied frog and cartoon face in the interior.
$700 £400

One of two chamber pots, circa 1750, 15.5cm. wide, 12.5cm. diam. (Christie's)
$3,754 £2,438

A Royal Doulton Aubrey chamber pot decorated with Art Nouveau designs. $85 £50

Staffordshire floral china chamber pot. $70 £40

Early 19th century pewter chamber pot. $175 £100

CHARACTER JUGS

The firm of Doulton started producing character jugs in the 1930's and continue to do so today. They have been modelled by a succession of skilful artists and often depict famous characters from history or legend. For example it is possible to buy a character jug of Anne Boleyn and another of her husband Henry VIII. Character jugs were made of famous actresses like Mae West and of actors like W.C. Fields. There's a character jug of William Shakespeare as well as many of the characters he created. The great Doulton designer Charles Noke was responsible for many jugs including a masterly Touchstone first issued in 1936. Some character jugs can be bought for around £60 but anyone who finds one of Sir Francis Drake without a hat has a jug worth £2000. A clown with red triangles on his cheeks is worth £1250 and an uncoloured jug featuring Sir Winston Churchill which was produced in 1940 but withdrawn because, it is said, the great man didn't like it, is worth at least £5000.

RONALD REAGAN D6718
Designer: E. Griffiths
Size: Large
Issued: 1984
Price: $375 £250

CHURCHILL (White) D6170
Designer: C. Noke
Size: Large
Issued: 1940-1941
Price: $7500 £5000

CLARK GABLE D6709
Designer: S. Taylor
Size: Large
Issued: 1984-
Price: $3300 £2200

SIMON THE CELLARER D5504
Designer: C. Noke and
           H. Fenton
Size: Large
Issued: 1935-1960
Price: $90 £60

OLD CHARLEY D5420
Designer: C. Noke
Size: Large
Issued: 1934-1983
Price: $52 £35

GRANNY (Toothless version) D5521
Designer: H. Fenton &
           M. Henk
Size: Large
Issued: 1935
Price: $675 £450

APOTHECARY D6567
Designer: M. Henk
Size: Large
Issued: 1963-1983
Price: $57 £38

GONDOLIER D6589
Designer: D. Biggs
Size: Large
Issued: 1964-1969
Price: $300 £200

DRAKE D6115
Designer: H. Fenton
Size: Large (Hatless)
Issued: 1940-1941
Price: $3000 £2000

JOHN BARLEYCORN D5327
Designer: C. Noke
Size: Large
Issued: 1934-1960
Price: $90 £60

MAE WEST D6688
Designer: C. Davidson
Size: Large
Issued: 1983-1985
Price: $52 £35

SMUTS D6198
Designer: H. Fenton
Size: Large
Issued: 1946-c.1948
Price: $1020 £680

JIMMY DURANTE D6708
Designer: D. Biggs
Size: Large
Issued: 1985-1986
Price: $52 £35

MEPHISTOPHELES D5757
Designer: H. Fenton
Size: Large
Issued: 1937-1948
Price: $1350 £900

JOCKEY D6625
Designer: D. Biggs
Size: Large
Issued: 1971-1975
Price: $225 £170

VETERAN MOTORIST D6633
Designer: D. Biggs
Size: Large
Issued: 1973-1983
Price: $57 £38

'ARRIET D6208
Designer: H. Fenton
Size: Large
Issued: 1947-1960
Price: $150 £100

'ARD OF EARING D6588
Designer: D. Biggs
Size: Large
Issued: 1964-1967
Price: $675 £450

PARSON BROWN D5486
Designer: C. Noke
Size: Large
Issued: 1935-1960
Price: $90 £60

CLOWN D5610
Designer: H. Fenton
Size: Large (Red Haired)
Issued: 1937-1942
Price: $1875 £1250

MIKADO D6501
Designer: M. Henk
Size: Large
Issued: 1959-1969
Price: $285 £190

LORD NELSON D6336
Designer: G. Blower
Size: Large
Issued: 1952-1969
Price: $240 £160

SIMPLE SIMON D6374
Designer: G. Blower
Size: Large
Issued: 1953-1960
Price: $390 £260

MAORI
Designer: Unknown
Size: Large
Issued: c.1939
Price: $11250 £7500

CHARITY BOXES

Charity boxes have been used for collecting from the public since the mid 19th century. The Church Missionary Society was one of the first organisations to use the boxes which were given the nickname "Poor Boxes" in the 1880's because they were used for collecting for the poor and needy. Some boxes had long handles so that they could be thrust into a crowd and no one donor would be missed out. During the First World War the use of charity boxes became more widespread because collecting for war funds was at its peak and they continue to be used today. The R.S.P.C.A.'s box in the shape of a lifesize dog is very popular. Charity boxes can be found in a variety of materials from tin to papier mâché and also in a wide range of shapes. There are Sooty, Noddy and Basil Brush charity boxes but the rarest include the one used by the Lifeboat Society. When a penny was put in its slot a lifeboat could be seen sliding down a ramp.

Guide Dogs for the Blind charity box. $130 £75

The Spastics Society, 'Helping people with cerebral palsy in your area'. $125 £70

An R.S.P.C.A. papier mache 'Puppy' charity box. $60 £35

World Wildlife Fund, Panda with baby. $80 £45

Composition R.S.P.C.A. charity box, 2ft.6in. high. $130 £75

Basil Brush says 'Please help the blind, boom! boom!' $90 £50

CHEESE DISHES

In the days before health scares about food, milk, butter and cheese were bought from the town dairy where there was often a cow tethered in the back and the cheese was cut with a cheese wire off a huge slab that lay on the marble counter. There were all sorts of pieces of equipment and domestic ware associated with the preparing and keeping of dairy products – butter moulds, paddles for making butter balls, lidded dishes, strainers and particularly cheese dishes which range in size from small ones for a special little titbit of cheese to huge ones big enough to accommodate an entire Stilton. Those which were going to be presented on the dining table were often beautifully painted, and the blue and white ones are especially attractive to collectors, but the ones that were used for storing cheese in the kitchen were made of fine china and plain white, in order to give a feeling of cleanliness and freshness perhaps.

A majolica glazed Stilton cheese dish and cover, probably by George Jones & Sons, late 19th century. (G. A. Key) $140 £85

Stilton cheese dish and cover in the style of Wedgwood, circa 1900, 12in. high. (Lots Road Galleries) $160 £100

A George Jones 'majolica' circular cheese dish and cover, circa 1880, 28cm. diam. (Christie's) $577 £330

Wilkinson Ltd. 'bizarre' cheese dish and cover, 1930. $130 £75

Shelley rectangular shaped cheese dish with matching handled cover 'Cloisello ware', 8in. long. (Giles Haywood) $106 £65

Staffordshire pottery cheese dish with floral decoration. $25 £15

A Minton majolica cheese dish and cover with reclining bull finial, 29cm. high. (Christie's) $1,285 £770

A Cheese dish in the form of a bull's head. (Worsfolds) $184 £110

A George Jones majolica cheese dome and stand. (Dreweatts) $604 £360

91

CHEQUES & BILLS OF EXCHANGE

Banks as we know them today began in Venice in the 16th century but the Bank of England was not founded until the beginning of the 18th century. Many other banks large and small, sprang up all over the country in the succeeding years but failures and crises eliminated many of them and in 1927, there were ten major clearing banks in Britain, all of them dealing with cheques. That is why there is plenty of scope for would-be collectors of old cheques and bills of exchange. It is a field that should attract anyone wanting to get in on the ground floor. Cheques and bills of exchange are still quite cheap and it is best to pick a theme, a particular bank, or group of banks in a special local area. Some old cheques are exceptionally attractive and well printed with fine Victorian script.

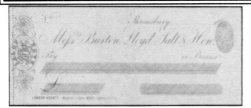

Burton, Lloyd, Salt & How, unused cheque from the 1870's. $9 £5

Eyton, Burton & Co., Shrewsbury, 1901, one of the last of the private Country banks. $7 £4

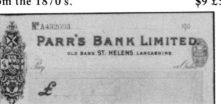

Parrs Bank Ltd., St. Helens, unused cheque of 1904. $5 £3

Grant, Gillman & Long, small branch or agency at Gosport from 1880. $9 £5

Gurneys & Turners, Bungay, famous banking group which became part of Barclay in 1896. This cheque dated 1811. $25 £15

Cooper & Purton, Bridgnorth, 1849, an example of one of the many private banks that failed during the last century. $14 £8

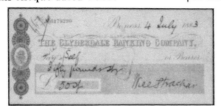

Clydesdale Banking Company, 1883, with overprint of new bank name, Clydesdale Bank Limited, when it was re-registered under Limited liability laws. $7 £4

Birmingham, Town & District Banking Company, 1870's, with Town replaced by Dudley on amalgamation with a competitor, this cheque also unusual as it sports a fine vignette of the bank building. $14 £8

(M. Veissid & Co.)

When buying children's books it is important to remember that condition is of paramount importance. A child's book in pristine condition is hard to find and when they do turn up, they are invariably expensive. The earliest children's hornbooks or chapbooks are usually bought for high prices by libraries or museums and ordinary collectors stick to more recent books, sometimes specialising in those they read themselves when children. The nostalgia factor plays a large part in this collecting field.

Illustrated books are the most highly prized and those with plates by artists like Arthur Rackham, Kay Neilsen, E.H. Detmold or Jessie M. King are always eagerly sought after. There are artists whose work sells a book — Edward Lear for example, but also Cruikshank, Tenniel and Ernest Shepherd who illustrated A.A. Milne's Winnie the Pooh books. Arthur Lang's fairy tale books make good prices if they are illustrated by Austen Dobson, Linley Sanbourne, Kate Greenaway, T. Bowick or Randolph Caldecott.

Another good selling point is an attractive cover, especially for Victorian children's books which tend to be on the stuffy, righteous side as far as content is concerned. The colourful covers of Henty's adventure stories however are more refreshing. Some collectors tend to buy all the books by one author or about a special character. For example Arthur Ransome's books or Richmal Crompton's William books. A battered "William" second edition might change hands at £1 while a first edition with its dust cover will cost £20. Alphabet books, Mabel Lucie Attwell books; the novels of Enid Blyton, W.E. Johns, creator of Biggles; and Frank Richards who dreamed up Bunter of Greyfriars are also highly prized.

Hans Anderson's Fairy Tales — ill. Harry Clarke. $9 £5

The Children's Treasury. $9 $5

Grand Jubilee Volume of Little Folks 1921. $18 £10

Gulliver's Travels — ill. John Hassall. $25 £15

Infants Magazine 1903. $20 £12

Blackie's Girls' Annual 1930. $12 £7

(Lynn Private Collection, Tyne & Wear)

93

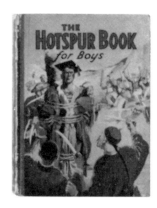

Child's Companion Annual 1934. $18 £10

Cassell's Children's Annual 1920 — illustrations include Anne Anderson, Harry Rountree and C. E. Brock. $25 £15

Hotspur Book for Boys 1937. $20 £12

Blackie's Granny's Old Stories — ill. Hassall 1939. $25 £15

Modern Boy's Book of True Adventure. $18 £10

Aldine Robin Hood Library. $2 £1

Blackie's Children's Annual 1922 — illustrations include Honor Appleton, H. M. Brock, Ruth Cobb, A. E. Jackson. $25 £15

Madge Williams Children's Annual. $12 £7

The Jolly Book 1919. $25 £15

(Lynn Private Collection, Tyne & Wear)

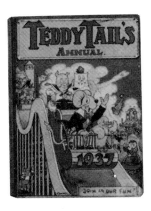

Teddy Tail's Annual 1937. $20 £12

Peek-a-Boo Japs — ill. Chloe Preston 1916. $35 £20

School Girl's Annual volume 3. $15 £10

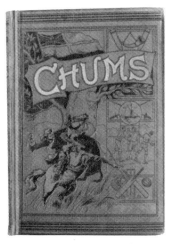

Les Vacances de Nane 1924. — ill. Henry Morin. $14 £8

Chums Volume 1, 1892. $70 £40

Noah's Ark Annual 1935. $14 £8

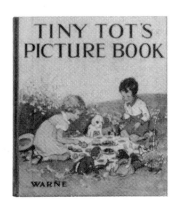

Pets and Playmates. $20 £12

Tiny Tot's Picture Book 1934 — 80 pages of pictures including Rountree, Beaman and Gordon Robinson. $25 £15

Make Believe Story Book 1924. $35 £20

(Lynn Private Collection, Tyne & Wear)

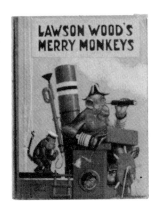

Lawson Wood's Merry Monkeys. $20 £12

Master Charlie 1899. $25 £15

Nister's Holiday Annual. $45 £25

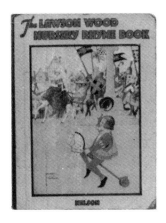

Lawson Wood Nursery Rhyme Book. $20 £12

The Bunty Book — published by G. Heath Robinson & J. Birch Ltd. Illustrations include Louis Wain and Gordon Browne. $45 £25

Sunbeam Annual 1933. $20 £12

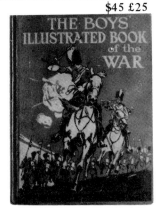

Musical Box Annual. $12 £7

Boys Illustrated Book of the War 1917. $14 £8

Cicely Mary Barker's Flower Fairy Picture Book. 40 illustrations. $14 £8

(Lynn Private Collection, Tyne & Wear)

96

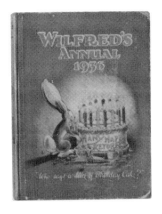

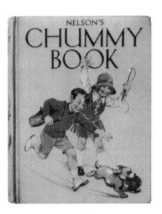

Wilfred's Annual 1936. $20 £12 Sunbeam's Picture Book 1926. Nelson's Chummy Book 1933.
$9 £5 $25 £14

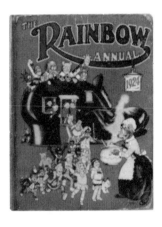

Rainbow Annual 1924. $25 £15 Adventure Land 1938. $20 £12 Book of Great Adventurers.
$14 £8

Children's Stories from the
Poets 1940 — ill. Frank Adams.
$20 £12

Mrs Strang's Annual for Child- The Prize for Boys and Girls
ren 1914. $35 £20 Volume 66. $12 £7

(Lynn Private Collection, Tyne & Wear)

CHINA

China is a truly enormous subject, and countless books have been written on every type and aspect of it. Porcelain was introduced into Europe from China in the 16th century and became an instant collectable for moneyed classes. The secrets of its manufacture were discovered in France and Germany in the early 18th century, and during the next few decades the Sevres, Meissen and Dresden factories produced most of the cabinet ware of the period. England at this time lacked the ingredients and skills for making fine porcelain, and it was not until the 19th century that such factories as Worcester, Swansea and Derby began manufacturing in any quantities.

During the Victorian times, fine porcelain became affordable for the middle classes also, and its popularity has persisted to the present day.

A model of a roistering Dutchman astride a Dutch gin cask, 37.5cm. high. (Christie's)
$52,360 £30,800

A Frankenthal group of chess players modelled by J. F. Luck, blue crowned Carl Theodor mark, circa 1765, 17cm. high. (Christie's)
$11,583 £7,150

A Whieldon tortoiseshell coffee pot and cover, of baluster shape with domed cover, circa 1760. (Phillips)
$8,010 £4,500

A Berlin two-handled campana vase painted in the neo-classical taste, 1803-1810, 45cm. high. (Christie's) $13,365 £8,250

Coloured Parian bust of The Beautiful Duchess, who was Georgiana, Duchess of Devonshire. (Goss & Crested China Ltd.) $2,250 £1,250

A Wedgwood solid pale-blue and white jasper cylindrical sugar bowl and cover, circa 1785, 10.5cm. diam. (Christie's) $673 £385

A stoneware 'spade-form' vase by Hans Coper, circa 1972, 23.4cm. high. (Christie's)
$16,720 £10,450

One of a pair of Yorkshire models of cows, one with a gardener, the other with a woman, 14.5cm. long. (Phillips) $4,676 £2,800

A Ralph Wood Vicar and Moses group, circa 1780, 24.5cm. high. (Christie's) $866 £495

A Bow spirally moulded cane handle of tapering form, circa 1750, 5.5cm. high. (Christie's) $1,942 £1,110

A Derby baluster jug, painted by Richard Dodson, 17cm. high, crown, crossed batons and D mark in red. (Phillips) $2,865 £1,500

A Maw & Co. pottery vase, the body painted in a ruby red lustre with large flowers and foliage all on a yellow ground, 13in. high. (Christie's) $644 £352

A Doulton Lambeth style stoneware conservatory planter in the form of a weathered tree trunk. (Locke & England) $978 £600

A Minton white and celadon glazed centrepiece modelled as three putti holding a basket, circa 1868, 26cm. high. (Christie's) $731 £418

A glazed ceramic grotesque face jug, by H. B. Craig, N. Carolina, ovoid with two applied strap handles, 16½in. high. (Christie's) $330 £186

A Chelsea group of two children, naked except for a white and gold drapery, seated on a rocky mound, 17.5cm. high. (Lawrence Fine Art)
$1,539 £950

Late 17th century large Arita blue and white baluster vase and cover, 47cm. high. (Christie's) $8,800 £5,500

A pair of Derby figures of a sailor and his lass, Wm. Duesbury & Co., circa 1765, approx. 24cm. high. (Christie's) $1,996 £1,210

An Urbino maiolica wet drug or syrup jar, workshop of Orazio Fontana, 1565-70, 34cm. high. (Phillips) $22,920 £12,000

Pair of Royal Dux figurines, signed F. Otto, pink triangle to base, 17in. high. (Giles Haywood) $574 £350

A Rookwood pottery standard glaze portrait vase, decorated with portrait of a black African with a cap, 1897, 12in. high. (Robt. W. Skinner Inc.) $2,500 £1,351

A 19th century Liverpool transfer-printed pitcher of baluster form with pulled spout and applied C-scroll handle. (Christie's) $1,100 £665

A large Meissen group of Count Bruhl's tailor on a goat, blue crossed swords and incised numeral marks, circa 1880, 43cm. high. (Christie's) $4,041 £2,420

A Jervis Art pottery motto mug, 1906, 5¾in. high, 4in. diam. (Robt. W. Skinner Inc.) $200 £119

A Minton majolica-ware Neptune shell dish, 17cm. high, impressed Minton, shape no. 903 and date code for 1861. (Phillips) $462 £280

A pair of pearlware figures of Mansion House dwarfs, their costumes in shades of yellow, brick-red, lime-green and brown, 16cm. and 16.5cm. high. (Phillips) $1,375 £720

Royal Worcester Hadley-style footed vase, designed as a jardiniere, 1906, 5in. high. (Giles Haywood) $458 £240

A Pilkington Lancastrian pottery vase by Richard Joyce, impressed Bee mark and date code for 1909, 11¾in. high. (Christie's) $1,006 £550

A Linthorpe earthenware vase moulded on each side with grotesque fish faces, 17.9cm. high. (Christie's) $589 £385

A pearlware puzzle jug, the serpent handle with three spouts, circa 1820, 29cm. high. (Christie's) $689 £418

Shaped Canton shrimp dish, 19th century, typical Canton scene, diam. 10¼in. (Robt. W. Skinner Inc.) $275 £171

A mid 19th century Japanese Imari goldfish bowl. (Miller & Co.) $787 £440

Late 19th century German porcelain table centrepiece, underglazed blue 'R' mark, 11½in. high. (Peter Wilson) $704 £400

CHRISTMAS ORNAMENTS

The trappings of Christmas as we know them became popular in the Victorian period — everyone knows how Prince Albert introduced the Christmas tree to Britain, and such items as crackers (or bon-bons as they were known, because they always contained sweets) already have a devoted following of collectors. Early ornaments were produced by leading china factories such as Dresden, and were really exquisite — a far cry from the mass-produced baubles on sale today.

Late 19th century Dresden Christmas ornament, white poodle with red silk ribbon, 3¼in. long. (Robt. W. Skinner Inc.)
$280 £160

Late 19th century Dresden Christmas ornament of a three-masted ship, 4½in. high, 4.7/8in. long. (Robt. W. Skinner Inc.) $ 235 £135

Late 19th century Dresden Christmas ornament of a silver champagne bottle candy container, 3.5/16in. high. (Robt. W. Skinner Inc.) $130 £75

Late 19th century Dresden Christmas ornament of a rooster, brown wash over gold, 3.1/8in. high. (Robt. W. Skinner Inc.) $175 £100

Late 19th century Dresden Christmas ornament of a sitting silver retriever, 2¾in. high. (Robt. W. Skinner Inc.) $400 £225

Late 19th century Dresden Christmas ornament of a gold and rose iridescent cockatoo in a hoop, 3.3/8in. high. (Robt. W. Skinner Inc.) $230 £130

Late 19th century Dresden Christmas ornament of a silver three-quarter flat jockey on horse, 2in. high. (Robt. W. Skinner Inc.) $210 £120

A Hagenauer chromium-plated stylised figure of a polar bear, 20cm. long. (Christie's)
$1,301   £770

An Austrian chromium-plated ashtray and matchbox-holder, the circular tray with vertical sides and pierced grid decoration, 21cm. wide. (Christie's)
$523   £308

A Hagenauer wood and chromium plated figure of a cockerel on a round metal base, stamped marks wHw, Austria, 44.6cm. high. (Christie's)
$836   £495

A large Art Deco white metal and bakelite urn, the flared form on four disc-shaped feet, 27.5cm. high. (Christie's)
$1,115   £660

A Hagenauer carved wood and chromium plated bust of a woman in profile, 12½in. high. (Christie's)
$1,344 £880

A Hagenauer figure of a javelin thrower, the stylised male figure with a javelin in hand, stamped marks wHw, Franz Hagenauer, Wien, Made in Austria 1218, 31.6cm. high. (Christie's)
$1,159   £682

A Ronson 'Touch-Tip' petrol-fuelled table-lighter, shaped as a bar with a negro barman, partially chromium-plated and enamel painted, circa 1935, 15.3cm. long. (Christie's)
$836   £495

CIGARETTE CARDS

Cigarette cards were first used as stiffeners in packages of cigarettes in the days before slide packets. They probably made their first appearance in the 1860's in the United States. The oldest card known to exist is in the Metropolitan Museum in New York and dates from 1878. W.D. & H.O. Wills were the first British firm to give away cards with their cigarettes in 1885. Between then and the end of the Second World War more than 5,000 sets of cards were produced and they range over every aspect of life as their theme. Royalty, railway trains , wild flowers and footballers, film stars and circus clowns, gardening and how to swim all made their appearance on cigarette cards.

The earliest cards had blank reverses or were used as advertising space but towards the end of the 19th century, informative text began to fill the empty space. The golden age of the cigarette card is from the last decade of the 19th century until about 1910. In the main the cards and their information was extremely accurate and they have been used by film companies researching period backgrounds. The texts are regarded as some of the best examples of pared down prose.

TADDY'S CLOWN

When the production of cigarette cards began to dwindle from 1950 onwards, the collecting mania began and today a set of Taddy's "Clowns and Circus Artistes" cards featuring circus clowns are the "penny blacks" of the card world. A set of them has been sold for over £15,000. As in the case of all paper items and ephemera, condition is very important. Thumbed and bent edged cards will sell for much less than those in good condition.

Hignetts Pilot Cigarettes, 'Cabinet' 1900, set of 20. $1,750 £1,000

Ogden's, 'Owners racing colours and jockeys' 1906, set of 50.
$130 £75

Players, 'Gallery of Beauty Series' 1896, 50 in set. $1,500 £875

British American Tobacco Co. Ltd., 'Butterflies' 1928, set of 50.
$125 £70

Salmon and Gluckstein, 'Wireless Explained' 1923, set of 25.
$110 £65

W. A. Churchman, 'Sporting Celebrities' 1931, set of 50. $90 £50

(Border Bygones)

Ogden's, 'Soldiers of the King' 1909, set of 50. $260 £150

Rothmans Ltd., 'Beauties of the Cinema' 1939, set of 24. $60 £35

Woods Purple Heather Cigarettes, 'Yeomanry' 1902, set of 25. $700 £400

Wills Scissors Cigarettes, 'Drum Horses' 1909, set of 32. $300 £175

Carreras, 'Alice in Wonderland' 1930, set of 48. $35 £20

Nicolas Sarony & Co., 'Origin of Games' 1923, set of 15. $45 £25

Ogdens, 'Flags and Funnels' 1906, set of 50. $225 £125

Wills, 'Famous British Authors' 1937, set of 40. $25 £15

Ardath Tobacco Co., 'Film, Stage & Radio Stars', 1935, set of 50. $35 £20

(Border Bygones)

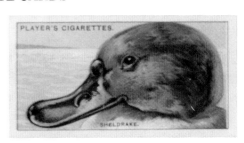

Wills, 'Borough Arms' 1906, set of 50.
$30 £18

Players, 'Curious Beaks' 1929, set of 50.
$12 £7

Players, 'Poultry' 1931, set of 50. $30 £16

Wills, 'Do you know', 2nd Series 1924, set of 50. $10 £6

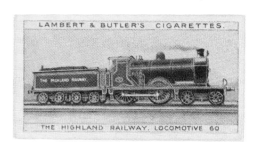

Ardath Ltd., 'Stamps' 1939, set of 50.
$60 £35

Lambert & Butler 'World Locomotives' 1912, set of 50. $260 £150

Wills 'Speed' 1930, set of 50. $50 £30

Wills, 'Household Hints' 1927, set of 50.
$10 £6

(Border Bygones)

Wills 'Military Motors' 1916, set of 50.
$55 £30

Wills, 'Historic Events' 1912, set of 50.
$55 £30

Players, 'Racehorses' 1926, set of 25.
$100 £60

Players, 'Everyday Phrases' 1900, set of 25.
$550 £300

Lambert & Butler, 'Motor Cars' 1922, set of 25.
$60 £35

Players, 'Drum Banners and Cap Badges' 1924, set of 50.
$35 £20

Bognal Tobacco Co., 'Luminous Silhouettes' 1938, set of 25.
$45 £25

Wills, 'Overseas Dominions', Australia 1915, set of 50.
$35 £20

(Border Bygones)

CIGARETTE CARDS

Cohen Weenen Co., 'Famous Boxers' 1912, set of 25. $260 £150

Stephen Mitchell & Son, 'Village Models' 1925, set of 25. $90 £50

W. A. Churchman, 'Wonderful Railway Travel' 1937, set of 50. $14 £8

Forcasta 'Racing Greyhounds' 1939, set of 25. $18 £10

Wills, 'Old Furniture' 1923, set of 25. $60 £35

Salmon & Gluckstein, 'Army and Navy Traditions' 1917, 25 in set. $260 £150

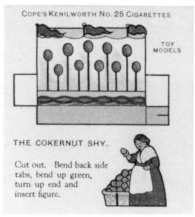

Ardath Ltd., 'Famous Film Stars' 1935, set of 50. $35 £20

Copes, 'Toy Models' 1925, set of 25. $7 £4

Hignetts, 'Modern Statesmen' 1906, set of 25. $160 £90

(Border Bygones)

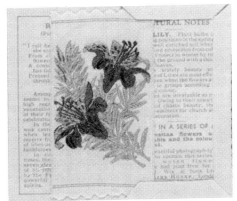

Taddys, 'Royalty Series' 1903, set of 25. $525 £300

J. Wix & Son Ltd., 'Kensitas Flowers' 1933, set of 60.
$160 £90

B. Morris & Sons, 'Golf Strokes' 1923, set of 25. $70 £40

Morris & Sons, 'Measurement of Time' 1924, set of 25.
$26 £15

Sunstripe Cigarettes, 'Wireless Telephony' 1923, set of 20. $55 £32

Ogden's, 'Football Caricatures' 1935, set of 50. $70 £40

Carreras, 'Birds' 1939, set of 50. $26 £15

Wills, 'Old Silver' 1924, set of 25. $60 £35

Hignett Bros., 'Dogs' 1936, set of 50. $55 £30

(Border Bygones)

CIGARETTE LIGHTERS

Cigarette lighters first made their appearance about 1900 and the most widely collected are those made by Dunhill some of which are highly decorative objects in the form of hunting horns or dancing maidens. Lighters made before 1920 worked on the flint principle and a well known maker was Orlik. In the 1920's table lighters became popular — some of them working by flint as well. They can be found incorporated in figures of birds or dancers. Others had a torch drawn from a fuel tank and struck on a strip of cerium to produce a flame. Wheeled pocket lighters made by Dunhill became popular in the 1930's and they were also made by Howitt, Parker Beacon, Polo, Thorens Oriflame, Imco and Beney. During both World Wars servicemen turned out lighters from scraps of shell or bullet cases and battered out coins. These lighters, known as Trench Art, sell today for between £5 and £25 each. Lighters are a good area for investment because they can still be found at reasonable cost.

A Dunhill electroplated table lighter, stamped Made in England, patent no. 143752, 9cm. high. (Christie's) $179 £110

Dunhill tinder pistol table lighter, 1934. $350 £200

A Dunhill white metal and enamelled watch lighter, 4.5cm. high. (Christie's) $717 £440

1920's plated metal table lighter in the form of a dancing nude. $85 £50

Chromium plated table lighter in the form of an aeroplane. $130 £75

A large 1930's gilt plaster table lighter. $260 £150

CIGARETTE PACKETS

Cigarettes began being sold in Britain in 1851. Initially they were sold in wrappers, but soon after, the cigarette packet was developed and since trade marks were first registered in 1876 over 30,000 different brands have appeared.

The hull and side packet came into use around 1890, and the flip-top, though it was invented in the USA in 1927, was not introduced into Britain until 1956, when it was first used for Churchman's No. 1. The collecting of cigarette packets is a fairly recent enthusiasm but there is infinite potential for exploration, and finds range from pretty Passing Clouds packets to the striking red packaging used for Du Maurier.

Many collectors specialise in themes, for example sports, or maritime, or perhaps restrict themselves to Players or Wills items only. Flip top or crushproof packs, mainly from the pre-Health Warning era, are also collected, while soft packs seem more popular with overseas collectors.

Foreign packs do not seem to be widely collected here, though there are many which are attractive, for example pre-1900 American packs, which have a lot of appeal.

Condition plays an important part in assessing the value of cigarette packets, and if they come complete with cigarettes this also attracts a premium.

Ogden's packet of 10 Robin cigarettes, circa 1920. $3.50 £2

The original Player's Weights, Made from pure Virginia Tobacco, packet of 10, circa 1920. $2 £1

Premier's packet of 10 Navy Cut medium cigarettes, made in England, circa 1930. $5 £3

Gunboat high class Virginia cigarettes, Lambert & Butler, England, circa 1920. $5 £3

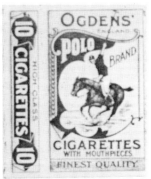

Polo brand, 10 packet Ogdens' finest quality cigarettes with mouth-pieces, circa 1915. $7 £4

Beechwood, packet of 10 cigarettes, C.W.S. Ltd., Manchester, circa 1930. $5 £3

The Clown Cigarettes, packet of 10, Ardath, circa 1915. **$9 £5**

Kits, packet of 20 cigarettes, W. Williams & Co. Chester, circa 1915. **$20 £12**

John Player & Sons, Anchor packet of 10 Virginia tipped cigarettes, circa 1958. **$3.50 £2**

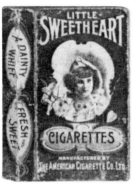  

Little Sweetheart cigarettes — A dainty whiff, fresh and sweet — manufactured by The American Cigarette Co. Ltd., circa 1900. **$26 £15**

Campaign '88, Bush for President, soft pack, 20 cigarettes, circa 1988. **$1 £0.50**

A. & M. Wix packet of Clock cigarettes, manufactured in England, circa 1930. **$5 £3**

  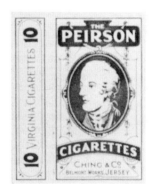

Air Mail, packet of 10 Golden Honeydew cigarettes, R. & J. Hill, circa 1925. **$5 £3**

Dandy Fifth cigarettes, 'We called them the Kid Gloves Dandy Fifth', packet of 10, Salmon & Gluckstein Ltd — Ever cigarette bears our name as a guarantee of quality — circa 1900. **$26 £15**

The Peirson Cigarettes, packet of 10, Ching & Co., Belmont Works, Jersey, circa 1915. **$7 £4**

Hignett's Golden Butterfly, 10 finest quality cigarettes, circa 1920. $5 £3

Twin Screw, special straight cut Virginia cigarettes, Thémens, circa 1915. $9 £5

United Service cigarettes, packet of 10, W. D. & H. O. Wills, Bristol & London, circa 1910. $18 £10

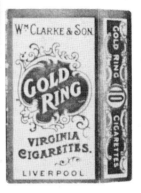

Darts, packet of 5, Gallaher Ltd., Virginia House, London & Belfast, circa 1930. $3.50 £2

Sweethearts cigarettes, tipped with Papier Ambre, Do not stick to lips, Salmon & Gluckstein Ltd., Largest tobacconists in the world, circa 1904. $20 £12

Gold Ring, packet of 10 Virginia cigarettes, Wm. Clarke & Son, Liverpool, circa 1900. $20 £12

Motor cigarettes, W. D. & H. O. Wills, Bristol & London, circa 1920. $10 £6

Russian Lauka, (first dog in space), 20 cigarettes. $1 £0.50

Rugger cigarettes, packet of 10, The United Tobacco Companies (South) Ltd., Cape Town, circa 1920. $9 £5

CLARICE CLIFF

The woman who set the style for the crockery of the 1920's and 30's was Clarice Cliff who began work as a painter at A.J. Wilkinson Ltd and went on to become art director at the Royal Staffordshire Pottery and Newport Pottery. Her work is distinguished by brilliant colour and clean lines. The pottery she painted in vibrant combinations of yellow, orange, red, purple, green and blue, was cheap and cheerful and was sold at Woolworths as well as at more prestigious stores. She had a refreshing way of combining avant garde styles with old fashioned almost childish themes − cottages tucked away on hillsides with smoke rising from their chimneys for example. The crockery she painted with crocuses brought life and colour to many a kitchen. Clarice Cliff was an innovator and her self portrait plaque and the designs she made inspired by Diaghilev's Ballet Russe which made its debut in London in the 1920's , now fetch high prices. Her most collected patterns are Bizarre, Crocus and Fantasque.

A Clarice Cliff 'Isis' shaped vase, painted with a central frieze of stylised leaves, 24.6cm. high. (Phillips) $1,169   £680

A Clarice Cliff Bizarre cubist breakfast set painted with geometric designs in red, blue, green and ochre, circa 1931. (Christie's) $835 £500

A Clarice Cliff vase, painted in blue, yellow, orange and green, with stylised leaf and triangular panels, 20.5cm high. (Phillips)
$1,215   £650

A Clarice Cliff Bizarre Latona vase of lotus shape with single handle, 30cm. high. (Osmond Tricks) $1,140 £610

A Clarice Cliff 'Bizarre' 17-piece tea-set painted in green, yellow, red and brown, with flowerbed, comprising; a teapot, milk jug, sugar bowl, honey pot, large plate, six side-plates and six teacups and saucers. (Christie's) $1,496 £880

A Clarice Cliff Fantasque lotus jug, 25cm. high, printed factory marks. (Phillips) $648 £450

A Clarice Cliff 'Bizarre' bowl, standing on four disc-shaped feet, painted in black, yellow, orange and green with climbing flowers on a geometric design, 12cm. high. (Christie's) $841 £495

A Clarice Cliff wall pocket in the form of a pair of budgerigars, 23cm. high. (Osmond Tricks) $93 £50

An early Clarice Cliff bowl, painted in green, orange and amber, with painted inscription and signature, *Bon Dieu, I think that I shall never see a form so lovely as a tree, Clarice Cliff, 1932,* 14cm. high. (Christie's) $743 £440

A Clarice Cliff 'Bizarre' circular charger, painted with a central house in yellow with a vivid orange roof, 42cm. diam., factory marks. (Phillips) $2,580 £1,500

A Clarice Cliff Fantasque pottery vase, painted in brown, black green, yellow and orange with a cottage and trees, 20.3cm. high. (Phillips) $216 £150

A large Clarice Cliff wall charger, painted with a band of acorns and acorn leaves in green red and black on a yellow and brown streaked ground, 45.7cm. diam. (Christie's) $1,481 £792

A Clarice Cliff Bizarre pottery mask, kite-shaped, 28cm. long. (Christie's) $1,793 £1,100

A Clarice Cliff 'Inspiration' charger, 'The Knight Errant', 45.5cm. high. (Phillips) $1,728 £1,200

A Clarice Cliff 'Bizarre' small two handled tureen and cover designed by Dame Laura Knight, the cover with a clown in full relief, 6in. high. (Christie's) $370 £198

CLOCKS

The word 'clock' is too comprehensive a term for a short description because it covers alarm, bracket, carriage, electric, grandmother, longcase, mantel, memorandum, miniature, pedestal, striking and wall clocks. They all have their following and they all have their stars and of course every household needs a clock so they are guaranteed their popularity. When buying a clock you either look for a fine horological instrument or something decorative – if not both. A Tompion timepiece can sell for around £500,000 while an Ebosa alarm made in 1960 will change hands at around £7. There is a fashion in clocks as in everything else and Victorian black slate clocks that could not find a buyer ten years ago are now changing hands at around £75. Some of the prettiest clocks on the market are those dating from the Art Nouveau and Art Deco period. There are some beautiful clocks set in glass surrounds by Lalique to be found and enamel alarm clocks dating from the 1930's are also popular.

An early Victorian maple wood lancet mantel timepiece, the dial with inscription Thos. Cole, London, 10in. high. (Christie's)
$2,178 £1,320

A silvered bronze mantel clock, by Edgar Brandt, 30.6cm. high. (Christie's)
$5,051 £3,080

A late 17th century ebony 'double six hour' grande sonnerie bracket clock, the 6½in. square dial now inscribed Tompion Londini, 35.5cm. high.   (Phillips)
$15,120   £9,000

A 19th century French brass mantel clock, the enamel dial signed for Payne, Tunbridge Wells, 1ft.8in. high. (Phillips) $2,062 £1,250

A Lalique square-shaped clock, Inseparables, the clear and opalescent glass decorated with budgerigars, 11cm. high. (Christie's) $1,584 £1,100

An 18th century striking Act of Parliament clock, signed Ino. Wilson, Peterborough, 56½in. high. (Christie's)
$1,881 £990

A 19th century French ormolu and porcelain mantel clock, the enamel dial signed Vieyres & Repignon a Paris, 11in. high. (Phillips) $990 £600

A Georgian giltwood wall dial clock, the 14in. enamel dial signed Geo. Yonge, London, 24in. diam. (Christie's) $2,217 £1,540

A brass chiming skeleton clock, on oval oak base with glass dome, English, circa 1900, 24in. high including dome. (Christie's) $5,500 £3,837

A French brass lantern clock, the circular chased dial with enamel numerals, 41cm. high. (Phillips) $1.008 £600

Breguet Neveu & Compie., No. 3992: a silver quarter striking carriage clock with alarm, 5½in. high. (Christie's) $33,264 £23,100

Federal mahogany pillar and scroll clock, E. Terry & Sons, Conn., circa 1825, 31in. high. (Robt. W. Skinner Inc.) $650 £454

A gilt brass and enamel striking carriage clock with uncut bimetallic balance to silvered lever platform, 5½in. high. (Christie's) $2,178 £1,320

An Arts & Crafts square oak mantel clock, by Seth Thomas Clock Co., 20th century, 12½in. high, 10½in. wide. (Robt. W. Skinner Inc.) $1,200 £648

A silvered bronze Art Deco table clock, signed R. Terras, 34.5cm. high. (Christie's) $1,623 £990

CLOTHES

It is not surprising that few clothes from very early times have survived but those that do generally find their way into museums where they make eye catching displays. The clothes that are more available to collectors date from Victorian times and baby dresses, christening robes, nightdresses and fur lined tippets from that period can be fairly easily found. More discriminating collectors however tend to prefer the clothes from the early part of the 20th century, from an age of ease and elegance which has perhaps never been surpassed. Rich women bought enormous wardrobes and changed their clothes frequently so that those which have survived often show little sign of wear. Shabby or damaged items do not fetch high prices but those in good condition certainly do. Clothes by well known dressmakers like Nina Ricci or Fortuny and, from a later date, by Dior, Jacques Patou or even early Mary Quant are eagerly sought after. As well as glamorous dresses and wrappers, hats, bags, shoes, shawls and even underclothes from the period are also fetching high prices.

An embroidered vest and pair of embroidered shoes, 18th century, the vest with floral sprays on ivory silk. (Robt. W. Skinner Inc.) $800 £559

A late 19th century bridal veil of tamboured net designed with flower sprays and sprigs, 2 x 2m. (Phillips) $320 £180

A late 18th century gentleman's double-breasted waistcoat of yellow silk brocade. (Phillips)
$119 £85

A late 19th century two-piece gown of mauve, grey and orange silk brocade of striped design, circa 1880. (Phillips)
$241 £160

A gentleman's banyan of printed worsted, circa 1820's. (Phillips)
$1,057 £750

A mid 19th century dress of cream and brown wool printed in mainly red, green and orange. (Phillips) $253 £180

A 1920's dress of black crepe, the skirt designed with grey and cream crepe insertions and ivory silk embroidery. (Phillips) $309 £170

A 1920's dress of brown chiffon embroidered in chain stitch with green and crimson silks, maker's label Gabrielle Chanel, Paris. (Phillips) $5,642 £3,100

A 1920's dress of black and pink chiffon and silk with silvered bead decoration to the hips and side bodice. (Phillips) $837 £460

A 1930's dress of cream crepe, having bias cut skirt and pleated attached scarf, bearing the maker's label Molyneux, 48 Grosvenor Street, London. (Phillips) $509 £280

A 1920's dress of dusty-pink velvet with full back bodice and bow trim, bearing the maker's label, Chanel. (Phillips) $2,002 £1,100

A 1910's dress of white net, having bauble trim, the bodice and upper skirt with cotton cutwork and filet lace overlay. (Phillips) $728 £400

A 1920's dress of black chiffon and silk with tie to the waistline, bearing the maker's label Molyneux, 5 Rue Royale, No.35767. (Phillips) $982   £540

A 1920's dress of black silk and gold thread brocade of striped design, the divided hem looped up to the back shoulder. (Phillips) $1,001   £550

A 1920's coat of burnt-orange silk with gold thread brocade, having deep cuffs and collar. (Phillips) $200   £110

A 1920's dress of sea-green and blue chiffon, having paprika chiffon and gold thread trim, after Poiret. (Phillips) $1,001   £550

A 1910's dress of ivory silk, having ivory chiffon and lace overlay of tiered design. (Phillips) $1,001   £550

A 1920's dress of midnight-blue chiffon and silk, the lower skirt of tiered petal design, bearing the maker's label, Chanel. (Phillips) $1,638   £900

COCA-COLA

Coca-Cola was originally sold from the back of a quack doctor's wagon as a cure-all. Nowadays you will find the ubiquitous Coke advert from Taiwan to Timbuctoo, and Coca Cola items are major collectables.

The classic waisted Coke bottle made its appearance in 1916 – hitherto, from about 1886 Coca Cola was sold in cylindrical bottles with sloping shoulders. A bottle with its name embossed in red or yellow dates from after 1933.

Enamel sign 'Drink Coca-Cola here'. $175 £100

Red, white and blue rhinestone brooch in the form of the American flag centrally set with a mini glass Coca-Cola bottle, dated 1976. (Robt. W. Skinner Inc.) $360 £240

An assortment of Coca-Cola badges with pin clasps. $1 50p

Coca Cola advertising tip tray, oval, America, circa 1907. (Robt. W. Skinner Inc.) $200 £155

Small red backed Coca-Cola sign. $35 £20

Enamel sign 'Refresh yourself! Coca-Cola sold here ice cold'. $210 £125

Enamel sign 'Drink Coca-Cola Strike Matches Here'. $75 £45

Enamel sign with thermometer 'Drink Coca-Cola, Thirst knows no season'. $350 £200

COINS

Condition is the name of the game in coin collecting, with gradings running from Fair, through Fine, Very Fine and Extremely Fine to Uncirculated. Value depends on condition; for instance to be graded better than Fine all detail has to be visible down to the hairs on Queen Victoria's head!

Never clean coins. This removes the lustre and patina of age and greatly reduces value. There are certain rare dates to look for, such as 1949 threepence, 1871 halfpence, 1844 farthings, 1905 halfcrowns, while a 1933 and a 1954 penny can fetch up to £20,000. Coins could be worth ten or even twenty times more than the prices shown, if they are in superb mint condition. Beware of replicas of early English hammered coinage and forgeries of rare pennies and gold guineas!

All coins shown are priced in fine condition unless otherwise stated.

Queen Victoria half farthing, 1839.
$3.50 £2

Maria Theresa Bohemian Thaler, 1780.
$14 £8

USA 'Kennedy' half dollar, 1967. $5 £3

George V halfcrown, 1923. $5 £3

George VI 'Scottish' shilling, 1937, uncirculated. $7 £4

USA silver dollar, 1885. $35 £20

George VI threepence, 1937. 35c 20p

George VI halfpence, 1937, uncirculated.
$3.50 £2

Queen Victoria halfpenny, 1866. $3.50 £2

Spanish Netherlands Albert & Isabella Ducatone, 1619. $175 £100

Charles II farthing, 1672.
$14 £8

William and Mary farthing, 1694. $30 £18

Meck-Schwein Taler, 1848. $18 £10

(Border Bygones)

122

COINS

Elizabeth II two-pence piece, 1981, uncirculated. 18c 10p

Venice gold zecchino, 1684-88. $140 £80

William IV farthing, 1837. $25 £14

Edward VII penny, 1907. $1 50p

George IV crown, 1821. $25 £15

George VI farthing, 1937, uncirculated. $2 £1

William III sixpence, 1700. $18 £10

Elizabeth II two pound coin, 1986, .916 Gold Proof. $525 £300

Queen Victoria, 1843, groat (four pence piece). $2 £1

James II halfcrown, 1686. $85 £50

Queen Victoria, 1854, threepence. $2 £1

William and Mary halfcrown, 1689. $60 £35

George V penny, 1927. 18c 10p

Charles II halfpence, 1675. $35 £20

Elizabeth I sixpence, 1561, mintmark 27. $45 £25

Italy Palerno Oncia, 1752. $125 £70

Queen Victoria halfcrown, young head, 1874. $10 £6

William and Mary crown, 1691. $350 £200

(Border Bygones)

COINS

George VI florin,
1937, uncirculated.
$9 £5

George V halfpenny,
1933.   50c 25p

Edward VII penny, 1904.
$1 50p

William & Mary five
guineas, 1691.
$1,600 £900

Edward VII crown,
1902. $50 £30

George V farthing,
1927.   70c 40p

George V halfcrown,
1923. $3.50 £2

George II sixpence,
1757. $7 £4

George III shilling,
1820. $3.50 £2

George III crown,
1818. $18 £10

Queen Victoria
double florin, 1887.
$10 £6

Elizabeth II three-
pence, uncirculated.
$7 £4

Queen Victoria
penny, 1853$3.50 £2

Charles II three-
pence, 1684. $7 £4

Queen Victoria half-
crown, 1895. $7 £4

Greece 20 APX, silver,
1960. $3.50 £2

Elizabeth II crown,
1981, Royal Wed-
ding, uncirculated.
$1 50p

Edward I penny,
1272-1307. $50 £30

George V florin,
1931. $2 £1

George V shilling,
1930. $3.50 £2

(Border Bygones)

COINS

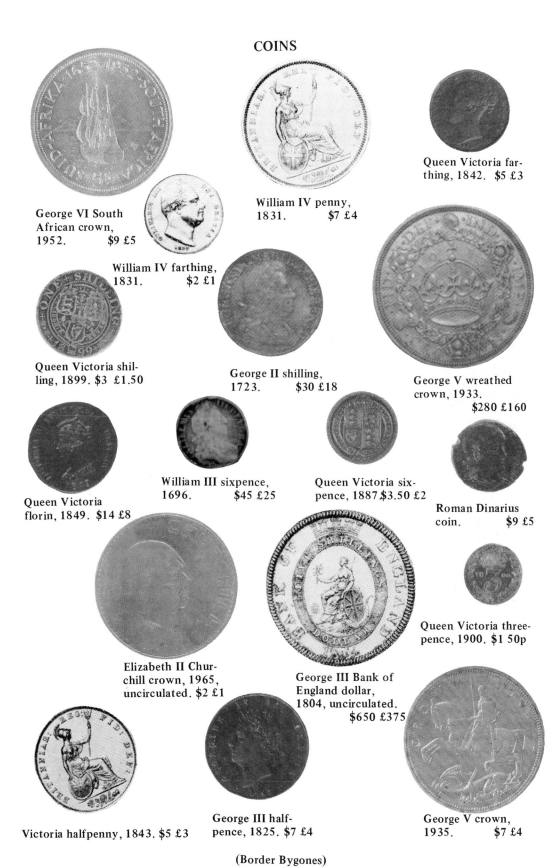

George VI South
African crown,
1952. $9 £5

William IV farthing,
1831. $2 £1

Queen Victoria shil-
ling, 1899. $3 £1.50

Queen Victoria
florin, 1849. $14 £8

William IV penny,
1831. $7 £4

George II shilling,
1723. $30 £18

William III sixpence,
1696. $45 £25

Queen Victoria far-
thing, 1842. $5 £3

George V wreathed
crown, 1933.
          $280 £160

Queen Victoria six-
pence, 1887.$3.50 £2

Roman Dinarius
coin. $9 £5

Elizabeth II Chur-
chill crown, 1965,
uncirculated. $2 £1

George III Bank of
England dollar,
1804, uncirculated.
          $650 £375

Queen Victoria three-
pence, 1900. $1 50p

Victoria halfpenny, 1843. $5 £3

George III half-
pence, 1825. $7 £4

George V crown,
1935. $7 £4

(Border Bygones)

125

COMICS, AMERICAN

Collecting American comics has boomed in the last few years owing to the popularity of films like "Star Wars" and "Superman" and the most recent screen outing for the now cult character Batman. Indeed both Superman and Batman have enjoyed their 50th anniversaries which has added to their historical and financial value.

Prices vary widely from a mint copy of "Action Comics" number 1 featuring the first appearance of Superman at £18,000 to dozens of titles at no more than 20p. In all cases condition is of the utmost importance, lesser condition bringing lesser values. Marvel comics from the 1960's featuring such characters as Spiderman and The Hulk are commanding high prices and for further reading another wise investment would be the Overstreet Comic Book Price Guide which concentrates on golden age comics (1930's to 1950's) and the Official Comic Book Price Guide for Great Britain which concentrates on selected British Comics and a complete listing of American Comics from when they were officially distributed in the U.K. from November 1959.

Detective Comics, No. 28, June 1939, 'Batman'. $4,900 £2,800

Action Comics, No. 1, June 1938, 'Superman'. $31,500 £18,000

New Book of Comics, No. 2, 1938. $1,300 £750

All Star Comics, No. 1, Summer Issue, 1940. $3,500 £2,000

The Big Book of Fun Comics. $2,600 £1,500

All-American Comics, No. 16, July 1940, 'Green Lantern'. $6,500 £3,750

(Duncan McAlpine)

Tillie Toiler, No. 184.
$26 £15

New Fun, No. 1.
$4,900 £2,800

Yellowjacket Comics,
No. 2. $60 £35

Movie Comics, No. 1,
April 1939. $1,000 £600

Action Comics, No. 15,
August 1939. $1,450 £825

The Purple Claw, No. 1.
$70 £40

New Adventure Comics,
No. 27, June 1938.
$300 £175

Batman, No. 1, Spring Issue
1940, 'The Batman and
Robin'. $8,750 £5,000

Adventure Comics, No. 72,
March 1942, 'Sandman'.
$1,150 £650

(Duncan McAlpine)

Walt Disney's No. 1.
$3,000 £1,700

Comics on Parade, 'Li'l Abner', No. 45. $45 £25

Billy the Kid and Oscar, No. 1. $25 £15

Action Comics, No. 5, October 1938.
$3,500 £2,000

More Fun, No. 8, 1938, D. C. Comics. $1,300 £750

More Fun Comics, No. 55, May 1940.
$2,100 £1,200

All-American Comics, No. 1, April 1939. $1,000 £600

All-American Comics, No. 2, July 1938, 'Superman'.
$4,900 £2,800

Spysmasher, No. 2. $350 £200

(Duncan McAlpine)

128

COMICS, BRITISH

The most valuable British comic is the first edition of the Beano, published by D.C. Thomson of Dundee, on 30th July, 1938 at the price of twopence. Today a copy in good condition could demand anything up to £2,000. Comics were often considered as waste paper the moment they were read and the waste paper drives of the Second World War swept them away in their thousands so early copies are valuable. The most sought after comics are the Beano, the Dandy, Film Fun, Radio Fun, Eagle and Knockout. Running them close are Magnet, Gem, Adventure, Hotspur, Rover, Skipper and Wizard. Most have now disappeared with the exception of the Beano and the Dandy which will keep alive memories of Desperate Dan and Lord Snooty, both creations of artist Dudley Watkins.

Other artists of note are Eric Parker and Frank Hampson who drew Dan Dare for the Eagle. Comics from more recent times are now achieving collecting status and one of the most highly regarded is 2000 AD, a science fiction comic strip which, though less than ten years old, commands over £2 a copy.

The Triumph, May 27th, 1933, 'The Boys Best Story Paper'. $4 £2.50

The Beano Comic, No. 1, July 30th, 1938, complete with it's free Whoopee Mask and in pristine condition. $3,500 £2,000

Detective Weekly, February 18th, 1939, The Big Smash. $5 £3

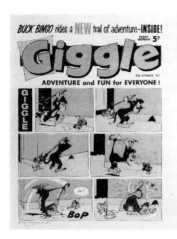

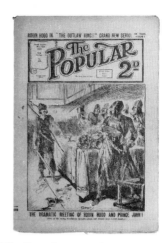

Giggle, 30th September, 1967, Adventure and Fun for Everyone. $1.50 75p

The Magnet, May 13th, 1939, Billy Bunters Own Paper. $4 £2.50

The Popular, May 12th, 1923, The Story Book for Boys. $2.50 £1.50

Dandy, March 31st, 1951, with Korky the Cat. $9 £5

Chips, November 3rd, 1951, Weary Willie and Tired Tim. $2.50 £1.50

Fantastic, 18th March, 1967, A Power Comic. $1.50 75p

The Ranger, September 7th, 1935, Thrill Stories of the Week. $2.50 £1.50

The Hornet, October 26th, 1963, The Wakefield Kicker. $1.50 75p

No. 1 Radio Fun, October 15th, 1938. $130 £75

The Rover, August 12th, 1950. $2.50 £1.50

Sun, December 18th, 1954, Billy the Kid. $2.50 £1.50

Young Britain, May 21, 1920, Prime of the Pictures. $4 £2.50

Knockout, May 14th, 1955, The Happy Family Fun Paper. $2.50 £1.50

The Champion, August 30th, 1947, '2 Brand New Thrillers Inside'. $2.50 £1.50

The Beano, July 31st, 1954, Biffo the Bear. $11 £6.50

The Union Jack, Xmas Number, December 22nd, 1923. $4 £2.50

Wonder, September 4th, 1948, The Comic Full of Laughter. $2.50 £1.50

Boys Cinema, The Lost City, 1923. $5 £3

COMMEMORATIVE MEDALLIONS

Although medallions have been made by hand hammering since the 16th century to commemorate important events, it wasn't until the advent of the mechanical screw press in 1662 that they became symmetrical and uniform in production.

They continued being made on a limited scale until the Great Exhibition of 1851 when they were manufactured in vast quantities to commemorate the event.

This triggered production of medallions to celebrate anything from the opening of a park to the launching of a great ship. As such, there is a wealth of subjects to specialise in be they sporting, transport or religious. Particularly sought after are medallions connected with railways or ships. They should be treated as coins when cleaning.

World's Columbian Exposition, Chicago 1893. Columbian half dollar. $18 £10

King George V and Queen Mary, Coronation Souvenir. $5 £3

S.C.C. 1949 cricket medallion by Pinches, London. $7 £4

Stephen and Joseph Montgolfier 'First Ascent of Man, 1783'. $3.50 £2

"To commemorate the 60th year of the Reign of Her Most Gracious Majesty, Queen Victoria, 1897', with inset photographs. $18 £10

'Tried for high treason, T. Hardy, 1794, Acquitted by his jury counsel, Hon. T. Erskine Gibbs Esq.'. $35 £20

Medallion commemorating Queen Victoria's Jubilee in 1887 from the Borough of Kidderminster. $9 £5

Medallion commemorating the unveiling of a statue, June 22nd, 1881, in memory of Sir Roland Hill, who founded the Penny Postage in 1840. $12 £7

To commemorate the Coronation of King George VI and Queen Elizabeth at Westminster Abbey, issued 12th May, 1937. $5 £3

(Border Bygones)

COMMEMORATIVE MEDALLIONS

To commemorate the visit of HRH The Prince of Wales to the Agricultural Show, Bristol, July 1878. $20 £12

Relay Race commemorative medallions. $2 £1

Talli — Oriental Good-Luck medallion. $2 £1

Guild of Servants of the Sanctuary. $7 £4

Edward VII Coronation medallion, June 26th, 1902, issued in Kidderminster. $10 £6

Holy Margaret O.P.N. 'My flesh is meat indeed'. $5 £3

To commemorate Her Majesty's Jubilee, 1887, 'Victoria, Queen and Empress of India', with gilt crown. $14 £8

Royal Society for the Prevention of Accidents — Safe Driving Award. $5 £3

National Society's Depot 'Feed my Lambs. For Regular Attendance' (to Sunday School). $7 £4

'For God, King and Empire', Empire Day medallion, May 24th, British Empire Union. $14 £8

French medallion commemorating the Universal Exhibition of 1878. $9 £5

Church of England Temperance Society medallion — bronze. $7 £4

(Border Bygones)

133

COOKERY BOOKS

Cookery or receipt books were fairly common in the early 19th century but some of the best were written in French and cooks tended to collect their own recipes. Cookery books written in the 17th and 18th centuries do exist but they are expensive and difficult to find. It was Mrs Isabella Beeton who revolutionised the British kitchen by producing her mammoth "Household Management" which was published in parts between 1859 and 1860. It covered not only cookery but all branches of domestic management and made her name a household word. Unfortunately she did not live long to enjoy her fame because she died young in 1864. Part of the appeal of Victorian cookery books, especially those of Mrs Beeton and Fanny Farmer, are the plates which show mammoth jellies and blancmanges and exotically trimmed dishes. Some collectors however prefer cookery booklets, especially those published during the Second World War when food economy was the order of the day and recipes describe how to make such delights as parsnip jam and turnip fritters.

Just read what you can make with Creamola. $2 £1

Ideal Milk, a book of recipes by Helen Tress. $3.50 £2

Edwardsburg Recipe Book, the Canada Starch Company Ltd. $5 £3

Golden Shred, some everyday dishes. $5 £3

Homepride Cookery Book. $2 £1

60 recipes for flavouring with Lyons Extract. $2.50 £1.50

Borwick's Baking Powder, 250 recipes by Elizabeth Craig. $3.50 £2

Two Hundred War-Time Recipes by Ambrose Heath, 1941. $3.50 £2

Potato Recipes by Elizabeth Craig. $3.50 £2

Yesterday's Paper

COPPER & BRASS

Brass is an alloy made basically from copper and zinc. In early times it was sparingly used but from the Middle Ages on it became popular for ornamental metal work like the chandeliers which were made in Holland, Norway and Sweden in the 16th and 17th centuries, many of which still hang in churches in Britain. It was also used for smaller objects in churches and private homes where it was turned into candlesticks, firedogs, warming pans, fenders and clock dials. The Victorians were very fond of brass ornaments and they were engraved or cast with a design in relief and the lines of the design filled in with enamel. Copper goes back to much earlier times because it was used in Egypt and Ancient Greece but its most common use today is in pots and pans for the kitchen which are still being made. The best ones from a collecting point of view are those produced during the 18th and 19th centuries but look out for signs of damage.

A 17th century brass candlestick engraved 'For the use of ye Company of Joyners and Carpenters', dated 1690, 9in. high. (Gorringes)
$7,920 £6,600

A George III brass and steel basket grate, 34¼in. wide, 30½in. high. (Christie's)
$7,047 £4,860

A copper and brass 'Bell Resonator' ear trumpet, English, mid 19th century, 6in. long. $227 £198

An early 17th century South German gilt brass and copper miniature casket, signed Michel Mann, 7.3cm. wide. (Phillips) $4,608 £3,200

A fine pair of 20th century brass candlesticks, 8½in. high. (Robt. W. Skinner Inc.)
$375 £202

An oval brass planter with gadroon embossed decoration, 13in. high. (Peter Wilson) $300 £190

Early 19th century copper coal helmet, also a matching shovel, 17½in. high. (Peter Wilson) $616 £390

A brass pen tray in the form of a roaring hippopotamus with hinged back, 12½in. wide. (Christie's)
$5,808 £3,520

An urn-shaped lidded coal bin fitted with two lion mask ring handles, 18in. high. (Peter Wilson) $189 £120

Benedict Art Studios hammered copper wall plaque, N.Y., circa 1907, 15in. diam. (Robt. W. Skinner Inc.)
$800 £560

Copper milk churn with cover. (Ball & Percival)
$95 £66

A Nara period copper gilt square plaque decorated in repousse with Amida, 7th/8th century, 11.3 x 11.3cm. (Christie's) $13,992 £8,800

A copper and brass diver's helmet, date 8.29.41, with clamp screws, valves, plate glass windows and guards, 20in. high. (Christie's)
$2,032 £1,210

A hammered copper chamberstick, by Gustav Stickley, circa 1913, 9¼in. high. (Robt. W. Skinner Inc.) $700 £378

An enamelled hammered copper humidor, by R. Cauman, Boston, circa 1925, 6½in. high. (Robt. W. Skinner Inc.) $425 £252

CREAM POTS

Cream pots, jars and jugs were used between 1880 and the 1920's for vending different forms of the product including 'thick', 'clotted', 'pure' and 'thin' cream. Those of particular interest to the collector still retain the original label printed on the pot — either with an inked rubber stamp or a paper transfer taken from an inked engraved copper plate — before application of the glaze. When fired in a kiln, the design was absorbed by the clay and protected by a glaze to give it permanence.

These stoneware containers vary in size from 2in to 6in, averaging about 4in, and were usually made airtight by inserting a cork or disc in the mouth of the pot and covering it with a tinfoil seal.

Creampots make attractive collectables, and many can still be picked up remarkably cheaply in junk shops and market stalls.

The Ayrshire Market, Galashiels and Selkirk, a grey pot with black printed label of Robbie Burns.
$45 £25

Bolesworth's Prize Dairy, Loughborough, Leicestershire, an extremely rare pot with a striking black label, although there is a slightly less rare example with a green top. $450 £250

Express Dairy, Finchley, a white earthenware pot with blue top and label. $60 £35

The Ulster Dairy, Belfast, an attractive and desirable pot with sharp sepia pictorial label and high glaze.
$175 £100

Carrick's Dairy, Cumberland, a cylindrical white pot with black label, 5in. high. $175 £100

Huntly Creamery, Aberdeenshire, a sepia printed pot with brown shoulders and lip, common.
$15 £8

Minifie's, Weston-Super-Mare, a small cylindrical white pot made by C. T. Maling, Newcastle, 3¼in. high. $100 £60

J. E. Bannister, Huddersfield, a cream jug with pouring lip and handle, brown top and black printed label.$35 £20

The Creamery, a small white cylindrical pot with black printed label, 3¼in. high. $100 £60

Express Dairy, Finchley, a white earthenware pot with dark blue label. Cylindrically shaped pots were tradtionally used for clotted cream.
          $245 £140

The Imperial Creamery, Glasgow, a rare jar with green glazed top and black label with a pictorial trade mark. $260 £150

A mauve printed white pot thought to be an early version of Harris's Original Clotted Cream, 5in. high, circa 1880. $110 £65

The Newmarket Dairy Co., a rare Irish pot with fine transfer printed label.
          $175 £100

J. E. Bannister, Sheffield, an extremely rare pot with a green glazed lip and shoulder as opposed to the normal brown. $300 £175

Crystal Brook Brand, Theydon Bois, a rare pot with green top and label.
          $175 £100

CRESTED CHINA

The greatest name in crested china was Goss but there were some 200 other makers who copied the lead set by William Henry Goss and his enterprising son Adolphus. The names of their British rivals include Arcadian, Carlton, Foley, Fords China, Grafton China, Macintyre, Melba, Nautilus, Podmore, Savoy, Shelley, Tuscan and Victoria. There were also foreign competitors who often made mistakes with British coats of arms.

Crested china boomed as a result of the enthusiasm for day trips and holidays that overtook the British public at the end of the 19th century. Trippers wanted a souvenir of their trip away from home and the perfect solution was a cheap little piece of china with the holiday town's coat of arms on it. Several subjects dominate the china manufacturers' output – the Great War – one of the more unusual items was a figure of Old Bill produced by Shelley; animals and birds; transport; memorials including the Cenotaph; statues; cartoon and comedy characters; sport and musical instruments. A cup and saucer was one of the most common items sold and, as a result today the price for such an item would be considerably less than for an Old Bill or a model of the Cenotaph. The rivals to Goss never took such fastidious care about their products as the trail blazers and their china is never as fine. However when buying crested china it is important to remember that imperfections of manufacture do not affect the price so much as subsequent damage. Cracks or chips can affect the value of a piece considerably.

Arcadian Black Cat sailing yacht. (Goss & Crested China Ltd)　$107 £60

Arcadian plump lady on weighing scales, inscribed 'Adding Weight'. (Goss & Crested China Ltd) $59 £33

Carlton Jenny Jones. (Goss & Crested China Ltd)　$63 £35

Carlton Monoplane with moveable propellor. (Goss & Crested China Ltd)　$100 £55

Arcadian Parian bust of King George V on glazed base . (Goss & Crested China Ltd)　$63 £35

Arcadian Banjo. (Goss & Crested China Ltd)　$16 £9

Arcadian ball vase with cartoon. (Goss & Crested China Ltd) $18 £10

Corona Renault Tank. (Goss & Crested China Ltd) $116 £65

Grafton Monkey wearing coat. (Goss & Crested China Ltd) $23 £13

Arcadian Traffic Policeman on point duty. (Goss & Crested China Ltd) $45 £25

Cyclone Cenotaph. (Goss & Crested China Ltd) $11 £6

Willow Art Burns and Highland Mary. (Goss & Crested China Ltd) $54 £30

Willow Art Guildford Castle. (Goss & Crested China Ltd) $54 £30

Carlton Drunkard leaning on lamppost, ashtray, striker and holder, lustre. (Goss & Crested China Ltd) $107 £60

Alexandra Westminster Abbey, West Front. (Goss & Crested China Ltd) $39 £22

CUCKOO CLOCKS

Cuckoo clocks originated in the Black Forest, when local farmers used their woodworking skills to supplement their income in winter. Early movements were of wood apart from lantern pinions and some use of wire. The theme of the cuckoo is said to have been introduced by Franz Ketterer around 1730. Trumpeter clocks have a trumpeter sounding instead of a cuckoo. These date from around 1857 and are choice collectors' pieces.

Black Forest shelf mounted German cuckoo clock with spring driven movement, striking on a gong and cuckoos. $525 £300

A fine Black Forest clock with two train movement striking in a wire gong and with cuckoo, 48in. high. $3,000 £1,700

A small 1950's decorated carved wood clock with two cuckoos and a weight driven movement. $45 £25

Combined cuckoo and weather clock, complete with thermometer. $35 £20

German Black Forest carved cuckoo clock. $50 £30

A small 1980's Black Forest cuckoo clock with weight driven movement. $25 £15

A finely carved Black Forest cuckoo clock decorated with a stag and dead game. $1,225   £700

CUPS & SAUCERS

Collecting cups and saucers is an excellent way to begin a lifelong fascination with antiques. There was no need for cups and saucers until tea drinking became fashionable and the earliest examples have saucers without wells for resting the cup and the cups themselves have no handles but look like large mouthed bowls. Many of these were products of the Worcester factory from around 1750 and were often painted with variations of Chinese designs. From that date, the manufacturing of tea services boomed and every pottery produced them. A tea set has been a traditional wedding gift for many years and the recipients often proudly displayed their best sets in glass fronted cabinets. It is possible to trace the development of artistic trends through the tea sets that have survived. The Victorians loved ornate cups and saucers with flourishes on the handles and embossed gilding round the rims.

Bizarre by Clarice Cliff

The designs they preferred were flowery and one of the most popular manufacturers was Rockingham. In the 20th century, cups and saucers often took on an angular look and among the best examples are those painted by Clarice Cliff in her Bizarre range especially the Summer House pattern which had sharp wedge handles sticking out of the sides of the cup without a hole for the fingers. Collectors tend to stick to cups and saucers by the same pottery, from the same period or in the same style — blue and white is very popular for example. Others collect moustache cups with a little draining ledge for wet moustaches. They were popular gifts in Victorian times.

Derby handled cup and saucer, white ground with floral and gilded decoration, red mark to base, circa 1815. (Giles Haywood) $70 £42

A Sevres hard-paste cup and saucer, blue crowned interlaced L mark enclosing date letter U for 1773. (Christie's) $675 £385

A Chelsea flared and fluted coffee cup with scroll handle, circa 1750, 7.5cm. high. (Christie's) $3,250 £1,870

A Minton pink-ground cabinet cup and saucer, circa 1825. (Christie's) $272 £165

A Wedgwood blue jasper dip cylindrical coffee cup and deep saucer, impressed mark. (Christie's) $444 £300

A Paris (Nast) green-ground cabinet cup and saucer, gilt marks, circa 1810. (Christie's) $220 £132

A Berlin cylindrical coffee-cup and saucer with garlands of flowers between blue bands gilt with foliage, blue sceptre mark and gilt dot circa 1795. (Christie's) $1,260 £779

A Berlin Celadon ground Tasse D'Amitie the saucer inscribed Le tems s'envole; votre amour est bien plus constant, circa 1805. (Christie's)$2,468 £1,320

A Sevres bleu nouveau cylindrical coffee cup and saucer, blue interlaced L marks enclosing the date letters EE for 1782. (Christie's) $766 £540

An early Worcester reeded coffee cup with a scroll handle, painted in Kakiemon style, circa 1753-55. (Phillips) $1,302 £780

A jewelled Sevres cylindrical cup and saucer, gilt interlaced L marks and painter's marks LG of Le Guay, circa 1783. (Christie's) $12,150 £8,100

A Paris (Jacob Petit) two-handled cup, cover and trembleuse-stand, blue JP marks, circa 1840, the stand 16.5cm. diam. (Christie's) $580 £352

CURTAINS

When rummaging around among the bundles of old curtains in salerooms or at jumble sales, keep an eye open for old curtaining for some can be worth fair sums of money. The Victorians tended to favour dull coloured, heavy curtains to keep out the cold, but a new interest in interior decoration was created by William Morris who revolutionised the art of furnishing and house decorating in Britain. With the co-operation of fellow artists from the Pre-Raphaelite Brotherhood, he opened his first decoration company which was to become Morris & Co in 1861. They designed everything for the home from cutlery, wallpapers, curtaining and furniture to carpets. Due to Morris, the old clutter beloved by the Victorians became unfashionable and was replaced by more simple, less cluttered rooms based on Morris' idealised ideas about Mediaeval life. The furnishing fabrics that he designed matched many of his wallpapers and had stylised, flowing plant and animal bird patterns which still fit in very well with modern furnishing schemes.

One of two pairs of Morris & Co. printed cotton curtains, designed by Wm. Morris, 'Corncockle' design, 1880's, 216 x 139cm. $340 £264

One of a pair of crewelwork curtains, one signed Mary Fincher 1703, 65 x 86in., another pair 41 x 52in. and two pelmets. (Christie's)
$2,887 £1,650

One of a pair of Morris & Co. wool curtains and match-ing pelmet, designed by Wm. Morris, 1880's, 'Bird' pattern, 250 x 240cm.
$3,547 £2,750

One of a set of three wool and silk Templeton's curtains, designed by Bruce Talbert, circa 1880, together with two pelmets. $3,121 £2,420

A printed velvet curtain designed by C. A. Voysey, 262 x 239.5cm. (Christie's)
$3,965 £2,592

One of a set of four Jacobean crewel-work bed hangings, embroidered in coloured wools, 3ft.1in. wide. (Lawrence Fine Art) $4,250 £2,450

CUSHIONS

Worked cushions were popular in the 19th century with Berlin woolwork finding favour between the 1820's and 1870's. This was similar in concept to the modern painting by numbers kit with designs first painted on squared paper and then transferred to the canvas by the needlewoman. By the 1830's designs were being printed directly onto the canvas and 14,000 patterns were available for the British market alone by 1840. Many such cushions can still be found for a few pounds in second hand charity shops.

A Berlin woolwork cushion with a large central medallion and sprays of flowers, 18in. square. (Christie's) $1,409 £972

A Berlin woolwork cushion, the central medallion worked with raised plush roses, circa 1860, 18in. square. (Christie's) $2,035 £1,404

One of a set of five cushions worked in coloured wools with sprays of flowers and edged with pink and yellow wool fringe. (Christie's) $3,132 £2,160

A feather cushion covered in purple and gold brocade woven with a displayed eagle, 15¼in. square. (Christie's) $1,250 £700

A 17th century needlework cushion, silk and metallic yarns in a variety of stitches, England, 8 x 10in. (Robt. W. Skinner Inc.) $3,000 £2,097

A rectangular needlework cushion with summer flowers on a brown ground, 18in. wide. (Christie's) $311 £180

A tapestry cushion cover woven with a classical scene, Dutch, 17th century, 12 x 23in. (Christie's) $982 £750

DINKY TOYS

The name 'Dinky' has passed into the English language as almost a generic term for model vehicles. Collecting early or even not so early examples is becoming a passion with an increasing number of people, with the major auction houses now devoting entire sales to these.

Dinky toys are something of which almost everyone will have one or two in their attic. Most are worth only a few pounds, though one from the 30's could be worth as much as £500. Generally speaking, if they come with an original box, the value leaps upwards. One of the most sought-after Dinkys is the No. 24 set of motor cars, which includes a Vogue Saloon, Sports Tourer 4-seater and 2-seaters, and will fetch, if boxed, around £5,000.

Ships of the British Navy, set no. 50, complete with box. (Phillips) $354 £200

Rare Gift Set no. 3, comprising a Standard Vanguard, Austin Taxi, Morris Oxford, Rover, Estate Car and a Daimler Ambulance. (Phillips) $1,680 £950

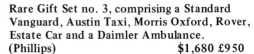

No. 24 Set of Motor Cars, comprising an Ambulance, Limousine, Town Sedan, Vogue Saloon, Super Streamlined Saloon, Sportsman's Coupe, Sports Tourer 4 Seater, Sports Tourer 2 Seater, boxed. (Phillips) $8,850 £5,000

998 Bristol Britannia Air Liner, Canadian Pacific, boxed. (Phillips) $250 £140

Gift Set no. 4, Racing Cars, comprising a Cooper Bristol, Alfa Romeo, Ferrari, H.W.M. and a Maserati, boxed. (Phillips) $1,200 £680

A Willeme Tractor and covered Trailer, boxed. (Phillips) $210 £120

198 Rolls Royce Phantom V, in metallic green and white, boxed. (Phillips) $170 £95

28N Delivery Van, Meccano 1st Type. (Phillips) $2,300 £1,300

239 Vanwall Racing Car, No. 35, boxed.(Phillips) $195 £110

27Y Studebaker 'Commander', red with tan roof, boxed. (Phillips) $175 £100

280C Delivery Van, Shredded Wheat, 2nd Type. (Phillips) $800 £450

941 Foden 14 ton Tanker, Mobilgas. (Phillips) $1,150 £650

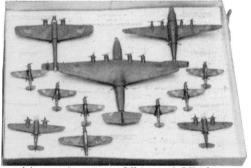

Pre-war No. 68 Set Camouflaged Aeroplanes, comprising an Armstrong Whitworth Whitley Bomber, Frobisher Liner, 3 Hawker Hurricane Fighters, 3 Vickers Supermarine Spitfire Fighters, Armstrong Whitworth Ensign Liner, 2 Bristol Blenheim Bombers and a Fairey Battle Bomber, boxed. (Phillips) $11,500 £6,500

137 Plymouth Fury Convertible, metallic green, boxed. (Phillips) $195 £110

514 Guy Van, Weetabix, boxed. (Phillips) $2,500 £1,400

180 Packard Clipper Sedan, orange and grey, boxed. (Phillips) $170 £95

DINKY TOYS

No. 12 Postal Set comprising a Royal Mail Van, Pillar Box, Pillar Box Airmail, Telephone Box, Telegraph Messenger and Postman, boxed. (Phillips) $1,150 £650

299 Post Office Services Gift Set, boxed. (Phillips) $1,000 £600

42 Set Police Hut, Motor Cycle Patrol and Policemen, boxed. (Phillips) $920 £520

934 Leyland Octopus Wagon, yellow and green, boxed. (Phillips) $740 £420

Pre-war No. 64 Set French Factory Avions comprising a Dewoitine, Bloch, Amiot, Potez 662 and a Potez 63, boxed. (Phillips) $3,900 £2,200

No. 24 Set Motor Cars, comprising an Ambulance, Limousine, Town Sedan, Vogue Saloon, Super Streamlined Saloon, Sportsmans Coupe and 2 Sports Tourers, boxed. (Phillips) $5,300 £3,000

Rare 675 Ford Sedan Staff Car for U.S. Market. (Phillips) $495 £280

DISNEYANA

Walter Elias Disney was born in Chicago in 1901 and by the time he died in 1966 his name was famous worldwide because he was the man who created the Disney World with its characters Mickey Mouse, Donald Duck and hundreds of others. His greatest creation, Mickey Mouse appeared on film in 1928. Pluto and Goofy made their first appearances in 1930 and Donald Duck in 1934. After that, as they say, Disney never looked back. Today there are two main streams of Disneyana collecting — firstly, studio ephemera which ranges from stills of films, original watercolours and the hand painted celluloid sheets used in the animation process. Memos or notes signed by Walt Disney fetch very high prices indeed.

The second, and more accessible field for collecting, and one in which good things can still be found, concentrates on the millions of things that appeared either under the Disney label or based on his characters. There are Seven Dwarf dolls; tin plate toys of Mickey Mouse and his mates; Pluto dogs; books by the million; comics like Mickey Mouse Weekly; playing cards; pottery; babies' feeding spoons, soap....the list is endless. And prices are remarkable, for a six inch high figure of Mickey Mouse as an organ grinder, dating from 1930, has been sold for £3,000. There were certain Disney illustrators whose work is prized above the rest and they include Gustave Tenggren, Al Taliaferro, Floyd Gottfredson and Carl Barks, the man who drew Donald Duck.

Walt Disney's 'The Jungle Book' souvenir brochure, 1967. $7 £4

Eight polychrome moulded terracotta figures of Snow White and the Seven Dwarfs: Sneezy, Sleepy, Bashful, Doc, Grumpy, Dopey and Happy, 10in. and 6in. high. (Christie's) $185 £99

Walt Disney's Snow White and the Seven Dwarfs. $5 £3

Walt Disney, a polychrome woollen rug depicting Mickey and Minnie Mouse performing in a circus arena, 46¾ x 71in., circa 1930's. (Christie's) $700 £385

Marx, Walt Disney's Donald Duck Duet, boxed. (Phillips) $396 £240

Walt Disney Studios, Snow White and the Seven Dwarfs, 1937 — 'Five Dwarfs in a heap', pencil and coloured crayon animation drawing, 10 x 12in. (Christie's) $650 £352

'Mickey Mouse Organ Grinder', tinplate toy with clockwork and musical mechanisms, by Distler, circa 1930, 6in. long. (Christie's) $975 £650

Walt Disney Studios, Snow White and the Seven Dwarfs, 1937 — 'The Seven Dwarfs', gouache on full celluloid applied to a wood veneer background, 10½ x 13¾in. (Christie's) $3,050 £1,650

Four Disney stuffed figures, comprising a velveteen Mickey Mouse and Pluto; two corduroy 'Widgets', late 1930s-40s. (Christie's) $440 £286

Walt Disney Studios, Sleeping Beauty, 1959 — 'Briar Rose, woodland animals, and Prince Phillip', gouache on celluloid, a compilation of seven celluloid pieces stapled onto paper, 11½ x 13½in. (Christie's) $445 £242

Mickey Mouse soft toy by Deans Rag Book Ltd., 1930's, 6¼in. high. $260 £150

Walt Disney Studios, Snow White and the Seven Dwarfs, 1937 — 'Five dwarfs peering into a water trough', gouache on full celluloid applied to a wood veneer background, 9½ x 12½in. (Christie's) $3,850 £2,090

Snow White and the Seven Dwarfs, circa 1937 — eight celluloids: 'Doc', 'Sleepy', 'Sneezy', 'Snow White', 'Three Running Dwarfs', 'Happy', 'Grumpy' and 'Woodland Animals', each gouache on celluloid, one inscribed '1936 Walt Disney Productions'. (Christie's) $710 £385

Marx tin wind-up toy 'Merry Makers', 1930's, 9in. high. (Robt. W. Skinner Inc) $525 £300

Robin Hood, 1973, and the Rescuers 1977 — three celluloids, 'A Vulture', 'A Hen' and 'A Small Child', each gouache on celluloid, stamped 'Walt Disney Productions Certified Original Hand-Painted Movie Film Cel'. (Christie's) $445   £242

Lead model Mickey and Minnie Mouse barrel organ group. (Hobbs & Chambers) $58 £38

Mickey Mouse Corporation 'Minnie Mouse' watercolour, pen and ink, initialled W.D.P. with 'Micky Mouse Corpora-tion Produktions-Afdelingen' ink stamp 9¼ x 6¼in. (Christie's) $325 £176

Glazed earthenware musical jug depicting the Three Little Pigs, circa 1935, 10in. high. $260 £150

Pelham Puppets, Mickey Mouse and Minnie Mouse. $175 £100

Pinnochio doll by Ideal Novelty & Toy Co., circa 1945, 7¼in. high. $260 £150

German tinplate Mickey Mouse mechanical bank, circa 1935, 6¾in. high. $435 £250

DOG ITEMS

Collectors of dog items are likely also to be fans of the real thing, and where the dog is actually depicted, it is usually in the role of the faithful friend. The scope is vast and varied, encompassing everything from Edwardian feeding bowls to car mascots and jewellery.

Interestingly, the auction house, Bonham's, hold an annual sale of dog pictures and related works of art timed to coincide with the Crufts Dog Show.

A Meissen pipe bowl modelled as a recumbent sheep-dog with hinged neck, circa 1745, 8cm. long. (Christie's)　　　$1,303 £918

Cast zinc St. Bernard dog figure, probably Mass., circa 1880, 45in. wide. (Robt. W. Skinner Inc.) $2,600 £1,818

One of a pair of Meissen pug dogs modelled by J. J. Kandler and P. Reinicke, one with blue crossed swords mark on base, circa 1745, 15cm. high. (Christie's) $4,600 £3,240

Late 19th century match striker 'Waiting for Orders', made by Conte & Boehme. $45 £25

Composition advertising figure for Spratt's 'Tracey, Witch of Ware', supreme champion 1948, 1950.
$130 £75

A papier mache model of Nipper with electrically operated wagging tail, 17in. high, in EMI wooden dis-patch case. (Christie's)
$950 £550

Late 19th century American moulded zinc mastiff figure, 48in. high, 48in. wide. (Robt. W. Skinner Inc.)
$1,650 £945

DOMESTIC EQUIPMENT

One of the best fields for investment is the early mechanical devices put onto the market as labour savers. As improvements were made, the old ones were almost invariably thrown away with the result that, nowadays they have considerable rarity and curiosity value. After a while, it was realised that many of the old gadgets still actually worked. And worked well. Many will swear that their old Victorian coffee mill grinds coffee far better than the brand new electric jobs, that the heavy iron or copper saucepans are far better than their modern counterparts, that bean slicers, apple peelers and cherry stoners add interest to the most mundane of preparatory tasks in the kitchen.

In saying this, I am referring to Victorian appliances. However, it must be said that it is well worth looking out for the now outdated gadgets of the 30's, 40's and 50's. This is a market still in its early stages and with many intriguing contraptions still modestly priced.

Pajot's midwifery forceps, signed Charriere a Paris, late 19th century, 34cm. long. (Christie's) $286 £199

The 'Improved Phantasmagoria Lantern, by Carpenter & Westley, with patent argand solar lamp with a quantity of lantern slides. (Christie's) $369 £220

A 19th century bone saw and three dental elevators. (Christie's) $153 £93

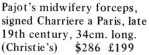

A London Stereoscopic Co. Brewster-pattern stereoscope with brass mounted eye pieces, in fitted rosewood box, 13in. wide. (Christie's) $513 £380

A late 18th century pocket dental scaling kit, with mirror in a shagreen case, 2¼in. wide. (Christie's) $286 £176

A mutoscope in cast iron octagonal shaped case, electrically lit, 22in. high. $822 £715

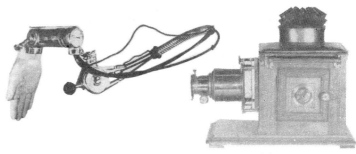

A cradle-mounted stereographoscope in black ebonised finish with lens panel, 16in. high. (Christie's) $248 £200

A chromium plated automatic traffic warner, stamped 'Birglow Auto Signal Pat. 375944, Pat. 376564, Reg. design 767816', 42in. long. (Christie's) $198 £160

A wood and brass magic lantern with brass bound lens and chimney with a slide holder and a small quantity of slides in wood box. (Christie's) $277 £165

A set of early Victorian mahogany jockey scales with ivory plaque De Grave & Co., Makers, London, 39in. wide. (Christie's) $4,329 £2,640

A Wimshurst pattern plate machine by Philip Harris Ltd., Birmingham, 21.5/8in. wide, and a pair of brass and ebonite discharge forks. (Christie's) $811 £495

A late 18th century 'Ladder Scale', the 1oz. and 2oz. beams stamped De Grave & Co. London, 16.1/8in. wide. (Christie's) $811 £495

A 19th century single cupping set by J. Laundy, with lacquered brass syringe and shaped glass cup, the case 5in. wide. (Christie's) $422 £264

A cast iron sundial by E. T. Hurley, circa 1900, 10¼in. diam. (Robt. W. Skinner Inc.) $425 £295

A 19th century walnut thunder house, the chimney carrying electrical wire, 19.5cm. long. (Christie's) $770 £531

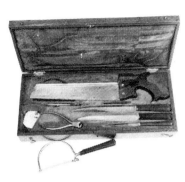

A Simpson part amputation set, in a fitted mahogany case. $835 £572

A Bonds Ltd./Kinora, pedestal Kinora viewer on moulded wood stand and base inlaid with wood. (Christie's) $1,143 £605

A Baird televisor, No. 204, in typical arched brown painted aluminium case with disc, valve and plaque on front. (Christie's) $1,848 £1,400

A brass stamp box by W. Avery & Son, 2½in. high. (Christie's) $396 £242

A Pascal's apparatus, unsigned, 14in. wide, with three different shaped glass vessels mounted in brass collars to fit the limb. (Christie's) $811 £495

A late 19th century desk calendar compendium, 3¼in. diam. (Christie's) $270 £165

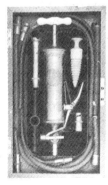

Rosewood stereo viewer, table top, manufactured by Alex. Becker, N.Y., circa 1859. (Robt. W. Skinner Inc.) $400 £325

An Ive's Kromskop colour stereoscopic viewer, in wood carrying case. (Christie's) $868 £700

Mid 19th century S. Maw, Son & Thompson enema or stomach pump apparatus, English, 12½ x 7½in. $202 £176

DOOR KNOCKERS

'Rappers', to use their old name, have been popular collectables for many years. Many early ones, in the form of dolphins or lion's head and ring, show Chippendale or Adam influence. Smaller decorative knockers, mostly produced since the 1880's, are now in demand and are made in many forms. Older, well-patinated examples are the most desirable. Look out for a clear registration number on the reverse, as many modern reproductions are made using old moulds.

One of a pair of inlaid bronze mask and ring handles, Warring States/Western Han Dynasty, the masks 9.5cm. wide, the rings 9cm. diam. (Christie's) $86,515 £60,500

An 18th century wrought-iron door knocker, 10½in. high. $558 £385

William Shakespeare brass door knocker, 6in. high. $35 £20

Harrow School brass door knocker with 'May the fortunes of the house stand' in Latin. $50 £30

A small 20th century brass door knocker depicting the devil. $18 £10

A Victorian heavy bronze door knocker of Regency design, circa 1850, 5in. diam. $85 £50

Robert Burns door knocker in brass, 3½in. high. $18 £10

DOORS

Victorian and Edwardian stripped pine and panelled doors are currently much in vogue, and old doors can add much character and security to a house, given the featureless and flimsy nature of their modern counterparts.

Look for unusual doors of all sorts, depending on the image you wish to create. Studded old oak church doors, or even those from a bank vault or prison cell can all be found. Late 19th century doors are among the best quality products and are still quite common.

A late 19th century leaded stained and coloured door window, signed W. J. McPherson, Tremont St., Boston, Mass. (Robt. W. Skinner Inc.) $800 £490

Pair of carved Gothic-style oak doors, 100in. high, 30in. wide. (Robt. W. Skinner Inc.)
$1,000 £909

Late 19th century Police cell door, from Bromyard Jail, made by C. Smith, Birmingham.
$350 £200

A late 19th century English brass doorway, each door 209 x 77.5cm. (Christie's)
$23,925 £16,500

A pair of Rowley Gallery silvered wood doors, 1920's, 216cm. high. $1,000 £600

Late Victorian Church oak side door with iron fittings.
$50 £30

Pair of doors by Jean Dunand for a Normandie liner.
$12,250 £7,000

157

DOULTON FIGURES

Doulton really started to be noted for figure making when Charles Noke joined the company in 1889. Early examples, however, though finely modelled, were quite drab and did not sell well, so production was suspended until 1912, when he introduced a figure range, one of which, 'Bedtime' (later rechristened 'Darling') found instant favour with the visiting Queen Mary.

The new range featured bolder colours, and a very talented group of designers worked on them. Many are still in production today. Later talents include Margaret Davies, whose work is notable for its meticulous research and attention to detail. Even figures currently still in production can command high prices among collectors, with, for example, the third version of 'St George', by W. K. Harper which was introduced in 1978, fetching £3,000 at auction.

'Pierette' HN644, designed by L. Harradine, issued 1924-38, 7¼in. high. $525 £300

'Balloon Seller' HN583, designed by L. Harradine, issued 1923-49, 9in. high.
$220 £125

'Helen' HN1509, designed by L. Harradine, issued 1932-38, 8in. high.
$520 £295

'Masquerade' HN599, designed by L. Harradine, issued 1924-49, 6¾in. high. $610 £350

'Old King' HN2134, designed by C. J. Noke, issued 1954, 10¾in. high. $350 £200

'Rosamund' HN1497, designed by L. Harradine, issued 1932-38, 8½in. high. $700 £400

DOULTON FIGURES

'Mask Seller' HN1361, designed by L. Harradine, issued 1929-38, 8½in. high. $610 £350

'Lady Fayre' HN1265, designed by L. Harradine, issued 1928-38, 5¼in. high. $400 £225

'Mask' HN785, designed by L. Harradine, issued 1926-38, 6¾in. high.$1,000 £600

'Priscilla' HN1340, designed by L. Harradine, issued 1929-49, 8in. high. $240 £135

'Sylvia', HN 1478, designed by L. Harradine, issued 1931-38, 10½in. high. $315 £180

'Wee Willie Winkie' HN2050, designed by M. Davies, issued 1949-53, 5¼in. high.$225 £130

'Stitch In Time' HN2352, designed by M. Nicholl, issued 1966-80, 6¼in. high. $100 £60

'Broken Lance' HN2041, designed by M. Davies, issued 1949-75, 8¾in. high. $315 £180

'Pierette' HN643 designed by L. Harradine, issued 1924-38, 7¼in. high. $610 £350

'Camille' HN1586, designed, by L. Harradine, issued 1933-49, 6½in. high. $315 £180

'Dinky Do' HN1678, designed by L. Harradine, issued 1934, 4¾in. high. $50 £30

'Pantalettes' HN1709, designed by L. Harradine, issued 1935-38, 8in. high. $250 £145

'Verena' HN1835, designed by L. Harradine, issued 1938-49, 8¼in. high. $435 £250

'Polly Peachum' HN550, designed by L. Harradine, issued 1922-49, 6½in. high. $260 £150

'Beggar' HN2175, designed by L. Harradine, issued 1956-72, 6¾in. high. $315 £180

'Bluebeard' HN2105 designed by L. Harradine, issued 1953, 11in. high. $260 £150

'Sibell' HN1695, designed by L. Harradine, issued 1935-49, 6½in. high. $480 £275

'Centurion' HN2726, designed by W. K. Harper, issued 1982-84, 9¼in. high. $110 £65

EGG CUPS

Egg stands were originally crude wooden stands designed to be kept in the kitchen. As they developed, simple egg cups were often created to sit in the holes and these became more decorative when egg stands found their way into the breakfast rooms of the nation.

Silver examples ususally date from the last quarter of the 18th century but it wasn't until the 19th century, when members of the household could boil their own eggs on a little spirit stove set on the sideboard, that egg cups came into their own. The variety is endless as is the price range, yet it is interesting to note that the boiled egg and its accompanying container has yet to find widespread popularity in America.

An egg cup stand by Mary Davies, the ochre stand with incised green foliate scrolls, r.m., 1884, 6in. diam. (Abridge Auctions) $300 £175

An egg cup by Frank Butler with incised blue leaves on a buff ground, circa 1872, 3½in. high. (Abridge Auctions) $130 £75

Clarice Cliff egg cruet with six cups and central duck handle, circa 1930. $430 £250

A pair of oak egg cups with silver plaques inscribed NB (Napoleon Bonaparte) 1798, 3in. high. (Christie's) $1,353 £825

1950's 'Chaste Makes Waste' china egg cup. $10 £6

Pair of late 19th century treen duck egg cups of good patina. $35 £20

EQUESTRIAN BOOKS

The horse, having been essential to civilisation since earliest times, has featured in literature throughout the ages. Anyone interested in horses must have a collection of equestrian books. Text books are available on just about every facet of the subject. Equestrian fiction, too, has entered the mainstream of English literature through such classics as 'Black Beauty', 'The Irish RM' and 'Memoirs of a Foxhunting Man'. Early, well-illustrated editions with coloured hunting prints are eagerly sought after.

Dixon (W.S.): Loose Rein, 11 orig. parts, col. plates, 1887. (Phillips) $787 £440

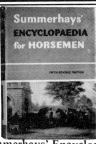

Summerhays' Encyclopaedia for Horsemen, fifth revised Edition, published by F. Warne, 1970. $14 £8

The Irish R.M. Complete, by E. Somerville and Martin Ross, 1973. $12 £7

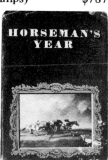

The Horseman's Year 1949, 1950, edited by W. E. Lyon. $12 £7

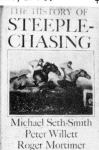

The History of Steeplechasing published by Michael Joseph, 1966. $12 £7

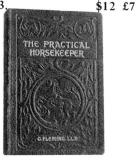

The Practical Horsekeeper by G. Fleming. $28 £16

Steeplechasing by Lord Willoughby de Broke, circa 1955. $20 £12

Lester, A Biography by Sean Pryor. $18 £10

Black Beauty by Anna Sewell illustrated by Cecil Aldin. $55 £30

Hoof Beats by Homer Hawkins, 1st Edition, 1932. $30 £18

(Andree Oughton)

162

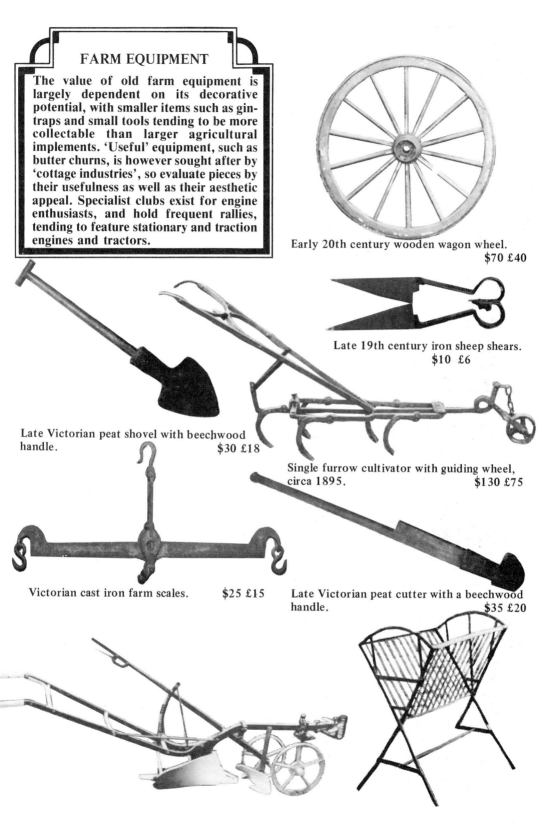

FARM EQUIPMENT

The value of old farm equipment is largely dependent on its decorative potential, with smaller items such as gin-traps and small tools tending to be more collectable than larger agricultural implements. 'Useful' equipment, such as butter churns, is however sought after by 'cottage industries', so evaluate pieces by their usefulness as well as their aesthetic appeal. Specialist clubs exist for engine enthusiasts, and hold frequent rallies, tending to feature stationary and traction engines and tractors.

Early 20th century wooden wagon wheel. $70 £40

Late 19th century iron sheep shears. $10 £6

Late Victorian peat shovel with beechwood handle. $30 £18

Single furrow cultivator with guiding wheel, circa 1895. $130 £75

Victorian cast iron farm scales. $25 £15

Late Victorian peat cutter with a beechwood handle. $35 £20

A single furrow plough, circa 1905. $175 £100

An iron standing hay rack, circa 1900. $60 £35

163

FILM MAGAZINES & BOOKS

Film goers in the years before the war could take their pick of a wide range of magazines and books dedicated to the movies and the stars that appeared in them. There was a huge industry in Hollywood given up to producing material, much of it false, to fill the pages of those publications and stars could be made or broken by them. There were two main types as far as magazines were concerned – firstly those dedicated to a professional audience like cinema owners or distributors who were responsible for booking films for their picture houses and had to be persuaded that this was one they could not miss. The second type of magazine was addressed to the fans who were fed all sorts of mollifying stories about the lives of the stars and in which films were glowingly reviewed. They were also lavishly illustrated with pictures of lovely, leggy girls and handsome men. The magazines that are most valuable today are those dedicated to stars who have become cult figures particularly Marilyn Monroe and James Dean.

Publications featuring either of them sell for around £5 each. Also collected are the huge range of magazines published by the Walt Disney organisation and featuring the well known cartoon characters. Most of these magazines produced year books with pictures on every page. In recent years there has been a more realistic and sceptical attitude about movie publicity and magazines like *Films and Filming* or the French *Cahier du Cinema* are worth collecting for the future.

Picture Show, 'Stars Whom Stars Admire', January 26th 1929. $5 £3

Screen Pictorial, Charles Laughton and Dolly Mollinger cover, September, 1938. $4 £2.50

Picturegoer, 'The Screen's Most Popular Magazine', January 9th, 1937.
$3.50 £2

Movie Life Year Book, 1955, 'Brando's True Love Story'. $2.50 £1.50

Yesterday's Paper

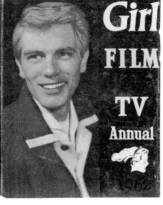

Inside Filmland, 'Life with the Stars', Liz Taylor and Montgomery Clift cover. $7 £4

Girl Film and TV Annual, 1962, Adam Faith cover. $18 £10

Picture Show Annual, 1957, 'The King and I' cover. $20 £12

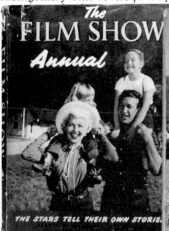

The Film Show Annual, Betty Grable and Harry James cover. $9 £5

The Boys' and Girls' Cinema Clubs Annual, by Associated British Cinemas Ltd. $7 £4

The New Film Show Annual, 'The Stars tell their own stories'. $9 £5

Film Parade, sold exclusively by Marks & Spencer Ltd. $12 £7

Picture Show Annual, 'For people who go to the pictures', 1955. $10 £6

The Film Star Weekly, April 7th, 1934, inside story, 'The Crime on the Hill'. $2.50 £1.50

(Yesterday's News)

165

Shadowland, 'Expressing the Arts', November 1922. $5 £3

Photoplay, 'World's Top Film Magazine', Belinda Lee cover, September 1956. $3.50 £2

Picturegoer, December 11th, 1943, Bob Hope cover. $7 £4

Pictures and the Picturegoer, 'All the latest and best photographs', August 22nd, 1914. $6 £3.50

Film Pictorial, 'Secrets of Charlie Chaplin', March 14th, 1936. $3.50 £2

The London Pictorial, 'Picks the Pictures that Please', May 29th, 1933. $2.50 £1.50

Yesterday's Paper

One of the most fascinating and profitable areas of collecting to emerge over recent years is that concerning film memorabilia. It would appear that virtually any artefact connected with the stars of the profession has a marketable value, but if you should chance upon the silk blouse worn by Marilyn Monroe in the film 'Bus Stop' or the red shoes worn by Judy Garland in the 'Wizard of Oz' you really would be into a fortune.

A polychrome film poster, 'Inn of the Sixth Happiness', 20th Century Fox, printed by Stafford & Co. Nottingham, 30 x 40in. (Christie's) $50 £30

Sergio Gargiulo, 'Clark Gable and Vivien Leigh in 'Gone with the Wind', original poster artwork, signed and dated '44, pastel, 16¼ x 12in. (Christie's) $700 £385

A stetson of fawn coloured hatter's plush, accompanied by a letter of authenticity from Gerald A. Fernback stating that 'John Wayne presented . . . his personal stetson when visiting London in February 1951'. (Christie's) $4,000 £2,200

Metro-Goldwyn-Mayer Studios Tom and Jerry — 'Barbecue Brawl', gouache on full celluloid applied to a water-colour background, 8½ x 11¼in. (Christie's) $1,320 £715

An original Paco Rabanne 'chain mail' dress, accompanied by a letter of authenticity and a film still of Audrey Hepburn wearing it in the 1966 Twentieth Century Fox film 'Two for the Road'. (Christie's) $2,035 £1,100

Dexter Brown, 'Portrait of Steve McQueen', signed, oil on board, 25½ x 17½in., framed. (Christie's) $1,830 £990

James Dean, '. . . Denn Sie Wissen nicht Was Sie tun (Rebel Without A Cause)' a German polychrome film poster, Warner Bros., printed in Heidelberg, 33 x 23¼in. (Christie's) $150 £88

Ronald Reagan, 'Law and Order' and 'Tropic Zone', two polychrome film posters, Universal productions and Paramount Pictures, both 30 x 40in. (Christie's) $1,425 £770

R. R. Bombe, 'Portrait of Marlene Dietrich', signed, ink inscription dated 15.11.59, watercolour and pencil, 18 x 14in. (Christie's) $185 £99

Cecil Beaton 'Liza, after Delacroix', signed and titled pencil sketch of Audrey Hepburn as Eliza Doolittle in 1964 CBS/Warner film 'My fair lady', 13 x 10in., window mounted, framed and glazed. (Christie's) $900 £495

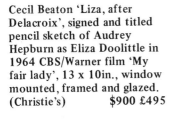

Two luggage labels each stamped 'S.S. President Roosevelt, Hong Kong to Yokohama, 12 Jun 1964', one inscribed with passenger's details 'Judy Garland', both signed by Judy Garland, signed by Alfred Hitchcock on reverse and annotated with a self-portrait caricature. (Christie's) $325 £176

A 1920's style sleeveless evening dress of black silk chiffon, worn by Betty Grable for publicising the 1940 Twentieth Century Fox film 'Tin Pan Alley'. (Christie's) $120 £66

A photographer's contract comprising a typescript receipt form acknowledging payment and authorising 'Earl S. Moran, . . . to use my photograph for advertising purposes . . . ' inscribed in blue ink with payment details, '$15.00', date 'Los Angeles 26 April '49', and model's name and address, 'Marilyn Monroe, 1301 Nr Harper'. (Christie's) $4,885 £2,640

A page from an autograph book with manuscript inscription 'Love and Kisses Marilyn Monroe'; with a collection of thirty-two clipped signatures and autographs. (Christie's) $1,320 £715

Charlie Chaplin autographed menu, for the 'Critics' Circle Film Section, Luncheon to Charles Chaplin Esq, Empress Club, W.1., 10.X.52', signed 'Charlie Chaplin'. (Christie's) $110 £65

A 'translucent' evening dress of 'gold' and 'silver' sequins, the bodice with shoe-string straps, the skirt slit to the thigh, worn by Joan Collins as Alexis Colby, 1981. (Christie's) $1,220 £660

Edith Head 'Ginger Rogers in Tender Comrade', signed, charcoal, pencil and coloured crayon costume design, titled by artist and inscribed 'Embroidered organdie', 11¼ x 8¾in. (Christie's) $530 £286

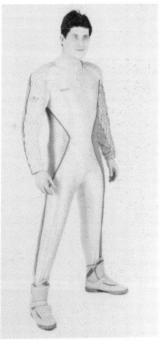

A pair of elaborate costumes of various materials, worn by dancers in the 1978 Universal Studios film 'The Wiz', accompanied by a still showing similar costumes. (Christie's) $325 £176

A rare album containing ninety-four snap-shots of film stars and film studios in Los Angeles, California, 1917-1918, subjects include Charlie Chaplin, Mary Pickford, and various camera-men and directors. (Christie's) $1,300 £715

A one piece running suit of yellow, grey and scarlet 'lycra', and a colour still of Arnold Schwarzenegger wearing the suit in the 1987 Tri Star film 'The Running Man'. (Christie's) $650 £352

A page from an autograph book signed and inscribed 'Rudolph Valentino, London Aug 2 1923', additionally signed by Valentino's wife 'Natacha Valentino'. (Christie's) $400 £220

Ronald Reagan, a single breasted tweed jacket, fully lined, with 'Warner Bros.' woven label, accompanied by a still of Reagan wearing the jacket in the 1947 Warner Brothers film 'Stallion Road'. (Christie's) $1,730 £935

A complete set of eight 'Gone with the Wind' front of house stills; with two promotional programmes and two poly-chrome film posters. (Christie's) $265 £143

Three unpublished portrait photographs of Peter O'Toole by Bryan Wharton taken in Bagehot St., Dublin, 1976, 10 x 8in. (Christie's) $285 £154

A page from an autograph book with manuscript inscription 'To Marilyn — Love and Kisses Marilyn Monroe'. (Christie's) $1,120 £605

Marilyn Monroe 'Let's Make Love', a polychrome film poster, 20th Century Fox, printed in England, 30 x 40in. (Christie's) $610 £330

An ornate headdress of gilt metal, paper, and fibre and an autographed photograph of autographed photograph of Ava Gardner wearing the headdress in the 1976 Twentieth Century Fox film 'The Blue Bird'. (Christie's) $305 £165

A tailored blouse of pink rose silk, with '20th Century Fox' woven label inside; the blouse reputedly worn by Marilyn Monroe in the 1960 Twentieth Century Fox film 'Let's Make Love'. (Christie's) $4,884 £2,640

A tiara of simulated diamonds and pearls set in white metal; with a quantity of ornate hair pins, allused to decorate Ava Gardner's hair in her role as the Empress Elizabeth of Austria-Hungary in the 1968 Corona film 'Mayerling'. (Christie's) $610 £330

A painted sign applied with cardboard cut-out letters 'W. C. Fields . . . Poppy', and photomontage portrait of W. C. Fields, advertising the 1936 Paramount Pictures film 'Poppy', 29¾ x 39½in. (Christie's) $160 £88

A U.S.A. Air Corps officer's peak cap with manufacturers details 'Fighter by Bancroft' stamped inside, the cap worn by Clark Gable in the 1949 Metro-Goldwyn-Mayer film 'Command Decision' and a typescript letter from the editor of Picture Show to Mr Browne, congratulating him on his '. . . postcard entry which wins this unique prize of Clark Gable's uniform cap'. (Christie's) $970 £528

An autograph album, containing twenty-five signatures including Glynis Johns, Bela Lugosi, Walt Disney, H.R.H. Edward, Duke of Windsor and Wallis Windsor, Charles Cahplin, Stan Laurel, Oliver Hardy, Bing Crosby, Rex Harrison and others. (Christie's) $1,100 £605

A two piece 'pant suit' of gold lurex reputedly worn by Marilyn Monroe, and given to Jean O'Doul, the wife of Joe Di Maggio's personal manager; accompanied by a copy of a letter from James Gold O'Doul. (Christie's) $2,850 £1,540

Van Jones, 'Portrait of Grace Kelly', signed, oil on canvas, with inscription 'To Edie, Bucks County Playhouse — from Your Friend Grace Kelly — Dec 25th '49', 18¼ x 14½in. (Christie's) $810 £440

A stand-in model of Boris Karloff as Frankenstein's monster in the 1935 Universal Pictures film 'The Bride of Frankenstein', modelled by Jack Pierce with Karloff's features, the square head with metal clamps circumventing the flattened top. (Christie's) $30,500 £16,500

FILM STAR POSTCARDS

The most popular period is 1920-39, though stars of the 40's-60's are also in increasing demand. Interestingly, plain-back, postcard size stills of stars fetch virtually as much as actual postcards issued by publishers and film companies. These are known in the trade is Red Letter Cards.

Hand-coloured, real photo examples are especially popular with collectors. Condition, as always, is very important. Hand-autographed cards are also worth more. Look out for rarer cards of, for example, 'horror' stars like Karloff and Peter Cushing, also of such performers as James Cagney, Charlie Chaplin, W. C. Fields and most of the Walt Disney stars (including cartoon characters).

It's worth noting, too, that postcards of the old cinemas (often now bingo halls) where these stars appeared can fetch £15-£40, depending on condition and the location of the photograph.

RANDOLPH SCOTT, born 23rd January 1903, debut in 'Sky Bridge' (1931). Pictures include: 'Follow the Fleet', 'The Nevadan Colt 45', 'Sugarfoot'. $3.50 £2

RITA HAYWORTH, real name Margarita Cansino, born 17th October 1919. Pictures include: 'Cover Girl', 'Seperate Tables', 'The Happy Thieves'. $2 £1

RAY MILLAND, real name Reginald Truscott-Jones, born in Neath, Wales, 3rd January 1908. Pictures include: 'Beau Geste', 'Ebb Tide', 'Reap the Wild Wind'. $5 £3

JANE WITHERS, child star. Pictures include: 'Bright Eyes', 'North Star', 'Danger Street'.
                                    $5 £3

CHARLES BOYER, born France, 28th August 1899. Pictures include: 'Caravan', 'Fanny', 'Hold back the dawn'.
                            $3.50 £2

FREDDIE BARTHOLOMEW, child star, born London, 28th March 1924, debut in USA in 'David Copperfield' (1935). Pictures include: 'Kidnapped', 'Swiss Family Robinson', 'Little Lord Fauntleroy'. $7 £4

(Border Bygones)

HUMPHREY BOGART, one of the most sought after cinema stars, famous as a gangster. $10 £6

MAE WEST, Paramount Pictures No.10. $9 £5

DON AMECHE, pictures include: 'Sins of Man', 'Ramona', 'Alexanders Ragtime Band'. $3.50 £2

GENE RAYMOND, born New York City, 13th August 1908. Pictures include: 'Red Dust', 'Flying Down to Rio', 'Plunder Road'. $3.50 £2

GINGER ROGERS, real name Virginia Katherine McMath, born 16th July 1911. Pictures include: 'Top Hat', 'Swing Time', 'Perfect Strangers'. $5 £3

RUDY VALLEE, born 28th July 1901, real name Hubert Prior Vallee, band leader turned actor. Pictures include: 'Gentlemen Marry Brunettes', 'Man Alive'. $3.50 £2

CLARK GABLE, born 1st February 1901. Pictures include: 'Hell Divers', 'Mutiny on the Bounty', 'Gone with the wind'. $5 £3

RICHARD ARLEN, born 1st September 1900, in Charlottesville, USA, served in British RAF. Pictures include: 'Alice in Wonderland', 'Sea God', 'Grand Canyon'. $5 £3

FRED ASTAIRE, born 10th May 1900, dancer. Pictures include : 'Holiday Inn', 'Ziegfeld Follies', 'Blue Skies'. Won nine Emmy awards in 1958. $7 £4

(Border Bygones)

SPENCER TRACY, born Milwaukee, 5th April 1900, screen debut in 1930 in 'Up the River', Academy award in 1937. $5 £3

BETTE DAVIS, born 5th April 1908. Pictures include: 'Of Human Bondage', 'The Little Foxes', 'Deception'. $5 £3

NELSON EDDY, born 29th June 1901, actor/singer. Pictures include: 'Phantom of the Opera', 'Rose Marie'. $7 £4

BARBARA STANWYCK, real name Ruby Stevens. Pictures include: 'Annie Oakley', 'Walk on the Wild Side', 'Ladies of Leisure'. $3.50 £2

OLIVIA DE HAVILLAND and ERROL FLYNN, famous romantic duet. Olivia de Havilland was born in Tokyo, Japan, 1st July 1916. $7 £4

JOAN CRAWFORD, born 23rd March 1908, ex dancer. Pictures include: 'Sudden Fear', 'Johnny Guitar', 'Queen Bee'. $3.50 £2

HENRY FONDA, born 16th May 1905, screen debut in 'Farmer Takes a Wife' (1935). Pictures include: 'Jesse James', 'War and Peace', 'Young Mr Lincoln'. $5 £3

GRETA GARBO, real name Greta Gustafson, born Sweden, 18th September 1906. Pictures include: 'Temptress', 'Mata Hari', 'Flesh and the Devil'. $15 £9

GARY COOPER, born 7th May 1901, Academy award 1952 for Best Performance in 'High Noon'. Pictures include: 'Return to Paradise', 'Sergeant York', 'For whom the bell tolls'. $5 £3

(Border Bygones)

174

FILM STAR POSTCARDS

INGRID BERGMAN, born Sweden, 1917. Pictures include: 'Joan of Arc', 'Casablanca', 'Indiscreet'. $7 £4

VIVIEW LEIGH AND LAURENCE OLIVIER, starred together in Shakesperean works. $9 £5

CLAUDETTE COLBERT, born Paris, 13th September 1907. Pictures include: 'Bride for Sale', 'Secret Fury', 'Texas Lady'. $5 £3

ANNA NEAGLE CBE, actress-producer, real name Marjorie Robertson. Pictures include: 'Nell Gwyn', 'Nurse Edith Cavell', 'Peg of Old Drury', 'A Yank in London'. $5 £3

SHIRLEY TEMPLE, born 23rd April 1929, child star. Pictures include: 'Bright Eyes', 'Wee Willie Winkle', 'Heidi', 'Stow-away', 'Little Princess'. $7 £4

MARGO, real name Maria Castilla, born Mexico, 10th May 1918. Pictures include: 'Lost Horizon', 'Crime without Passion', 'The Leopard Man'. $3.50 £2

DAVID NIVEN, born Scotland, 1st March 1910, served in Highland Light Infantry in Malaya, became Colonel. Pictures include: 'Rose Marie', 'Charge of the Light Brigade', 'Guns of Navarone'. $7 £4

ROBERT TAYLOR, born 5th August 1911, Lieutenant in US Navy. Pictures include: 'Ivanhoe', 'Quentin Durward', 'Ambush', TV star in 'The Detectives'. $3.50 £2

MARLENE DIETRICH, real name Maria Magdalene Von Losch, born Berlin, 27th December 1904. Pictures include: 'Dishonoured', 'Blonde Venus', 'Desire'. $12 £7

(Border Bygones)

FISHING TACKLE

Fishing is the most popular outdoor sport in Britain and since there are reckoned to be three million anglers in the country, there is a huge market for collecting anything connected with fishing. Because they tend to deteriorate rapidly and are often in poor condition, rods are not greatly in demand except for lightweight split cane rods, but reels, landing nets, gaffs and flies are all eagerly collected. Some of the best names among fishing tackle makers are Hardy Brothers of Alnwick which was established in 1872; Mallochs of Perth; Allcocks of Redditch and Farlows of London. Fishing reels in particular fetch high prices and one of the best is a Silex Reel made by Hardy's of Alnwick in the 1930's which has the advantage of not getting tangled. Its price today is over £1,000. As well as tackle, fishing books have a strong following and, of course, one of the most desirable is Izaak Walton's "The Compleat Angler" first published in 1653 and republished in many editions since.

Hardy's Anglers' Guide 53rd Edition, 1931 issue with 20 colour plates. $60 £35

A selection of salmon flies by Allcocks, Redditch, in original packets, circa 1938.
                              $5 £3 each

Anglers' Guide of Foster Bros. of Midland Works, Ashbourne, England, 1945, 94 pages of fishing tackle. $18 £10

A line dryer made of wood, brass and alloy used for drying silk lines, circa 1940.
                    $25 £15

Allcocks & Co. Ltd., catalogue No. 44 wholesale price list of fishing tackle for USA and Canada, circa 1927.
                    $85 £50

A medium size alloy trout wet fly box and cast carrier, to hold 75 flies, a cast compartment in the lid, 1938. $35 £20

(Robert C. Coley)

FISHING TACKLE

Albert Smith & Co., Anglers catalogue No. 19, 1939, 176 pages. $25 £15

A set of bait boxes, circa 1870, of hammered brass construction with small copper name plates on the top of the lids. $50 £30

Smith & Wall Ltd., tackle catalogue, circa 1927, 38 pages of tackle. $80 £45

An alloy small trout dry fly box with celluloid windows and a washable slate on the lid, 3½in. wide, 1935. $35 £20

A Hardy Nottingham Starback 'Silex' reel made in mahogany, the drum fitted with turned cow horn handles on brass mounts, 5in. across back, circa 1905. $260 £150

A salmon alloy fly box with clips on both sides to hold 30 salmon flies, circa 1930. $35 £20

A nickel plated brass side-mounted American trotting reel with twin wooden handles, 4¾in. diam., circa 1920. $80 £45

An alloy trout dry-wet box with celluloid windows and clips in the lid for wet flies, 1939. $45 £25

An ebonite sea casting reel in the style of a Scarborough reel, marked Pownall, circa 1935. $85 £50

(Robert C. Coley)

FOLEY

The Foley pottery was established in Fenton, Staffordshire in the mid 19th century and was operated from 1903 by E Brain & Co. Its porcelain is noted for the simplicity of its design. That said, in the 1930's work was commissioned from leading contemporary artists such as Graham Sutherland and Laura Knight and is marked with the maker's name and the signature of the artist and decorator. The Foley marks include the brand name Peacock Pottery, with a peacock in a rectangle and Staffordshire knot.

A Foley 'Intarsio' 'Kruger' teapot and cover, designed by Frederick Rhead, modelled as the South African Statesman, 12.7cm. high. (Phillips) $563 £320

Early 20th century Arts & Crafts ceramic umbrella stand, stamped with logo, 'The Foley "Intarsio" England', 27½in. high. (Robt. W. Skinner Inc.) $700 £416

A large Foley Intarsio circular pottery plate painted with sunflowers, 12½in. diam. (Christie's) $224 £170

A Foley Intarsio tapering cylindrical vase with bulbous rim, 8½in. high. (Christie's) $294 £200

A Foley 'Intarsio' tobacco jar and cover, 14.3cm. high, no. 3458, Rd. no. 364386 (SR). (Phillips) $203 £140

A Foley 'Intarsio' earthenware clock case in the form of a miniature longcase clock, circa 1900, 33.8cm. high. (Lawrence Fine Art) $706 £484

A Foley 'Intarsio' earthenware vase of ovoid shape with two handles, England, circa 1900, 26cm. high. (Christie's) $562 £450

FOOTBALL CLUB LAPEL BADGES

In recent years these badges have become very popular resulting in an Association of Football Badge Collectors with around 100 members

Official badges always have the maker's name and address on the reverse and names to look for are Gladman and Norman, Fattorini, Reeves, Lewis, Vaughtons, Millers, Parry, Marples and Beasley, Firmin, Pinches and Butler. Especially sought after are badges from clubs which are no longer in existence or early badges from clubs which went on to become the giants of the game such as Liverpool or Manchester United. Some collectors confine themselves to Scottish or English badges while others collect across the board. Badges of recent date sell for around £1 but if they date from the 1920's and are still in good condition, the price can be as high as £50. Approximate prices are as follows — 50p to £2 for 1970's badges; 50p to £5 for 1960's badges; £3 to £8 for 1950's badges; £5 to £10 for 1940's badges and £5 to £20 for 1930's badges. The price for badges dating before 1930 starts at £10.

Watford Supporters Club 87-88. $2 £1

Liverpool FC League Champions, 1921-22, by Tiptaft. $50 £30

Accrington Stanley Division III Northern Section by Vaughtons. $40 £25

Abbey United Supporters Club by thomas Fattorini, pre-1949. $35 £20

English Schools' Football Association, England v. Rest, by Thomas Fattorini, 1950's. $18 £10

Aston Villa FC English Cup Final 1920. $40 £25

Aston Villa London Lions Club by Reeves. $5 £3

Llanewst United FC, by Lewis, issued 1987. $2.50 £1.50

Tottenham Hotspur Canada Tour, 1952. $25 £15

Buckingham Town FC Supporters Club. $18 £10

(Keith Wilkinson)

FOOTBALL PROGRAMMES

Earliest examples of football programmes date back to the 1880's when they were simple teamsheets with marginal advertising. There is a trade association, a monthly magazine and several clubs for devotees of this branch of collecting. It is not a rich man's hobby though there are some very special programmes that change hands for three figure prices. An example of one is the programme for the first Wembley Final in 1922/23 when West Ham United played Bolton. It is priced at around £140 if in good condition. Most programmes however cost below £10. Some collectors try to specialise in the programmes relating to games played by a specific team while others concentrate on Cup Final or International programmes. One of the great games of all time was played between Great Britain and Europe at Hampden Park, Glasgow, in 1946/47 and the programme for it now costs around £6. About twice that sum would be asked for a programme of the Victory International, played in 1945/46 between Scotland and England also at Hampden Park.

1973 Celtic playing Vejle in Denmark, away games in Europe are always in demand.
$14 £8

1951 Portsmouth v Spurs, this early Pompey programme opens out to form one long sheet.
$7 £4

1929/30 FAC Final, Arsenal v. Huddersfield, pre-War FAC Finals are amongst the most eagerly sought programmes.
$150 £90

The 1973/74 F.A. Amateur Cup Final between Bishop's Stortford and Ilford was the last to be held. $3.50 £2

1945/46 Scotland v. England (Victory International) at Hampden Park, Glasgow.
$30 £18

Wolves v. Bangu of Brazil in the 60's, when British clubs were popular visitors to the USA and Canada. $25 £15

1948 Queen's Park v. Hearts at Hampden Park, 40's Scottish programmes are quite rare. $18 £10

1922/23 F. A. Cup Final between West Ham United and Bolton was the first Wembley Final. $350 £200

Hibs were due to play Barcelona in December 1960, but the game was called off due to fog. $60 £35

Accrington Stanley v. Darlington, 1960/61. Accrington are now no longer in existence. $18 £10

Everton v. Rangers in Dubai, the rich Arab States pay large sums to attract Western glamour clubs. $12 £7

1938/39 Scotland v. England and a 2-1 victory for the Scots at Hampden Park. $35 £20

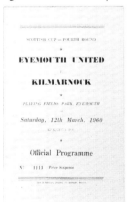

Eyemouth United, a Berwickshire fishing village play 1st Division Kilmarnock in the Scottish Cup. $18 £10

Derby defender Ray McFarland celebrated his Testimonial with a match against the Belgian club F.C. Bruges. $3.50 £2

Dunfermline Athletic v. Slovan Bratislava in the Cup Winners Cup semi final, a very rare programme. $45 £25

FURNITURE

Furniture is more than a collection of utilitarian objects for sitting on, lying on and eating off. It is an expression of the aspirations of the people who use it and the period in which they live. We all need furniture – it is the sort of furniture that we like which is significant. The Egyptians had chairs with rounded legs and ornamented backs; the Romans liked pieces to be heavier and more squat; French furniture during the years before the Revolution was light, curving, elegant and beautifully ornamented – the furniture of the rich and careless. In Britain, furniture has reflected the style of the age from the rough hewn solidity of the Tudor pieces that look as if they were cut by craftsmen from the same oak out of which they made the ships that routed the Armada to the elegance of Regency furniture with spindly legs and basket work chair backs. That was followed by the solemnity of Victorian furniture with bulbous legs on tables and masses of fussy detail on tops of cabinets. The 20th century has seen an enormous change in styles from the fake Mediaevalism of the Arts and Crafts Movement to the chrome and smoked glass styles of the 1970's. Collectors can take their pick of the style of furniture that appeals to them – bergere chairs, papier mache tables decorated with mother of pearl, wardrobes that look as if they are made of panels taken from castle walls or desks with elegant gilding and bayonet legs that look too fragile to carry any weight. The genius of designers like Chippendale, Sheraton, William Morris, Hepplewhite and Pugin can still be appreciated today.

A Regency mahogany canterbury with carrying handle and one division with spindle uprights, 18in. wide. (Christie's)
$4,123 £2,530

A dining table, the five legs joined by flared stretchers, by Gustav Stickley, circa 1905-1907, 54in. diam. (Robt. W. Skinner Inc.)
$6,800 £3,675

A Gustav Stickley oak 'Eastwood' chair with original rope support for seat, circa 1902. (Robt. W. Skinner Inc.)
$28,000 £16,666

A Sheraton Revival rosewood and marquetry small cylinder desk, 28in. wide. (Dreweatt Neate) $2,232 £1,200

A George II mahogany card table with folding top, 32¾in. wide. (Christie's) $3,227 £1,980

A painted and grained pine Empire cupboard, New England, circa 1830, 18¼in. deep. (Robt. W. Skinner Inc.) $900 £505

A Regency mahogany what-not with two tiers, ring-turned supports and two drawers, 24in. wide. (Christie's) $2,525 £1,540

A walnut chest-on-stand with moulded quartered top, basically early 18th century, 40in. wide. (Christie's) $2,345 £1,430

A Sheraton period two tier mahogany dumb waiter, the two tiers with hinged flaps, 37in. high. (Prudential Fine Art) $1,387 £750

A William IV burr-yew daven-port with three-quarter spindle gallery and green leather-lined sloping flap, 20½in. wide. (Christie's) $11,228 £6,380

A Regency mahogany library armchair, the cane filled back and seat with red leather squab cushions. (Christie's) $3,406 £2,090

A cane-sided plant stand, pro-bably Limbert, circa 1910, 23in. high, the top 16in. sq. (Robt. W. Skinner Inc.) $475 £282

A walnut side table with three drawers on cabriole legs and pad-feet, 30½in. wide. (Christie's) $2,402 £1,320

A Charles II oak chest-of-drawers with oyster walnut veneered front, 3ft.3in. wide. (Woolley & Wallis) $2,268 £1,400

Mid 19th century rosewood stool, the padded seat covered in floral needlepoint, 17¼in. wide. (Christie's) $902 £550

Edwardian inlaid mahogany music cabinet with four drawers and open shelf. (Lots Road Chelsea Auction Galleries) $495 £300

Early 20th century wicker arm rocker, 31in. wide. (Robt. W. Skinner Inc.) $200 £119

A George III brass bound mahogany cellaret with a lead-lined interior, 19in. wide. (Christie's) $3,968 £2,420

Mid Victorian figured walnut davenport with serpentine front and raised stationery box with hinged lid, 21in. wide. (Lalonde Fine Art) $1,650 £1,000

A George III mahogany breakfront bookcase with two pairs of geometrically glazed doors, 82in. wide. (Christie's) $16,137 £9,900

A set of Regency mahogany bedside steps with three red leather-lined treads, the top hinged, the middle sliding, previously fitted with a commode, 20½in. wide. (Christie's) $1,645 £880

Late 19th century lacquer cabinet formed in four sections, 216 x 135 x 44cm. (Christie's) $70,400 £44,000

Late 18th century North Italian walnut and parquetry commode, 50½in. wide. (Christie's) $6,265 £3,520

A Queen Anne walnut chest-on-stand, the drawers fitted with pierced brass handles, 40in. wide. (Chancellors Hollingsworths)
$2,754 £1,700

A figured walnut inlaid Sutherland table with four turned columns and turned gatelegs with porcelain castors, 35in. wide. (Peter Wilson)
$915 £520

A 19th century Italian blue-painted and parcel gilt four-post double bedstead, 71in. wide, 103in. high. (Christie's)
$1,996 £1,210

A George I walnut bureau inlaid with chequered lines, the slant lid enclosing a fitted interior, 41½in. wide. (Christie's) $20,493 £12,650

A mid Victorian parcel gilt, painted and sycamore work table with hinged top, 19½in. wide. (Christie's)
$1,633 £990

A 19th century French design mahogany breakfront side cabinet on bun turned feet, 3ft.10in. wide. (Woolley & Wallis) $3,300 £2,000

An early George III mahogany open armchair with padded back and seat upholstered in pink and brown cut velvet. (Christie's) $24,948 £15,400

GAMES

Anyone who was a child in the age before the television will remember evenings passed playing board games or doing jig-saw puzzles. The nostalgia element plays a large part in the enthusiastic collecting of games of which many survive. The jig-saw is a particular favourite, especially those from the 1930's when they were sold by railway companies, steamship lines and many other commercial businesses. The pictures have a period appeal, featuring landscapes or flower filled gardens with white doves on cottage roofs. Try to make sure that all the bits are in the box and that it is in good condition. Other favourite games were Ludo, Snakes and Ladders and card games like Happy Families. There were also general knowledge and word games which offered education as well as amusement. They should be complete and have their dice and shaking boxes where necessary. Even mechanical machines from pier ends are selling well now and 1970's pin ball machines have become collectors' items.

The Rose Chess Set with metal pieces. $40 £25

1950's game of Lotto, complete with cards and counters. $10 £6

1950's Zoo-m-Roo space pinball game. $18 £10

Wireless Whist Score Cards, P840. $7 £4

Oscar, the Film Stars Rise to Fame. $21 £12

Find the Car by Faulkner & Co. Ltd. $5 £3

GAMES

Happy Families by Chad Valley, circa 1910.
$15 £9

Drunken Coachman card game. $10 £6

Sport-a-Crest, Dennis's 'Dainty' Series
N. G829. $5 £3

Tops and Tails Around the World, made in
Austria. $2 £1

Lindy card game. $12 £7

The Cavalry Game. $10 £6

Bussey's Table Croquet game, complete with
balls. $85 £50

History of England card game. $10 £6

GARDEN GNOMES

The idea of 'little people' dates from earliest mythology, and gnomes were said to have guarded the treasures of the inner parts of the Earth. Perhaps it is a subconscious echo of this belief which prompts so many people to populate their gardens with these little figures.

Look out for early gnomes carved out of hardwood or stone. Later 'cast' gnomes with enamelled hats, beards and eyes can still be quite valuable, however, as can some of the handpainted small pottery examples.

1930's garden gnome with red jacket and blue trousers, 12in. high. $18 £10

Early 20th century terracotta garden gnome, 14in. high. $35 £20

An unusual 1940's garden gnome 'spraying the weeds', 7in. high. $50 £30

1960's cast concrete painted gnome with closed eyes. $10 £6

Early 20th century stoneware garden gnome with white enamelled beard. $50 £30

1950's German gnome tying his shoes, A629. $35 £20

1960's cast painted gnome with pipe. $10 £6

A Victorian stoneware garden gnome wearing a pointed red hat and green shorts, 2ft. 3in. high. (Heathcote Ball) $300 £250

Artistic gnome painting a toadstool with spots, 1950's. $35 £20

Sand filled Pebmarsh gnome, circa 1968. $20 £12

(Fred Price)

GLASS

Glass is made primarily from a combination of silicic acid and an alkali, potassium or sodium. Added ingredients make possible the huge variety in glass – for example lead, calcium, metallic oxides or gold. Since the Middle Ages people have been collecting glass and today it is one of the most interesting of the collecting categories.

The Venetian glass making industry dates back to the 11th century and in the 13th century the glassmaking ovens were removed to Murano. It was the German glassmakers who developed the skill of cutting glass which was practised with much success in Bohemia. Ruby glass Bohemian goblets are today highly prized by collectors.

Throughout the centuries and in every country there have been skilled and experimental glassmakers. In the late 19th and early 20th centuries, the Art Nouveau and Deco periods produced artists like Galle, Daum, Tiffany and Lalique whose work changes hands today for astronomical prices. Lalique in particular brought the craft of glass moulding to a high art and he did not only create very expensive objects but also produced utilitarian objects like bottles for perfume manufacturers which made his art accessible for a wide range of people and greatly influenced public taste. Collectors also seek out pewter mounted glass articles produced for the London store Liberty's under the trade name of Tudric.

Glass is essentially a utilitarian material and therefore can be found in many guises – flagons, figurines, plates, beakers, goblets and ewers, chandeliers, vases, perfume bottles and, of course, paper weights. Those made by Baccarat, St. Louis and Clichy are among the most beautiful.

A double eagle historical pint flask, GII-40, bright green, sheared mouth-pontil scar, 1830-38. (Robt. W. Skinner Inc.)
$275 £193

A faceted stemmed portrait wine glass, by David Wolff, The Hague, 1780-85, 15.8cm. high. (Christie's)
$6,946 £5,184

A Patriz Huber liqueur set, white metal and glass, stamped with 935 German silver mark and PH, circa 1900, decanter 18.4cm. high. (Christie's)
$4,099 £2,808

A baluster toastmaster's glass, the funnel bowl wet on an inverted baluster stem, circa 1710, 12cm. (Christie's) $630 £352

Mid 19th century Bohemian engraved cylindrical beaker with scenes and quotes from The Lord's Prayer, 5½in. high. (Christie's) $550 £314

'Three Dahlias', a Lalique
blue opalescent circular bQx
and cover of clear and satin
finished glass, 20.9cm. diam.
(Christie's) $469 £324

'Lys', a Lalique opalescent
bowl moulded with four
lily flowers, 24cm. diam.
(Christie's) $902 £550

A Mount Washington magnum
pink dahlia weight, 4¼in. diam.
(Christie's) $28,600 £16,342

A Baccarat double medal
cylindrical tumbler with cut
foot and sunray base, 10.5cm.
high. (Christie's) $1,378 £770

A Lalique frosted glass figure
on bronze base, Suzanne,
23cm. high without base.
(Christie's) $6,019 £4,180

'Martins Pecheurs', a black
Lalique vase, with impressed
signature R. Lalique, 23.5cm.
high. (Christie's) $8,659 £5,280

An early serving bottle, the
compressed globular body
with a kick-in base,
circa 1700, 14.5cm. high.
(Christie's) $1,530 £850

Late 19th century two-part
cut glass punch bowl,
America, 14½in. high, 14¾in.
diam. (Robt. W. Skinner Inc.)
$900 £629

A Baccarat close millefiori
wafer dish, the base with a
cane inscribed 'B1848',
10cm. high. (Christie's)
$1,533 £1,080

Mid 19th century Bohemian overlay and enamelled casket, the body in opaque white, 5¼in. wide. (Bermondsey) $600 £400

An Almaric Walter pate-de-verre paperweight designed by H. Berge, 8cm. high. (Christie's) $15,334 £9,350

Mid 19th century cobalt blue blown glass cuspidor, American, 5in. high, 9in. diam. (Robt. W. Skinner Inc.) $250 £156

Pair of 19th century cut glass lustres, 11½in. high. (Du Mouchelles) $700 £421

A Dimple Haig clear glass bottle, decorated with pierced plated mounts depicting Chinese dragons, original stopper, 10½in. high. (Peter Wilson & Co.) $120 £80

A Stourbridge olive-green opaline vase on four gilt feet detailed in white and black enamel, 12¾in. high. (Christie's) $228 £160

A Guild of Handicrafts silver and glass box and cover, designed by C. R. Ashbee, with London hallmarks for 1900, 21cm. high, 16oz. 15dwt. gross weight without cover. (Christie's) $6,894 £4,536

An Archimede Seguso 'Compisizione Piume' carafe, circa 1960, 29cm. high. (Christie's) $7,920 £4,950

'Danaides', a Lalique vase moulded with six nude maidens pouring water from urns, 18.3cm. high. (Christie's) $2,525 £1,540

191

GLOVES

Not so long ago no lady would be seen out of doors without gloves. With the disappearance of the fashion, they were carefully laid away and now collectors seek them out in second hand clothes shops because gloves are coming back. Some of the earliest gloves to be found date from the 17th and 18th centuries, and they were heavily decorated, fringed and scented, some elbow length and others with slit fingers to show off the wearer's rings. They were worn by both sexes and made of animal skin, embroidered satin, velvet knitted silk, worsted cloth or cotton. Long gloves were secured at the elbow by a ribbon or a plait of horsehair. In Victorian times gloves became more demure, hand stitched of finest suede or leather or made of crocheted silk or cotton. Some of them were fingerless. The dashing leather gloves, often with high stiff gauntlets like aviators' gloves, worn by ladies in the 1930's, are very desirable today and collectors also seek out long black or white suede gloves which were essential wear with evening gowns only forty years ago.

A pair of white kid gloves with deep cuffs of white satin embroidered in silver thread and sequins, mid 17th century. (Christie's) $3,744 £2,600

A pair of late 19th century American Woodlands Indian gauntlets of brown leather, probably Cree. (Phillips) $672 £400

A pair of gloves of pale cream chamois leather, engraved under the thumb, F. Bull & Co., Jan 4th 1791. (Christie's) $288 £220

Pair of men's kid gloves saide to have belonged to Edward VII. $175 £100

A pair of mid 19th century North American Eastern Woodlands Indian gloves of light brown leather, lined, probably Cree. (Phillips) $235 £140

A lady's glove of white kid, the deep cuff of ivory satin lined with pink silk, early 17th century. (Christie's) $366 £280

GOLFING MEMORABILIA

Some amazing prices have been chalked up for golfing items because that game seems to attract more well heeled collectors than any other sport. Anything to do with golf fetches money – books, china, clubs, balls, bags, jewellery, figurines – the demand seems insatiable. Even balls and clubs that can no longer be played with sell for enormous sums. For example, Victorian "feathery" golf balls made of stitched leather stuffed with chicken feathers are worth over £4000. One of the best known makers of those balls was William Gourlay who would be thunderstruck if he knew what present day enthusiasts are prepared to pay for them. Even feathery golf balls with no maker's name on them sell for over £700. The golfer's shopping list sounds literally baffling to the outsider for he seeks out baffy spoons (applewood clubs used for lofting); cleeks; trouble irons and scared head putters. In the evenings the golfing enthusiast will relax and read a golfing book like 'Golfiana', a little book of poems on golf which was sold in a Scottish saleroom for nearly £17,000.

Copeland Spode water jug with golfing scene on a dark blue ground, 8in. high. $1,300 £750

Silver manicure set contained in a miniature golf bag, circa 1910. $435 £250

Doulton flared mug applied with golfing vignettes of 'The Drive' and 'The Lost Ball', circa 1900, 5in. high. $435 £250

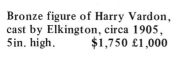
Bronze figure of Harry Vardon, cast by Elkington, circa 1905, 5in. high. $1,750 £1,000

Set of six silver spoons with golf head finials. $130 £75

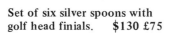
The Bushey Challenge Medal 1907, with the winners names and scores on the silver bars, by Elkington. $210 £125

GOLFING MEMORABILIA

Salt and pepper shakers in the form of a golf ball, E.P.N.S. circa 1930. $70 £40

'The Home Press', for remaking damaged Gutty balls, circa 1900. $1,000 £600

Golf club badges and buttons in silver with enamel decoration. $25 £15 each

Silver King advertising man in papier mache, circa 1920. $525 £300

'Golf Terms' cigarette cards by W. F. Faulkner, 1901, set of twelve. $700 £400

A composition painted caricature figure carrying a golf bag of clubs advertising the 'Dunlop' golf balls, 17in. high. $525 £300

American O'Hara Dial lidded mug with enamel decoration, circa 1900. $1,750 £1,000

19th century Dutch delft tiles decorated with golfing scenes. $175 £100 each

Doulton golfing jug with panels, 'Lost Ball', 'Putting' and 'Driving', impressed Lambeth mark, circa 1880. $700 £400

GOSS CHINA

Goss china was the first and finest crested china created for the burgeoning tourist trade of Victorian times. It was produced by an enterprising firm called W.H. Goss & Sons − which later became W.H. Goss Ltd. The firm was owned by William Henry Goss, a Londoner born in 1833 who started making Copeland style china in 1858 but in the 1880's he took up the suggestion of his clever son Adolphus and concentrated on producing miniature pieces of china at low prices to be sold to the day trippers who were flocking to every pretty part of the country.

Goss printed towns' crests or coats of arms on each piece made so the buyer had an instant souvenir. By a clever stroke, the crest of any town was only in that town itself so anyone aiming to start a collection − and many did − had to travel all over the country to complete it.

The porcelain made by Goss was ivory coloured with simple crests printed on. It was turned out in a vast number of shapes − Roman vases, tombs, shoes, clocks, crosses, lighthouses, replicas of famous buildings and cottages to name only a few. Today the cottages are particularly popular with collectors. Some of them were designed as nightlights so that a candle could glow through the windows and smoke rise from the chimney. They were hardly ever more than six inches long. Goss models of Anne Hathaway's cottage or Robert Burns' cottage at Alloway are particular favourites with collectors. The Goss mark was a goshawk with its wings outstretched and though other potteries copied his pieces, their marks were always different.

Goss Buckland Monachorum Font with Buckland Abbey arms. (Goss & Crested China Ltd) $770 £430

Orknie Craisie by Goss. (Goss & Crested China Ltd) $36 £20

First period figurine 'Ophelia', marked Goss & Peake, dated 1867. (Goss & Crested China Ltd) $2,685 £1,500

Durham Sanctuary Knocker flower holder wall pocket in brown, by Goss. (Goss & Crested China Ltd) $72 £40

Goss Waterlooville Soldier's Water Bottle, with matching arms. (Goss & Crested China Ltd) $45 £25

Coloured Goss parian bust of Shakespeare from the tomb in Stratford-on-Avon church. (Goss & Crested China Ltd) $152 £85

Goss Rhinoceros on oval base. (Goss & Crested China Ltd) $940 £525

Goss eggshell first period cup and saucer, white with violets in relief. (Goss & Crested China Ltd) $179 £100

Second period Goss model of Dutch Sabot. (Goss & Crested China Ltd) $36 £20

Third period Goss England Flower Girl 'Miss Julia'. (Goss & Crested China Ltd) $376 £210

First period parian 'Think Thank and Thrive' bread plate by Goss, decorated in enamels. (Goss & Crested China Ltd) $448 £250

Goss doll (No.31) child with real hair, glass eyes, china arms and stuffed legs. (Goss & Crested China Ltd) $895 £500

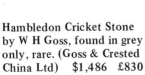

Hambledon Cricket Stone by W H Goss, found in grey only, rare. (Goss & Crested China Ltd) $1,486 £830

Goss three-handled Loving Cup invented by King Henry of Navarre, 38mm. high. (Goss & Crested China Ltd) $20 £11

Goss Old Gateway on Monnow Bridge, white glazed. (Goss & Crested China Ltd) $134 £75

GRAMOPHONE NEEDLE TINS

The collecting of gramophone needle tins developed from the separate hobby of collecting gramophones and phonographs. The tins, which are small, easy to store and cheap to buy, are often found inside the machines or in the lids. They can also sometimes be discovered in boxes of mixed lots at car boot sales or jumble sales. There are also occasional auction sales in London at which needle tins can be bought.

In the early days of gramophones, each needle could be used only once so there was a tremendous demand for them. Because there was no volume control on early gramophones, the tone was set by the needle. Popular tones were medium, loud and extra loud. Needles were sold in boxes of 100 or 200. The boxes were often attractively printed with the trade marks or special designs of the gramophone manufacturer. The principal machine manufacturers and needle producers were HMV, Songster, Columbia, Decca, Embassy and Edison Bell. More information on needle tins can be found from the City of London Phonograph and Gramophone Society which has members in Australia, America, Holland, Germany and the United Kingdom.

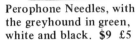

Perophone Needles, with the greyhound in green, white and black. $9 £5

Judge Brand, Test for fair trial, British tin in pale turquoise. $5 £3

Songster Supertone in pale and dark green with Songster in gold. $9 £5

Bohin, French tin in yellow and green with a black face. $10 £6

Imperial, large shaped tin in orange with black lettering, 250 needles. $5 £3

Columbia, an early tin in pale blue and gold, 300 needles. $7 £4

Herold Electro, a large four compartment German tin in red and green. $60 £35

Merchantship, a rare large Japanese tin which originally held a wrapped razor blade. $30 £18

Herold Tango, square German tin in pale turquoise, one of a series of five. $10 £6

197

GRAMOPHONES

Thomas Alva Edison launched the phonograph in America in 1876 and in 1887 Emile Berliner patented the first gramophone, also in U.S.A. The first machines were jerky because of hand cranked powering but in 1896 the techniques of clockwork mechanisms were worked out and shellac discs replaced the old zinc coated rubber discs. From the time of the First World War, every family wanted a gramophone in the parlour and there were many manufacturers vying for their business. They gave their machines wonderful names like Aeolian, Vocalion, Deccalion and Oranoca. These early machines had big horns, some of which looked very elegant and could be made of brass, painted tin (sometimes decorated with flowers inside), or papier mâché, but as people began to look on the gramophone as a piece of furniture, the horns shrank and were concealed inside the sets which were disguised as cabinets. Collectors also seek out gramophone accessories like record cleaners, needle sharpeners and needle cutters.

A G. & T. double-spring Monarch in oak case, the oak horn 18in. diam., the gramophone circa 1906. (Christie's) $1,232 £800

A horn Pathephone with chequer-strung oak case, horn 22in. diam., (Christie's) $924 £600

A Gramophone Co. mahogany Junior Monarch ('Doric') with single-spring motor, the horn 21½in. diam., circa 1908. (Christie's) $1,001 £650

A Decca Dulcephone horn gramophone with fine tin flower horn. (Onslows) $268 £180

Early HMV wind-up table gramophone with original gilt pleated circular diaphram. (Lawrence Butler & Co.) $820 £500

An HMV Intermediate Monarch gramophone with mahogany case and horn, 1911 (soundbox replaced). (Christie's) $1,158 £715

A Gramophone & Typewriter Ltd. New Style No. 3 gramophone, with 7in. turntable and concert soundbox, circa 1904. (Onslows) $834 £560

An early Kammer & Reinhardt Berliner gramophone with gilt-lined japanned cast iron base. (Christie's) $691 £480

A gramophone with 'The Gramophone Co., Maiden Lane, London, W.C.' label, a 7in. diam. turntable and four single sided E. Berliner's 7in. diam. records, circa 1900-10. (Hobbs & Chambers)$1,600 £1,000

An HMV Model 203 cabinet gramophone, 5A soundbox and re-entrant tone chamber, the mahogany case with gilt internal fittings. (Christie's) $3,564 £2,200

An early Kammer & Reinhardt 5in. Berliner Gramophone, with three Berliner records. (Phillips) $2,080 £1,300

An EMG gramophone of compact Mark 10 design, with papier mache horn, 25in. diam. and approx. 300 classical records. (Christie's) $748 £462

A Gramophone & Typewriter Ltd. Style No. 6 gramophone in panelled oak case and Concert soundbox, travelling arm and brass horn, circa 1901. (Christie's) $1,603 £990

A G. & T. single-spring Monarch gramophone with Morning Glory horn, 24in. diam., circa 1903-04. (Christie's) $492 £320

A Gramophone & Typewriter Ltd. New Style No. 3 gramophone with 7in. turntable, now with Columbia soundbox and brass horn. (Christie's) $1,452 £880

GUINEA GOLDS

Guinea Gold cigarette cards, produced by Ogdens Ltd., were introduced in 1894 and issued up to 1907. Forty two sets were issued between 1899 and 1902, with between fourteen to three thousand cards in a set. They range in value from 25p to £10 *per card*, and are identified by variations of lettering on the base.

Guinea Golds show actual photographs of actresses, prominent people, places and topical events of the day.

Boer War, 1901, 'Loading a 15 pounder field gun', Ogden's Guinea Gold Cigarettes. $2 £1

No. 458 Miscellaneous set 1902 (2974 cards in the set), M. Fournier's 'Mors' the winner of the race from Paris to Berlin 1901. $5 £3

No. 495 General Interest set, 1900, Miss E. Goodall's 'Gypsy Princess'. $2 £1

Large format Boer War 1900 Base D, 'The Boer Prison in the Happy Valley, Ceylon by permission of Black & White'. $2 £1

No. 210 New Series B 1902, 'The Three Daughters of King Edward VII (Princess Victoria, The Duchess of Fife and Princess Charles of Denmark)'. $2 £1

No. 144 General Interest 1899, HMS Ramillies 'First Class armoured twin screw battleship, 14,150 tons'. $3.50 £2

Denumbered group 1900, 'A group of Chinese boxers'. $2 £1

(Border Bygones)

General Interest 1899, 'King — Manager of Chinese Telegraphs who witheld despatches from European legations'. $3.50 £2

No. 200 Actresses 1900. Lily Langtry, her latest creation and success in 'The Degenerates'. $9 £5

General Interest, white panel base D 1900, H.R.H. The Prince of Wales. $2 £1

Large format Boer War Base D 1900, Admiral Kempff, U.S. Commander in Chief on China Station. $3.50 £2

Large format Theatre Artistes 1899, Monnie Emerald by Webber, Lancaster. $5 £3

General Interest unnumbered 1898, Col. Baden-Powell. $3.50 £2

No. 839 1900, Actresses, Alexandra Dagmar. $2 £1

No. 254 1899, General Interest, Statesman and Leaders, The Rt. Hon. Sir Frank Cavendish Lascelles, G.C.B. $2 £1

Cricketers 1898, A. Greenwell, Northumberland. $14 £8

(Border Bygones)

HAIR COMBS

Combs have been used for grooming the hair since the days of the Pharoahs – one was found in Tutankhamun's tomb. Roman combs which have turned up on archaelogical sites were made of wood, antler, ivory or bone, the teeth were cut by a fine saw and the combs were usually double sided. It was not till Renaissance times that the comb as we know it today evolved with teeth of a uniform size on only one side. Before women began bobbing their hair during the Jazz Age, combs were a necessity for keeping tresses in place. The large Spanish style comb became very popular after the huge success of Bizet's opera 'Carmen' which opened in 1875. Large upstanding tortoiseshell combs became very fashionable. They were copied in other materials and decorated with gold and silver or semi-precious stones. During the Art Nouveau period, when loosely dressed hair was an ideal of womanhood, the comb became smaller, often in a foliate design and decorated with enamelling.

An early French boxwood folding H-comb, 4¼in. long.
$4,375 £2,500

An Edwardian engraved tortoiseshell hair comb.
$35 £20

An early 16th century boxwood double-sided comb, 6¾in. long.
$2,625 £1,500

A Maori bone comb, 12.7cm. high. (Phillips) $254 £140

A carved horn, gold, enamel and mother-of-pearl hair ornament by Lalique, circa 1900, 17.5cm. wide.
$4,375 £2,500

A French hair comb of horn adorned with silver lilies in the Art Nouveau style.
$700 £400

HANDKERCHIEFS

Fashionable Italians in the Middle Ages were the first to flourish handkerchiefs and they were copied by the well to do in the rest of Europe who before that had found their sleeves perfectly adequate for the purpose of blowing the nose. Early handkerchiefs could be any shape but it was Queen Marie Antoinette of France who thought they should be square and a Royal decree to that effect was actually pronounced in January 1785 – not long before the Queen lost her head at the guillotine.

The handkerchief is not just a utilitarian object, it is a thing of beauty as well. Collectors find good examples in a wide variety of materials ranging from printed gauze to lace edged silk often for very little money. Handkerchiefs printed with pictures, rhymes, verses or comic stories turn up; so do initialled handkerchiefs, beautifully embroidered handkerchiefs and even some painted with scenes from various foreign places brought home as souvenirs.

Early 19th Century printed handkerchief apotheosis of George Washington, England, 26 x 19½in. $1,200 £700

'The Reformers attack on the Old Rotten Tree – of the Foul Nests of our Morants in Danger', handkerchief printed in colour on silk, circa 1830. (Christie's) $316 £220

1930's floral design silk handkerchief in pink, green and white. $25 £15

A large Edward VII silk handkerchief with transfer printed design. $25 £15

'A faithful representation of Her Most Gracious Majesty, Caroline Queen of England in the House of Lords, 1820', a handkerchief on linen, 22in. wide. (Christie's) $576 £400

Copper plate printed handkerchief, England, circa 1800, 18½ x 21in. $875 £500

'A representation of the Manchester Reform Meeting dispersed by the Civil and Military Powers. August 16, 1819', handkerchief on linen, 20 x 22in. (Christie's) $504 £350

Souvenir of the Great War with woven silk pictures. $85 £50

A printed George Washington handkerchief, probably England, circa 1800, 12½ x 11½in. $700 £400

Early 19th century printed handkerchief, printed in red on linen, 32 x 25½in. $1,000 £600

HATS

If you want to get ahead, get a hat! Hats are high fashion and some of the most splendid models can be found in second hand clothes shops for those with the courage to wear them.

Large hats trimmed with feathers which were popular from the late 18th till the early 20th centuries, are difficult to find in good condition because they were so fragile but often feathers alone turn up, dyed in a wide variety of colours and carefully curled. Cloche hats from the 1920's and the elegant little straw hats with eye veils of the 30's and 40's make splendid buys. Victorian silk bonnets can often be found as well as hats trimmed with artificial flowers made of silk or with flourishes of artificial fruit. Men's hats from the past times are bought by both sexes — straw boaters, trilbys and toppers in gleaming plush. Even if you don't want to wear these dashing hats, they can be displayed on bentwood hat or wig stands indoors.

A lady's flat wide-brimmed hat of plaited straw edged with ivory silk ribbon, circa 1770, 14in. diam. (Christie's) $3,000 £1,800

A large round black hat with pale drab cotton cover bearing a large elaborate badge in wire embroidery of the Bersaglieri. (Christie's) $127 £70

Iroquois beaded velvet cap with floral designs, on black velvet. $435 £250

A Nazi Naval officer's cocked hat with silk lining. (Wallis & Wallis) $192 £120

A 1920's rubber bathing cap. $45 £25

A post-1902 R.N. Flag officer's dark blue peaked cap. (Wallis & Wallis) $352 £220

A silk embroidered linen based nightcap, circa 1600. $5,250 £3,000

An interesting WW1 steel helmet in the form of a tropical helmet, khaki painted overall. (Wallis & Wallis) $100 £55

An Italian grey-green felt Alpini style hat bearing black embroidered badge of Alpine Artillery. (Christie's) $110 £60

English early 17th century man's neglige cap in white linen worked with gilt chain-stitch. $10,000 £5,750

A black satin bonnet trimmed with pleating, circa 1880. (Christie's) $26 £20

A child's or young lady's hat of ivory silk quilted with a scale design and trimmed with a rosette of ivory ribbons, circa 1820. (Christie's) $655 £500

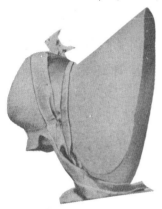

A straw bonnet with deep brim, trimmed later with satin with chine silk ribbon and artificial flowers, circa 1830. (Christie's) $340 £260

Moss Bros. grey felt top hat, complete with box. $52 £30

A bonnet of brown striped plaited straw trimmed with brown figured ribbons, edged with a fringe, circa 1850. (Christie's) $65 £50

A 16th century man's embroidered cap embellished with sequins and gold lace trim, England, 8in. high. (Robt. W. Skinner Inc.) $10,000 £6,993

Dunn & Co. felt bowler hat. $28 £16

A lady's flat wide-brimmed hat of black figured silk laid over plaited straw, circa 1770, 15¼in. diam. (Christie's) $876 £600

A top hat of brown felt, with black ribbon, by A. Giessen, Delft, circa 1870. (Christie's) $688 £462

A boy's cap of black moleskin with peak of patent leather, circa 1845. (Christie's) $114 £77

A top hat of black beaver, with black silk ribbon, 7in. high, circa 1840. (Christie's) $360 £242

A mourning bonnet of black crepe, circa 1830. (Christie's) $163 £110

A top hat of grey beaver, possibly 1829, labelled M. Strieken, 8in. high. (Christie's) $1,065 £715

A bonnet of black satin trimmed with a large bow and rouleaux, circa 1830. (Christie's) $360 £242

A top hat of grey beaver with narrow ribbon of cream ribbed silk, 5½in. high, circa 1830. (Christie's) $426 £286

A pearl grey bowler hat, made in Italy by Borsalino for Cecil, 112 rue de Richelieu, circa 1800, together with two others and a bowler. (Christie's) $65 £44

A top hat of grey beaver, 7½in. high, circa 1830. (Christie's) $426 £286

HMS INVINCIBLE ARTEFACTS

HMS Invincible started life in the French Navy in 1744 and was captured by the British Channel Fleet under Anson in 1747 at the Battle of Cape Finisterre. Commissioned into the British Navy, the revolutionary 74-gun Invincible was to have been Admiral Hardy's flagship in the expedition against the French in Canada in 1758. She ran aground on Horsetail Sandbank in the Channel, where, despite attempts to refloat her, she went down on 22 February.

A wooden gun tackle single block with 1¼in. sheave, stamped 'X', 10in. long. (Christie's)
$744 £418

A gun cartridge piercing spike with turned beech wood handle, 4in. long, (spike broken). (Christie's) $509 £286

A leather shoe of welt construction, the uppers partially cut away, 9in. long. (Christie's) $1,076 £605

A stoneware jug complete with handle and lipped neck, 9½in. high. (Christie's) $1,468 £825

One of two wicker baskets, one with both handles. (Christie's) $117 £66

One of two cast iron grenades both with wooden fuses, one marked 'X' and one with canvas fuse cover. (Christie's)
$1,566 £880

An elm clew block, without pin or sheave, stamped 'XVI', 16in. long. (Christie's)
$881 £495

A single pulley block with 2¼in. lignum vitae sheave, stamped 'XVIII', 18in. long. (Christie's) $430 £242

Part of a set of parrel tackle comprising two bars of ash or elm, 12in. long, and two trucks, 2¾in. long, and another similar. (Christie's) $391 £220

A sailor's square wooden dinner plate, with fiddle, 11¾ x 11¾in. (Christie's) $1,664 £935

A spirit barrel of approx. 2 gals. capacity, built of fourteen oak staves originally bound with four iron hoops, 17½in. high. (Christie's) $430 £242

A stave built oak save-all or bucket, with wicker binding and pegged oak bottom, and remains of original rope handle, 10¼in. high x 14½in. diam. (Christie's) $352 £198

A 14-second sand glass, the case with turned oak ends, four pine struts and beech packing, 5½in. high. (Christie's) $5,482 £3,080

An elm clew block with 2in. lignum vitae sheave, stamped 'XVI', 16½in. long. (Christie's) $587 £330

A leather firebucket with stitched sides and bottom, complete with handle, 10in. high, (restored). (Christie's) $1,272 £715

A 32-pounder gun ramrod head stamped '32' and 'I', 6in. diam. (Christie's) $509 £286

HOLD TO LIGHT POSTCARDS

These cards reveal a 'surprise' when held to the light. There are transparencies, which appear 'normal' until held to the light, and cut-outs, which have cut out sections in the form of flames, moons, windows, etc. forming a source of light. Some noted publishers include Hartmann (transparencies), Samuel Cupples (particularly 1904 World's Fair cards) and Meteor Transparencies. Look for Father Christmas cards (£40 plus) and date letter and flame cut-out cards at about £15.

'Behind these naughty children throw a light and you will see them have their bolster fight'.
$18 £10

'A Happy Christmas', 1905. $12 £7

'A Merry Christmas', Cat hold to light.
$12 £7

'Hearty Wishes for Christmas', hold to light card printed in Germany. $10 £6

'A Happy New Year, With Best Wishes', printed in Germany. $9 £5

'A Bright and Happy Christmas', by D.R.G.M.
$9 £5

'A Merry Christmas', Windmill hold to light.
$10 £6

HORSE BRASSES

About thirty years ago there was a craze for buying old horse brasses, of which there were a large supply. Because farmers had been replacing draught horses with tractors for a couple of decades, they often had a glut of old harness cluttering up their premises and it was cleared out. The attractive old brasses which used to be mounted on the martingales, lames, straps and buckles of cart horses' harness proved so popular with the collecting public that enterprising manufacturers began producing hundreds of replicas which were often mistaken for originals. However, a genuine old horse brass is generally much heavier than a new one. It is also of a more mellow colour and is always well rubbed. New horse brasses were often artificially rubbed down on the front but the giveaway is the back which is still rough.

Old brasses were ancient symbols or amulets relating to pagan fertility gods. They were also thought to have the power of diverting the evil eye from the horse. They were handmade by gypsies and sold at fairs up and down the country for centuries until around 1830 when mass produced stamped brasses began to appear for the demand for them was immense by the end of Victoria's reign. The earliest designs were very traditional and showed acorns, flowers, wheatsheaves, stags, trees, foxes running or fox masks. By the mid 19th century new designs of portraits, geometric patterns and symbols representing events like Queen Victoria's diamond jubilee, began to appear and proved very popular. When buying horse brasses, bear in mind that those still mounted on their original leather straps are the most valuable.

Galloping horse cast brass, late Victorian. $18 £10

1950's pressed brass 'Tally-Ho'. $3.50 £2

Victorian cast dog horse brass. $20 £12

1920's cast brass parrot. $9 £5

Cast steam locomotive brass. $90 £50

Victoria 1870, a rare cast brass. $130 £75

Squirrel design horse brass, circa 1920. $10 £6

An early pierced horse brass of early design, circa 1820. $45 £25

HOSPITAL & NURSE BADGES

Florence Nightingale, who opened the first nurses' training school in 1860, disapproved of badges, so it was many years before they were issued to those who trained there. As the number of schools and training organisations increased, however, it became customary for them to issue their own medals on completion of training. Most pre-1960 badges were enamelled silver or bronze; later ones were mainly base metal. With fewer training schools, the variety of badges is no longer so great.

General Nursing Council for England and Wales, blue enamel on base metal. $7 £4

Clacton and District Hospital, blue and red enamel on base metal, 1950. $5 £3

Hartlepool School of Nursing, green, white and black enamel on base metal. $5 £3

Royal Hampshire County Hospical, red and blue enamel on silver, E. M. James, SRN. $14 £8

Royal College of Nursing, blue and red enamel on base metal, showing sun for day duty and stars for night duty. $7 £4

Glamorgan County Asylum Committee, hallmarked 1899, depicting a dragon on the front and hung on a green ribbon. $35 £20

Richmond Red Cross Hospital, red, green and white enamel on silver, awarded to Mabel Goldsmith, July 1915. $35 £20

St Marylebone Hospital, bronze and boxed, awarded retrospecitvely to Gertrude Morris, 1902-1905. $25 £15

Manchester Royal Infirmary, base metal showing Good Samaritan. $7 £4

Medway School of Nursing, grey, blue and gold enamel on base metal, showing the Medway Bridge. $3.50 £2

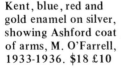

Ashford Hospital, Kent, blue, red and gold enamel on silver, showing Ashford coat of arms, M. O'Farrell, 1933-1936. $18 £10

St Luke's Hospital, Lowestoft, various enamels on silver, showing London County Council coat of arms. $20 £12

Salisbury General Hospital, blue enamel on base metal, showing local landmark, SEAN was only awarded between 1943 and 1961. $7 £4

London Fever Hospital, mauve enamel on silver. $5 £3

INDENTURES

Besides the fascination of their content, old indentures are often beautiful in their own right, hand-cut and adorned with seals and embossings. Some even included slivers of silver as part of the duty stamp. As a general guide to value, the more pictorial the better, smaller sizes are preferred, and anything pertaining to local history usually attracts a premium. Look out for documents with interesting signatures, and always check the interest of the content too.

The Last Will and Testament of William Wittle, including the Probate Certificate and large seal, dated 30th October, 1863. $18 £10

Indenture dated 5th August 1825, in respect of a 'parcel' of land for £45, in the name of William Tanner. $18 £10

Obligation Bond dated 29th April 1737, with three witness signatures and a seal, between James Cozen and Francis Jones. $50 £30

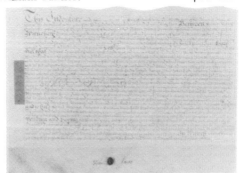

Indenture dated 24th August 1739 referring to a property transaction to William Baston. $35 £20

Indenture dated 28th April 1737, re the sale of a tenement and three acres of arable land for the sum of five shillings. $25 £15

(Border Bygones)

INK BOTTLES

Ink was expensive in the 19th century and to keep the price of their product down in a very competitive market, ink manufacturers made every effort to market it as cheaply — but as eye-catchingly — as possible.

Ink bottles can be found in glass, saltglaze pottery and occasionally porcelain. Among the rarest examples are 'sheered lip' glass bottles in which the glass bottle openings were not polished but only broken off and sealed with a cork and sealing wax.

There were ink bottles in the shape of turtles, cottages, locomotives, Bonaparte, Mr Punch, igloos, bird cages and grimacing clowns. Today there is a strong American interest in ink bottle collecting.

A Tiffany Studios bronze and glass inkwell, 18cm. diam., stamped Tiffany Studio New York, 69391. (Phillips) $518 £360

Staffordshire ceramic face ink bottle in the form of Sairey Gamp with the open mouth providing access to the ink reservoir. $100 £60

A Lowestoft square inkwell, the base inscribed in black, 'Eliz,th. Buckle 1775', 5cm. high. (Lawrence Fine Art) $4,306 £2,970

Aqua glass umbrella inkwell embossed with G. H. Fletcher, London. $45 £25

Mid 19th century 'Bonaparte' ink bottle, the hollow body forming the reservoir while the front hole acts as a quill holder. $260 £150

Aqua glass birdcage inkwell embossed with bars, a door and two feeders. $45 £25

A cobalt blue glass square shaped inkwell with cavity for free pen nib. $35 £20

An extremely rare deep green glass turtle or sunflower ink-well, possibly French. $350 £200

Blackwoods of London, aqua glass igloo inkwell with embos-sed Registry of Designs diamond. $25 £15

'Mr Punch' saltglaze ink bottle, incised on the back 'Gardeners Ink Works, Lower White Cross St., London', 4½in. high. $210 £120

American red and blue ceramic bottles known as 'MA' and 'PA', with removable heads forming the cork stoppers. $175 £100

A fine white china inkwell in the form of a dolphin, the open mouth providing access to the reservoir, with Perry & Co., London, printed on the base. $175 £100

Aqua glass cottage inkwell with water butt and stippled roof decoration, 6cm. high. $85 £50

An extremely rare circular cot-tage inkwell in aqua glass em-bossed on the base for August 1868, 6cm. high. $260 £150

Aqua glass inkwell in the form of a beehive made from coiled straw with opening at the base. $175 £100

215

INSTRUMENTS

There is a huge collecting market for scientific instruments. They range from architects' or surveyors' sets to ships' chronometers and many are appearing on the market now because they have been usurped by electronic gadgets which do the job but do not look nearly as decorative. Microscopes are particularly popular with collectors but they have to be at least early 19th century and made of brass to be worth serious money because later students' microscopes had cast iron bases and struts. Telescopes are much sought after, especially again if brass mounted and collectors long to find long pull-out telescopes dating from the early 19th century which we imagine Nelson raising to his blind eye. There is a huge range of instruments to pick from − theodolites, circumferentors, equatorial dials and graphometers as well as early telephones, typewriters and Morse telegraph keys which were made of brass as well. Some instruments date from early times like a writing duplicator that was in use in the 18th century and was used to copy letters in the days before carbon paper.

A brass transit theodolite by Cooke Troughton & Simms Ltd., London, in mahogany case, 5¼in. wide. (Christie's) $616 £385

An early 19th century lacquered brass and mahogany vacuum pump, 18¾in. long, with an extensive collection of accessories. (Christie's) $8,298 £5,060

A Country painted globe, New England, circa 1810, 15in. diam., 37in. high. (Robt. W. Skinner Inc.) $5,500 £3,273

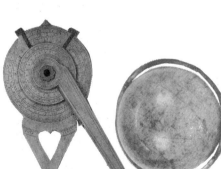

A 17th century fruitwood nocturnal, unsigned, main plate 4.1/8in. diam., index arm length 7.3/8in. (Christie's) $2,956 £1,760

A pair of early Victorian terrestrial and celestial globes, by Malby & Son, London, dated 1850. (Lacy Scott) $2,227 £1,350

Late 19th century sectional model of the eye, the plaster body decorated in colours and with glass lenses, 6¾in. high. (Christie's) $541 £330

A 16th/17th century Italian ship's drycard compass, 11cm. diam. (Phillips) $6,200 £4,000

A small one-day marine chronometer by John Roger Arnold, the dial 64mm. diam. (Christie's) $3,732 £2,592

An 18th century brass combined analemmatic and inclining dial, signed M:Semah Aboab tot Amsterdam, 185mm. long. (Christie's) $6,600 £4,551

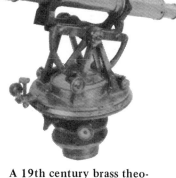

Late 18th century brass transit instrument, signed Lenoir (Paris), on circular base with three levelling screws, the telescope 53.5cm. long. (Christie's) $3,080 £2,124

A 19th century brass theodolite, signed by Troughton & Simms, 9½in. high. (Christie's) $811 £495

A lacquered brass compound monocular microscope, by Powell & Lealand, 1901, 49cm. high, in case. (Phillips) $4,650 £3,000

A gilt brass pedometer, German, possibly Augsburg, circa 1700, 65mm. long. (Christie's) $1,100 £759

A Cary brass sextant with gold scale, numbered 3856, 11¾ x 11¼in. (Lawrence Fine Art) $1,929 £1,595

A late 19th century oxidized brass surveying aneroid barometer, by Pidduck & Sons, Hanley, 6in. diam. (Christie's) $211 £132

INSTRUMENTS

A 17th century engraved silver and gilt brass geared astronomical dial, signed Ph. Dagoneau, Grenoble, 13.8cm. diam. (Christie's) $5,500 £3,793

Early 19th century lacquered brass universal equinoctial ring dial, signed Dollond, London, in original fishskin covered case, 9½in. diam. (Christie's) $5,772 £3,520

An early marine chronometer by John Arnold & Son, with 4½in. circular silvered dial, in mahogany box. (Phillips) $11,600 £8,000

An ivory diptych dial, with the thrush trademark of Hans Troschel, Nuremburg, dated 1649, 4¼in. long. (Christie's) $2,420 £1,688

A 19th century brass double-rack action twin cylinder vacuum pump, unsigned, 14in. high. (Christie's) $992 £605

A lacquered brass precision balance, the beam stamped To Weigh/To Grain, No. 5962, with electrical attachments in a glazed mahogany case, 14¾in. wide. (Christie's) $278 £176

A brass cased dip-circle by F. E. Becker & Co., on adjustable stand, 10¾in. high. (Christie's) $528 £330

Early 19th century brass compound monocular microscope, probably English, length of tube 17.3cm. (Christie's) $605 £417

A Betts's portable terrestrial globe arranged so as to fold like an umbrella, 15in. diam. (Christie's) $563 £352

IRONS

Victorian clothes were pleated, frilled, ruffled, crimped and goffered which meant that when they needed laundering, the ironing of them was a mammoth and painstaking task. To cope with it there were whole batteries of different irons for specific purposes and those which survive are highly regarded collectors' items. They range from tiny irons with long handles which were used for ironing hats to massive Tailors' Goose Irons which were capable of smoothing out the thickest materials and weighed up to 30 lbs. There were tiny curved irons only four inches long for ironing lace and heavy irons with exchangeable handles which were patented in America by a lady called Mrs Potts in 1871.

That was an excellent idea because since irons were really made of cast iron, the handles often became too hot to handle. They had to be heated on top of the fire or stove and for this reason too they were often sold in pairs so that there could always be an iron ready for use.

Towards the end of the 19th century, irons that were heated by gas, petrol or methylated spirits began to appear – the predecessors of today's electric irons.

A simple cast iron flat iron will only cost about £2 and they are often used as fireside decorations. Collectors can also find hollow irons complete with a heating stone, ornately cast iron stands and sometimes even old laundry stoves, many of which had the capacity of heating forty irons at a time.

Radiation Rhythm electric iron No.375 with a green enamelled base. $18 £10

A leaf iron in which silk is placed to receive an impression before being stitched to bonnets. $85 £50

Wooden handled hatters irons of various shapes. $35 £20 each.

Mid Victorian panel wrought charcoal iron with beechwood handle. $130 £75

19th century charcoal iron with chimney and wooden handle. $60 £35

An interesting late 19th century flat iron in the form of a horse. $70 £40

JIGSAW PUZZLES

A London map maker invented the first jig-saw puzzle in the 1760's by mounting a map on a sheet of mahogany and cutting it into small pieces with a fine marquetry saw. The reassembling of it was intended to help pupils learn geography. He sold his "dissecting maps" in wooden boxes with sliding lids and his idea was copied by other manufacturers. These early jig-saws were all hand made and quite expensive to buy but their popularity with the public was immediate. Pictures made into puzzles dealt with religious themes or history and mythology. The best known early makers whose work is eagerly sought after by collectors were J. Wallis, W. Darton, J.W. Barfoot, W. Peacock, Dean & Son and J. Betts.

At the end of the 19th century, coloured labels showing the finished puzzle were pasted on box lids and they ware worth collecting on their own. Mass production techniques and the use of plywood and fret saws meant that it was possible to turn out large numbers of puzzles at a fairly low cost and jig-saws became a craze in the 1920's and 30's before the advent of television. Some of the most famous firms who produced them were Raphael Tuck who made the Zag Zaw; Chad Valley who produced jig-saws for Great Eastern Railway and steamship lines like Cunard and the White Star Line; Frederic Warne who were also the publishers of Peter Rabbit; Victory; Holtsapffel whose puzzles were given the name 'Figure It Out'; Salman; Delta Fine Cut; Huvanco and A.V.N. Jones.

'Ireland' — for teaching youth geography, circa 1820. Unknown, probably William Darton, some replacement pieces and missing necks, 11 x 10in. $215 £125

'Venice', Vera Picture Puzzle, made in France, 1930's, and box, finely cut, with contour cutting and shapes, difficult. Made specially for Truslove & Hansen of London SW1, 9 x 12in. $35 £20

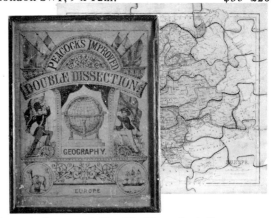

Peacocks Improved 'Double Dissection', Europe on one side, Nursery rhymes on the other. Puzzles cut in sympathy with the map (ie round borders) with large interlocking edge pieces to hold it all together, circa 1895, fine hand-coloured label to whitewood box lid, 11x12in.
$245 £140

(Trench Enterprises)

'Aladdin meets the Sultan's daughter', Huvarco puzzle, 1920's/30's, no box (often Huvarco puzzles were sold ready-made-up and without a box). $45 £25

'De Dame Te Amsterdam', Dutch made puzzle, 1930's. Amateur, but intricately cut (not a manufactured puzzle), difficult, 10 x 13in. $35 £20

'Cunard Liner Berengaria', Chad Valley for Cunard Steam Ship Co., 12 x 16in., with box. $60 £35

'Changing the Guard at Buckingham Palace', Raphael Tuck military puzzle, 1930's distinctive style of cut different to their two styles of zag zaw puzzle (one of which is interlocking, the other push-fit, but both of which include intricate shapes), 15 x 10in., with box. $35 £20

'Washington returning from Fox Hunt', Parker Brothers pastime puzzle and box (USA). 1920-1930's. Finely cut with shapes and colour contoured, a difficult puzzle, 10 x 13in. $50 £30

(Trench Enterprises)

'The History of Joseph and his Brethren', circa 1835. Unknown maker, possibly Edward Wallis. Hand coloured wood blocks, plain mahogany box, lacking original label, 9 x 10in.
$350 £200

'The Edge of the Common', Chandos puzzle (F. Hanse), 1920's/30's, 11 x 17in., and box.
$70 £40

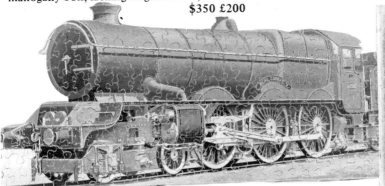

'King George V loco', Chad Valley for the Great Western Railway Co. 1930's, 8 x 22in. overall, contoured edge, hand coloured photographic print, and box.
$80 £45

'Daffodils', Chad Valley 1920's (early Chad Valley cutting style), 14 x 10in. with box. £45 £25

'At Pharaoh's Court', Victory artistic puzzle, 1950's, 14 x 18in. with box. No guide picture is supplied with these puzzles, which include strips of traditional victory shapes amongst the interlocking pieces.
$35 £20

(Trench Enterprises)

JUKE BOXES

The upsurge in nostalgia for the Rock 'n' Roll era has made its archetypal symbol, the juke box, into one of the most highly profiled of modern collectables. Collecting, however, does not come cheap, and the costs are not for the faint hearted, with prices starting at around £2,000 and extending well into five figures. The aesthetics have to appeal to you as well — few people are fortunate enough to have space for their own museum, and most collectors share their living rooms, bedrooms and even bathrooms with these large, often gaudy and never unobtrusive items.

One of the bonuses for the collector is that, hopefully, his treasure will be in working order, and may even come ready stocked with discs — an instant nostalgia trip at the touch of a button.

Chantal Meteor, produced England, 1958-1963, 200 selections at 45rpm.
$8,750 £5,000

Wurlitzer model 1015, produced USA, 1946-1947, 24 selections at 78rpm., plays A sides only. $19,250 £11,000

Wurlitzer model 2500S, produced USA, 1961, 200 selections at 45rpm.
$3,850 £2,200

AMI model B, produced USA, 1947-1948, 40 selections at 78rpm. $8,750 £5,000

AMI Continental 1, produced USA, 1961, 200 selections at 45rpm. $4,900 £2,800

Wurlitzer model 1400, produced USA, 1951, 48 selections at 78rpm.
$6,125 £3,500

(The Chicago Sound Co.)

Seeburg Symphonola 148, produced USA, 1948, plays A sides only, 20 selections at 78rpm. $7,875 £4,500

Wurlitzer model 1800, produced USA, 1955, 104 selections at 45rpm. $6,125 £3,500

Wurlitzer model 1550, produced USA, 1952-1953, 104 selections at both 78rpm. and 45rpm. $5,250 £3,000

AMI model I 200, produced USA, 1958, also in England as BAL AMI I 200, 200 selections at 45rpm. $5,250 £3,000

Wurlitzer model 1050, produced USA, 1973-1974, 100 selections at 45rpm. $8,750 £5,000

Rock-ola 1428, produced USA, 1948, plays A sides only, 20 selections at 78rpm. $10,500 £6,000

Mills Empress, produced USA, 1939, plays A sides only, 20 selections at 78rpm. $12,250 £7,000

AMI model A, produced USA, 1946, 40 selections at 78rpm. $9,625 £5,500

Wurlitzer model 1100, produced USA, 1947-1949, 24 selections at 78rpm., plays A sides only. $11,900 £6,800

(The Chicago Sound Co.)

KITCHEN EQUIPMENT

If time could be turned back and the kitchens of Victorian homes could be recreated in their entirety, antique collectors would be in heaven because there is no room more likely to yield treasures than the kitchen. From copper jelly moulds to apple corers, from wire baskets used to store eggs or boil potatoes to huge copper fish steamers, from black leaded ranges to pottery water filters, almost everything in an old kitchen is worth money today. Artistry and care marked the production of each piece, even the stamps used for making embossed butter balls were hand carved with the symbols of roses or thistles. Copper pots were beaten out by hand and when the cook set a rabbit mould it was left to cool in a copper mould in the shape of a crouching rabbit. The price of copper utensils has soared to a tremendous level but there are many other small items which can still be used today and can be picked up for very little. Look for prettily painted tin tea caddies; look for white enamel bread bins with pretty blue lettering; serving spoons with long curved handles; white pottery jelly moulds and wooden draining racks. Also desirable are old fashioned mincers and glass butter churns with a metal fly wheel mounted on the screw top lid. An early 20th century juice extractor with a long handle and a metal bowl for squeezing oranges is worth at least £5. More expensive are knife grinders with large wooden drums and iron crank handles which were turned to sharpen the kitchen knives placed blade down inside.

Plated tin Mouli grater. $9 £5

Victorian enamel slop bucket complete with lid. $35 £20

Victorian blue enamel kettle. $18 £10

A portable plated candle holder, 6in. high, circa 1915. $9 £5

Victorian white enamel jug. $9 £5

Set of three early 20th century tin shredders. $9 £5

(Border Bygones)

225

A late Victorian brass coal box with domed lid and pierced finial, 17in. wide. (Christie's) $551 £330

Late 18th century cast iron bake kettle, original fitted cover with deep flange, 13¼in. deep. (Robt. W. Skinner Inc.) $325 £225

Late 18th century wrought iron broiler, probably Pennsylvania, 20in. long. (Robt. W. Skinner Inc.) $360 £250

Victorian pressed brass bellows, circa 1880. (British Antique Exporters) $33 £25

An attractive butter crock manufactured by The Caledonian Pottery, Rutherglen, 5in. high. $260 £150

Pair of Georgian brass door stops, the moulded bases with weighted iron insets, 13¾in. high. (Woolley & Wallis) $736 £460

A mid Victorian black and gilt japanned tole purdonium, with shovel, 12½in. wide. (Christie's) $597 £418

A National currant cleaner by Parnall, Bristol. $85 £50

A Victorian copper oval jelly mold, orb and scepter mark, 5.5in. high. (Woolley & Wallis) $140 £85

KITCHEN EQUIPMENT

Victorian polished steel coal scuttle with a lifting flap and shovel. (Lots Road Galleries) $144 £90

Early 19th century copper coal helmet, also a matching shovel, 17½in. high. (Peter Wilson) $616 £390

A Regency brass tea urn with raised and pierced lid, 13in. high. (Christie's) $225 £130

An early coffee grinder by Parnall. $130 £75

A James I iron fireback. (Russell Baldwin & Bright) $500 £400'

A Benham & Froud brass kettle designed by Dr. C. Dresser, on three spiked feet, 24.5cm. high. (Christie's) $473 £324

Victorian brass preserving pan, 1850. (British Antique Exporters) $85 £50

Victorian copper kettle, circa 1850. (British Antique Exporters) $85 £50

An 18th century wrought iron bound salt bucket with swing handle, 7¼in. diam. (Christie's) $203 £121

LABELS

As everyone in advertising knows, it is the label that often sells the goods and they have to be designed as eye-catchers. The designers of some labels made a speciality of turning them into an art and collectors seek out colourful cheese or perfume labels because of that. Perfume labels from the 1920's and '30's are particularly attractive when they were designed in Art Deco styles. The labels on fruit crates are also often very colourful and designed to convey the feeling of country freshness and sunshine. Orange and apple growers in the '40's and '50's would often buy a ready designed label and have it overprinted with the name of their farm or product so the same picture can be found bearing different names. Textile labels are also very appealing though most of them tend to rely on script rather than pictures. Other labels that are eagerly collected are those used for the first appearance of certain items — soap powders for example — or for items which no longer exist or are now packaged in a different way.

Textile label Bayette, registered in South Africa. $5 £3

Columbia Belle Apples, Wenatchee, Washington, 1950's. $2   £1

Raspberryade, Haworth & Sons. $1 50p

Rosey Rapture, Cream Soda. $1 50p

Tic and Nerve Powders, W.K. Harrison. $1 50p

Elixir of Cascara Sagrada, John Baily & Co. $1 50p

Worm Powder, W. H. Laverack & Son. $1 50p

Haworth's Pineapple Crush. $1 50p

Seltzer Water, Hopkinson & Co.
$1 50p

Rowntree's Windsor Mixture, 4lb. Base, 1890's. $2 £1

Standard Jamaica Rum, Turnbull, Hawick, 1930's. $2 £1

Yesterday's Paper

Textile label Assegai
Fancy Prints, 1930.
$3.50 £2

Rowntree's Ping Pong Biscuits, 1890's. $13 £7.50

Turnbull's Scotch
Whisky, Hawick,
circa 1930. $2 £1

Habana, Flor de Lopez
Hermanos. $6 £3.50

Textile label Oubaas, 1930's. $4 £2.50

Tadcaster Tower,
Lime Juice Cordial.
$1 50p

Sparkling Cherry
Ciderette, non
alcoholic. $1 50p

Soda Water, sparkling
and refreshing. $1 50p

Haworth's Ginger
Ale, Pale Dry. $1 50p

Old Fashioned
Stone Ginger Beer.
$1 50p

Textile label Agrada,
registered in India,
1930's. $3.50 £2

Rowntree's Homoeopathic Cocoa, 1890's. $9 £5

The much improved
Fellon Drink, circa
1900. $3.50 £2

LADIES UNDERWEAR

The existence of ladies' underwear was first documented in Sumeria around 3,000 BC. About a dozen pairs of monogrammed bloomers purporting to belong to Queen Victoria do turn up every year, and sell for around £200 a piece. Maybe the good lady wore each pair only once, or maybe there's a secret factory somewhere.... Other underwear with personal associations also fetches a premium. A pink mesh bra left by Marilyn Monroe in a London hairdresser's(!) sold at auction for £520!

Late 19th century ladies padded corset, edged with lace. $100 £60

Edwardian tie-back petticoat, pleated lace edged, muslin lined and with pocket. $45 £25

Late Victorian nightdress with lace edging. $60 £35

Victorian 'combination' with floral lace edge. $70 £40

Dimety Bustle, with hide and fabric covered steel springs, circa 1880. $210 £120

Edwardian camisole with ribbon and lace inserts. $50 £27

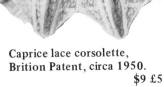

Caprice lace corsolette, Brition Patent, circa 1950. $9 £5

(Kaleidoscope)

LADIES UNDERWEAR

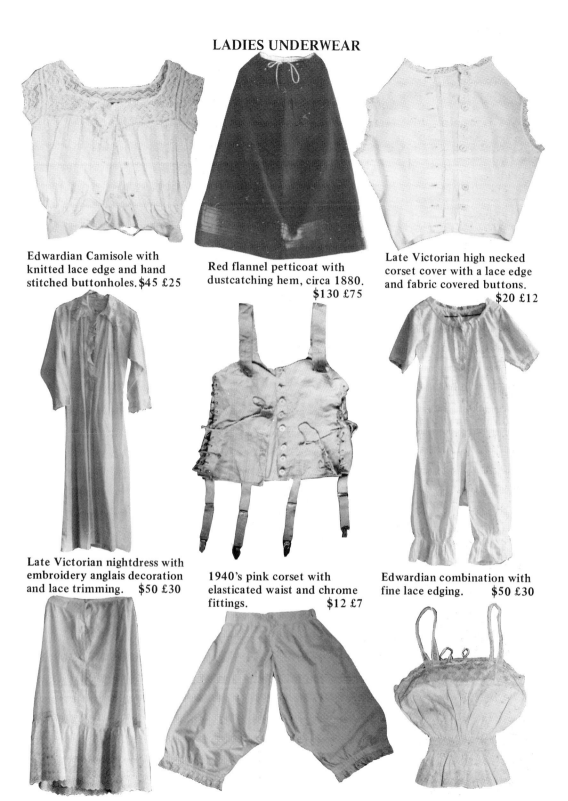

Edwardian Camisole with knitted lace edge and hand stitched buttonholes. $45 £25

Red flannel petticoat with dustcatching hem, circa 1880. $130 £75

Late Victorian high necked corset cover with a lace edge and fabric covered buttons. $20 £12

Late Victorian nightdress with embroidery anglais decoration and lace trimming. $50 £30

1940's pink corset with elasticated waist and chrome fittings. $12 £7

Edwardian combination with fine lace edging. $50 £30

Linen petticoat decorated with embroidery anglais, circa 1912. $14 £8

Victorian open gusset linen 'drawers' with embroidery anglais lace edge. $40 £22

1940's lace edged camisole top. $18 £10

(Kaleidoscope)

231

LAMPS

Victorian brass lamps with ornate glass bowls and the library lamps with shades like upturned flowers are worth a great deal of money but what are still sometimes overlooked are old brass carbide and Tilley lamps. About 1860 a popular lamp appeared that worked on acetylene. It had a small reservoir of water placed above a container filled with calcium carbide. Artists were always aware of the potential of lamps as objects of beauty but it was not until the arrival of glass workers like Daum, Galle and Tiffany that the art lamp really reached its highest point. These men with Gustav Girschner, Handel, Lalique and Loetz produced some beautiful lamps which fetch astronomical prices today. Tiffany's stained glass lamps decorated with flowers or his tall upstanding versions that look like clusters of lilies sell for thousands of pounds.

A Tiffany Studios enamelled copper electric lamp base, circa 1900, 15in. high. (Robt. W. Skinner Inc.)
$3,700 £2,202

A copper and amber glass lantern, style no. 324, by Gustav Stickley, circa 1906, 15in. high, globe 5¼in. diam. (Robt. W. Skinner Inc.)
$7,500 £4,054

A tall Galle cameo table lamp, the domed shade and stem overlaid with claret-coloured glass, 63.5cm. high. (Christie's) $12,584 £8,800

A Tiffany Studios 'lotus' leaded glass and bronze table lamp, 62.5cm. high. (Christie's) $15,048 £10,450

Rudolph, a robot light fitting, designed by Frank Clewett, 149cm. high. (Christie's)
$3,484 £2,420

A Stilnova painted metal lamp, by Gaetano Scolari, Italy, circa 1959, 67cm. high. (Phillips) $174 £120

A German Art Nouveau silvered pewter nautilus shell desk lamp, stamped M H 20, 27cm. high. (Christie's) $2,692 £1,870

LAMPS

A Tiffany Studio lamp with green-blue Favrile glass moulded as a scarab, N.Y., circa 1902, 8½in. high. (Robt. W. Skinner Inc.) $3,000 £1,875

A plated two-branch student's oil lamp with green tinted shades. (Peter Wilson & Co.) $244 £170

A Doulton Flambe figure by Noke, modelled as a seated Buddha, mounted as a lamp, circa 1930, 57.5cm. high. (Christie's) $1,252 £864

'Nymph among the bulrushes', a bronze table lamp cast after a model by Louis Convers, 28.1cm. high. (Christie's) $751 £518

A Galle blowout lamp, varying shades of red on an amber ground, signed, circa 1900, 44.5cm. high. (Christie's) $59,508 £41,040

One of a pair of Tiffany Studios three-light, lily-gold favrile glass and bronze table lamps, 33.2cm. high. (Christie's) $6,336 £4,400

A Continental porcelain oil lamp base in the form of a white owl with glass eyes, 17½in. high. (Dreweatts) $754 £520

An Almaric Walter pate-de-verre and wrought-iron lamp, the amber glass plaque moulded with a blue and amber mottled peacock, 27cm. high. (Christie's)$3,146 £2,200

A brass and tole painted table lamp, 20in. high. (Christie's) $330 £215

233

LAMPSHADES

The 20th century saw not only the introduction of electric lighting, but also a revolution in lighting fixtures. Lampshades have often aspired to works of art in their own right, through the designs of such masters as Lalique, Daum and Galle, while the Tiffany lamp has passed into standard parlance as a generic term. Through the 40's, 50's and 60's too, top designers have incorporated lamp fittings into their ranges, which have made these into the most exciting, practical and beautiful of collectables.

A Galle cameo glass flower form shade, the white body overlaid in deep pink/red/brown, circa 1900, 21.5cm. max. width. $1,237 £990

A Tiffany Studios leaded glass shade, inset with a floral design in deep blue and mauve glass, circa 1900, 46cm. diam. $3,750 £3,000

A Le Verre Francais cameo glass hanging lamp shade in the form of a strawberry overlaid in orange and blue, 30.9cm. high. (Christie's) $1,174 £810

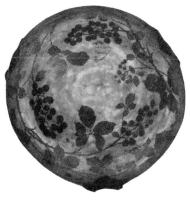

A large Daum cameo glass hanging lampshade of shallow domed form, 46cm. diam., signed. (Phillips) $3,024 £2,100

A pendant lamp shade of shallow bowl shape, signed 'Maxonade Paris', 1ft.6in. diam. (Capes, Dunn & Co.) $231 £190

A cameo glass hanging shade, attributed to Loetz, the mottled pink/white body overlaid in deep red, circa 1900/10, 40cm. max. width. $357 £286

A Lalique opalescent glass hanging shade moulded with swags of fruit, circa 1930, 31cm. diam. $343 £275

LEAD SOLDIERS

Toy maker William Britain launched his invention of hollow cast lead figures on the British toy market in 1893 and for the next sixty odd years until the use of lead in toys was discontinued for health reasons, his firm was first in the field of the production of toy soldiers. When the use of lead was banned, they became collectors' items and now they change hands for staggering sums, especially when it is considered that many of them cost only a penny when they were first bought.

Some of the most desirable are the mounted regiments of the British Army which Britain's introduced in the first year of production and also their sets of foreign regiments like South African Mounted Infantry, a set of which in its original box has been sold for £650. Britain's also made less usual sets like Salvation Army bandsmen which sold recently for £1000. They continued to make toy soldiers up till the time of the Coronation of Queen Elizabeth II in 1953.

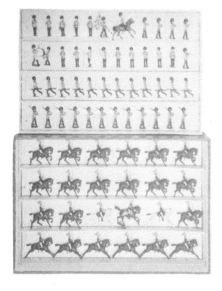

Large display box Set 93, containing Coldstream Guards with mounted officer, four pioneers, thirteen-piece band, two officers, twelve marching, twelve running, two trumpeters, six troopers and fifteen normal troopers, 1938. Britain's. (Phillips)
$11,550 £7,000

Britains extremely rare display set 131, including cavalrymen, infantrymen, bandsmen, sailors and Camel Corps soldiers, the largest set ever made by Britains. (Phillips)
$17,500 £10,000

Britains extremely rare Territorials in full dress standing at attention in red uniforms. (Phillips)
$5,103 £2,700

Britains very rare set 1904, Officers and Men of the U.S. Army Air Corps, four positions, in original green box, 1940. (Phillips) $3,024 £1,600

German made attractive first grade 52mm. hollowcast British Fusiliers at the slope with mounted officer, 1900. (Phillips) $283 £150

Britains special paint originally from the Poitier-Smith Collection, Royal Horse Guards, 1937. (Phillips) $1,549 £820

Rare set 1629, Lord Strathcona's Horse in original 'Types of the Canadian Forces' box, 1938. (Phillips) $3,402 £1,800

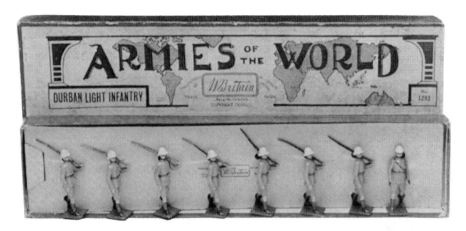

Britains rare set 1293, Durban Light Infantry at the slope, short trousers, unusual paint variation, 1934. (Phillips) $2,457 £1,300

Britains, unusual set of British Infantry in steel helmets based on the U.S. Marine marching figure, one slight dent, 1940. (Phillips) $2,835 £1,500

LIGHT BULBS

One Otto Von Guericke, a contemporary of Robert Boyle, is generally regarded as producing the first light from electricity back in the 17th century when he discovered that by holding the hands firmly against a revolving ball of sulphur, the friction produced a dull glow. It wasn't, however, until the electric arc was discovered early in the 19th century by Sir Humphrey Davy, that a practical source of artificial light was established.

Light bulbs themselves date from about 1841 when an American inventor named Starr found that a bright light could be produced by sending an electric current through a piece of carbon.

The first successful incandescent electric lamps produced in the U.K. were made by J. W. Swan of Newcastle and subsequently by several other inventors and pioneers including St. George Lane Fox, while in America the market was dominated by T. A. Edison.

All of these manufacturers used carbonised material as the filament, such as a cotton thread (Swan), a fibre of grass (Lane Fox) or a sliver of bamboo (Edison). Such light was regarded with fascination and carbon filament lamps were tremendously popular from 1880 until the turn of the century.

The big breakthrough came in 1906 when the General Electric Company found that by using a tungsten filament sealed in a glass bulb, it not only produced a clear white light but used very little electricity as well.

This revolutionised the whole industry and created a massive demand, though doubts were expressed at the time as to the adverse effect all this powerful light would have on the eyesight of future generations.

Dual Carbon Filament (dim/bright), circa 1905. $35 £20

Swan 'Pipless' light bulb, English, circa 1882. $525 £300

Nernst Lamp, circa 1900, 6in. high. $60 £35

1,000 watt 250 volt screw fitting ceramic based light bulb, 12in. high. $18 £10

Tantalum Lamp, probably German, circa 1906. $50 £30

Late 19th century 'Sunbeam Lamp' electric light bulb, with lobed element, 11in. high. $365 £210

238

LOCKS

The look of a lock can often date a piece of furniture for a specialist and most early cupboards, chests and boxes had locks for they date from the days before banks. Apart from being valuable for dating however, locks are collected in their own right because some of them were of ingenious design and superb workmanship. The earliest locks were used by the Egyptians and the Chinese. Chinese locks are particularly interesting because they work by using a long thin sliver of metal to push aside a clip inside a shell like clamp that holds two brackets together. The lock and key as we know it was generally in use in Europe from the Middle Ages onwards and they turn up made of iron, brass, steel, bronze or ormolu and are often finely chased. Locks range in size from tiny ones that were used for miniature pieces of furniture to enormous ones that fastened castle gates.

A 17th century William and Mary period brass door lock, keeper key escutcheon and key. $525 £300

A 17th century Spanish iron strongbox with hinged top, the sides with carrying handles, 20½in. wide. (Christie's) $1,460 £825

Late 17th/18th century South German steel lock and key, 6½ x 3.5/8in. $2,128 £1,650

English 18th century brass rim lock with ball-turned knob, 8¼in. long. $430 £250

Etas No.5 brass lavatory lock with 'engaged' display. $85 £50

An impressive iron 17th century 'Armada' chest with an intricate locking system in the lid, 37 x 19 x 20in. (Wallis & Wallis) $3,052 £1,850

LUGGAGE

The only drawback to period luggage is its weight. Air travellers are forced to stick to lightweight cases for practicality but it is difficult to beat the old style ones for style and appearance. In the days when weight did not matter, there was a huge market for suitcases and bags of all sorts made from real leather. The steamship cases made by Vuitton can sometimes be seen in films set on ocean liners, huge upstanding things like wardrobes. Smaller suitcases were also made by the same firm and they fetch high prices today. Other cases that are selling well are handstitched leather cases, those made of crocodile skin and others covered with shagreen, a nubbly looking sharkskin. Cosmetic bags, square shaped miniature cases, carried by model girls in the '50's are popular if they are made of real leather. Buyers are also keen on old Gladstone bags and carpet bags if in reasonable condition. Travelling trunks and chests which come up for sale are also rising rapidly in price, especially those bearing labels from distant places and exotic hotels.

Victorian metal uniform case with simulation crocodile skin design. $21 £12

Early 19th century wallpaper hat box, 'A Peep at the Moon', America, 12½in. high, 17in. wide. (Robt. W. Skinner Inc.) $200 £129

Late 19th century hessian covered wooden case with brass fittings by Lucas Collins, London, 21in. wide. $25 £15

Leather Gladstone bag marked 'Post Office'. $25 £15

A Louis Vuitton cabin trunk covered in brown hide, with brass lock plate, 114cm. wide. (Christie's) $1,404 £918

Items of leather luggage including a hat box, picnic case and suitcases. (Lots Road Galleries) $400 £250

A travelling dressing set with silver mounts, dated 1901, Birmingham, in an alligator skin case. (Lots Road Chelsea Auction Galleries) $680 £420

MAGAZINES

Much lamented magazines like *Picture Post* still have a large following among collectors who appreciate the remarkable quality of the pictures that appeared in them. Another magazine with a huge collecting following because of the scope and variety of the pieces it printed is the *Illustrated London News* for which some famous artists have worked since the 19th century. Old copies of *Vogue* and *Harper's Bazaar* cost more today than they ever did when new because they are highly prized for their beautiful illustrations and period covers, especially those from the 1920's and 1930's. Almost any magazine has a second hand value if collected in sequence and if in good condition. It is essential that magazines still have their covers and advertisements which form part of the period appeal. Many people buy old magazines simply for the advertisements which can be framed and displayed as pictures, especially those which appeared in the American *Ladies Home Journal* in the 1940's and 50's.

Lilliput, February 1959, 'Mike Hawthorn's dice with fate'. $5 £3

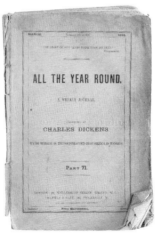

'Elvis in the Army', Fans Star Library. $14 £8

Up-to-Date, June 11th, 1927, 'The paper for the smart women'. $5 £3

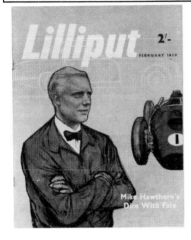

L'Indiscret, Le Lapin et Le-pine, 5th November, 1902. $9 £5

All the Year Round, March 1865, contains Dickens stories. $45 £25

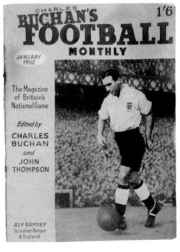

Charles Buchan's Football Monthly, January 1952, Alf Ramsey Cover. $9 £5

The Humorist, July 27th,
1935, Summer Number. $7 £4

Popular Science, June 1932,
Ocean Marvels seen from
underwater bus. $4 £2.50

Modern Home, October 1928,
the Magazine of New Ideas.
$5 £3

Woman, the National
Home Weekly, September
3rd, 1938. $3.50 £2

The Passing Show, April 14th,
1934, Four Pages of Humour.
$3.50 £2

To-day, the New National
Weekly, No. 1, May 28th,
1938. $4 £2.50

Yesterday's Paper

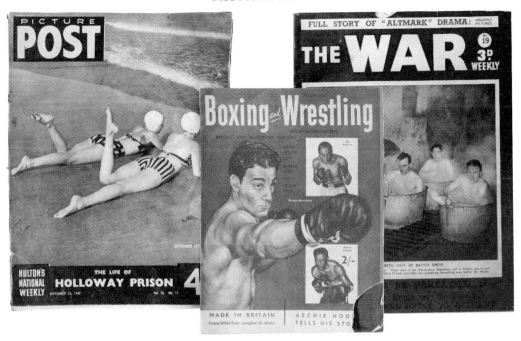

Picture Post, September 13th, 1947, The Life of Holloway Prison. $3.50 £2

Boxing and Wrestling, March/ April 1953. $3.50 £2

The War, 1st March 1940, 'The Dorsets — Out of Battle Dress'. $5 £3

Life, April 24th, 1950, Blouses under $5. $5 £3

Le Cri de Paris, 3rd January, 1904. $5 £3

Modern Wonder, December 2nd, 1939, Lifebelts and War-birds. $9 £5

The Studio, an illustrated magazine of Fine and Applied Art, March 16th, 1903. $9 £5

Cavalcade Weekly, September 27th, 1947. $3.50 £2

Rhythm, Modern Music Monthly, October, 1931. $12 £7

OZ — School Kids Issue. $130 £75

John Bull, June 27th, 1936. $5 £3

Punch, June 11th, 1859, with the original postal wrapper. $26 £15

Weekly Illustrated, November 27th, 1937, King and Queen's busy season. $12 £7

Farmer and Stock-breeder, 8th December 1959. $3.50 £2

Les Corbeaux, L'Emente clericale a Louvain, 26th June 1904. $9 £5

Woman's Journal, September 1954, 'Of Special Home Interest'. $3.50 £2

The Connoisseur, a magazine for collectors, November 1902. $7 £4

Private Eye, Friday 21st May 1971, 'That Wedding' souvenir issue. $10 £6

MAGAZINES

Football Favourites, 1952, Who's who in soccer. $9 £5

Courier, Fact, fiction, art, nature, March 1949. $3.50 £2

Lilliput, April 1949, Charlie Chaplin Cover. $2 £1

Poppy's Paper, February 2nd, 1924, 'Passionate Surrender'. $5 £3

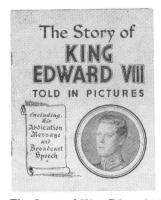

The Story of King Edward VII told in pictures, 1937. $12 £7

Uncensored, May 1957, 'Victor Mature, secret honeymoon without a bride'. $3.50 £2

Cycling, the leading cycling journal of the world, June 1st, 1938. $5 £3

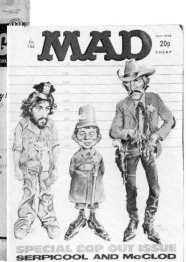

Mad, Special Cop Out Issue, No. 152. $5 £3

The Pele-Mele, Journal Humoristique Hebdomaire, 23rd September, 1900. $10 £6

MATCH BOX HOLDERS

Within a few years of the safety match being invented in Sweden they were brought into use in Britain. By 1900 many people found it a great convenience to carry a box of matches on their person and, since the boxes were produced with little regard for appearance, a decorative holder was devised. The pocket matchbox holder is a three-sided affair – constructed to leave the end free for the removal of matches and the side open to expose the striker. There are many purely decorative designs and some bearing military insignia or heraldic devices. Official holders were issued to the A.R.P. and C.D. as part of the kit. The household variety, designed to be placed on a mantel shelf or other convenient spot, was often the work of some of the better known porcelain factories of the day. Conta & Boehme, Doulton and Wedgwood all supplied this trade. The most common examples are the modest earthenware pieces made specifically for the souvenir trade.

An early pictorial match container made for the Lewis Stores in 1884. $50 £30

Enamelled match box holder with the insignia of the A.F.S., Auxiliary Fine Service. $10 £6

Patriotic enamelled grip 'Our deepest gratitude and admiration to the Allies who stood united in defeating the Greatest Tyrant in History.' $18 £10

2nd World War match box holder 'the Right Man in the Right Place'. $18 £10

Second World War metal match box holder decorated with 'peace' symbols. $14 £8

A Victorian brass match box holder in the form of a book. $20 £12

Enamelled metal match box holder 'The Wiltshire Regiment'. $10 £6

MATCH BOX LABELS

Matches were in use in Britain in the 18th century but they were originally sold in plain boxes without decoration. The Congreve match, invented by Sir William Congreve, the famous dramatist, made its appearance in the 1820's however and the labels from its boxes are highly prized and very rare. The next label to appear on any scale was for the Royal Patent Lucifer produced by a Mr Jones in 1829. His label showed a Scotsman and an Englishman and the boxes were collected from the time they first appeared. Since then the collecting of matchbox labels has been a hobby on a grand scale. There is even a name for it − phillumeny − and it has clubs, magazines and meetings all over the country. There are thousands of different labels to be found, some issued by manufacturers world wide and others bearing advertising slogans.

Polar Bear, Made in Belgium, 1925. $2 £1

An old label from a British Company no longer in existence, early 1920's. $50 £30

Wild Goose Chase, Made in Belgium, 1939. $2 £1

Two Rabbits Safety Matches, Made in Ceylon. $3.50 £2

'Koningin Wilhelmina' matches by Eras & Paulson, Holland.
$9 £5

Commemorative label made in Ceylon for the Coronation, 1937. $18 £10

Chinese match box label with 2000 contents. $5 £3

Bryant & May's Pearl Matches, 1886. $7 £4

'Fixed Stars' by R. Bell & Co., London, circa 1863. $50 £30

MATCH BOX LABELS

'God Bless Edward VII', Made in Austria. $1 50p

'All Rount The Box' label from a British Manufacturer no longer in existence, early 1900's. $25 £15

Squirrel Brand matches made in India, 1923. $9 £5

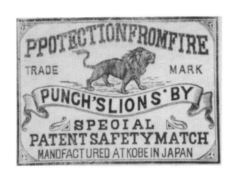

'Mammy' brand safety matches Made in Nigeria. $7 £4

An interesting Japanese label, with a host of spelling mistakes. $18 £10

Russian label commemorating Yuri Gagarin, 1961. $2 £1

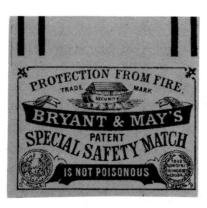

Pegasus, Foreign Made, 1930. $3.50 £2

One of Bryant & May's early labels, circa 1891. $18 £10

The North Star, Belgium, 1925. $2 £1

MATCH CASES

Because early matches were very volatile it was necessary to store them in containers that would restrict any accidental fire for they burst into flame at the slightest knock. By 1827 most friction matches were sold to the public in tin boxes by John Walker of Stockton on Tees and by the 1850's these safety tins were taking a wide variety of different shapes. Some of them were shaped like soldiers, historical figures or animals and as well as being made of tin, they were produced in iron, brass or even precious metals. If the containers were figures, their heads were hinged so that the matches could be placed inside the bodies. There was also a tiny hole in the case into which a single match could be stuck and allowed to burn for the full length of its wooden shaft. This was handy for holding a match steady when melting sealing wax.

Some match cases were made of ceramics or wood and most of them had roughened patches for the striking of the matches. Others had two roughened discs between which the match head could be pulled. Some matches ignited because the ends of them were tipped with chlorate of potash which burned when dipped into sulphuric acid. Contained within their match cases was a small cylinder for carrying the acid.

A Victorian fisherman's creel vesta case, the interior with Essex crystal depicting two trout, by Thos. Johnson, 1882, 5.5cm. long. (Phillips)
$3,062 £1,750

A Victorian enamelled silver vesta case, S. Mordan & Co., London, 1891, 2¼in. high.
$527 £462

An early Bryant & May's wax vestas pictorial case, circa 1875. $45 £25

An early Vesta case featuring the Marquis of Lorne by Bryant & May's, London, 1876. $45 £25

An enamelled silver vesta case, S. Mordan & Co., London, 1885, 1½in. high.
$527 £462

MATCHBOX TOYS

The Lesney Toy Co, manufacturers of the famous Matchbox range, started operating out of a London pub in 1947. At first it was primarily a commercial die-casting company, and the manufacture of toys was very much a sideline. Following the runaway success for their Coronation Coach model, of which over a million were sold in 1953, their future as a toy company was assured. Their popularity increased steadily during the 50's and 60's, and extended to America and Australia. In their heyday in the early 1970's they were turning out as many as 12 million models a week.

As always the condition of the models is very important, and the original box adds greatly to the value. The best places to find models for collection are still Toy Collectors' Fairs and Swapmeets. Experts advise collectors, wherever possible, to buy additional models as these can become exchangeable and thus help in obtaining items which may be necessary to complete a collection.

1934 Riley M.P.H., with blue bodywork, Y3. $18 £10

1930 Duesenberg, Model J, red bodywork, black roof, Y4. $18 £10

1945 M.G. Twin Carburetter, with green bodywork and red trim, Y8. $20 £12

Colman's Mustard, 1912 Ford T, Y12. $18 £10

25 years Silver Jubilee, 1956-1981, 1912 Ford T, Y12. $35 £20

Traystee Old Fashioned Enriched Bread, 1927 Talbot, Y5. $18 £10

Evans Bros., Coal, Coke, 1918 Crossley with red body, Y13. $20 £12

1929 Ford A Woody Wagon with yellow bodywork and black trim, Y21. $18 £10

Rolls Royce, yellow body, black roof and trim, Y6. $18 £10

Wright's Original Coal Tar Soap, 1927 Talbot, Y5, 1978. $18 £10

Cerebos Table Salt, 1912 Ford T, Y12. $25 £15

Lipton's Tea, City Road, London, E.C.1, 1927 Talbot, Y5, 1978. $35 £20

1920 Rolls Royce Fire Engine, Y6. $18 £10

Model Ford A with green body, No. 73, 1979. $18 £10

1938 Lagonda with yellow body and black trim, Y11, 1979. $20 £12

Royal Mail van with the crown and G.R. in gold, 1912 Ford T, Y12, 1978. $35 £20

British Petroleum Company Ltd., 1912 Ford T, Y3. $25 £15

Chivers & Sons Ltd., Jams, Jellies and Marmalade, 1927 Talbot, Y5, 1982. $18 £10

1930 Ford A van, Oxo, 'It's meat and drink to you', Y22. $25 £15

Captain Morgan, Ford Model T van, Y12. $45 £25

Menier Chocolat, 1927, Talbot with blue body, Y5. $18 £10

MENUS

The great hotels of the world and the vast liners that used to carry passengers across the oceans before air travel became usual, attracted customers by the quality and quantity of their food. The preparation of menus was an art form and these lists of delights were treasured by passengers as souvenirs. On the last night of a voyage or holiday it was common for all the people at a certain table to sign their menus as remembrances. The designs of menu cards were elegant and looking at them carries one back to the days of leisurely travel that will never come again. Always at the head of the menu would be the ship's or hotel's logo, often in colour. P. & O., Cunard and White Funnel Line all produced lovely menus and some of these turn up in folios or boxes of mixed cards. When they do, if they have been signed by some famous person, the price soars but generally they cost only around £2 each depending on the condition and the attractiveness of the decoration.

M.S. 'Terukuni Maru', N.Y.K. Line, Menu for Monday, 20th March, 1933. $7 £4

M.V. 'Reina Del Pacifico', Dinner Menu for 20th August 1932, a fine Art Deco design. $7 £4

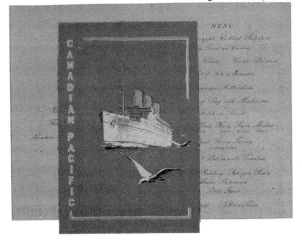

Cunard Breakfast Menu for R.M.S. 'Mauretania', June 12th, 1933. $3.50 £2

Canadian Pacific Dinner Menu, June 7th, 1934. $7 £4

MENUS

P & O Menu for S.S. 'Mongolia', May 18th, 1933, Fancy Dress Ball. $5 £3

Borough of Keighley Mayoral Luncheon, November 29th, 1929.
                              $2 £1

Cunard 'Carte du Jour', R.M.S. 'Mauretania', June 15th, 1933.
                              $5 £3

The Walton Walker No. 3847 Ladies Night Programme and Menu, 1926. $12 £6

Cunard Line 'Auld Lang Syne' Menu, R.M.S. 'Mauretania', 1933. $5 £3

Ye Palaontographical Society Menu, 1872, with fine engraving. $14 £8

MILK BOTTLES

The humble milk bottle has become a collector's item! With the demise of many small independent dairies, their old bottles, many bearing the embossed name and location of their origin, are eagerly sought after.

Milk first sold in glass bottles in the late 19th century, but they did not become common until after the First World War. Most were of clear glass, but amber and green examples can also be found.

A selection of cardboard disc closures in common use in the 1920's and 30's.
50c 25p each

Wensleydale Pure Milk Society Ltd., North-allerton. $9 £5

Bennetts of Worcester bottle with embossed cow. $2 £1

Reeces of Liverpool, unusual square bottle. $5 £3

Liverpool Corporation bottle embossed with the Liver Bird. $7 £4

Surrey Sterilised Milk Co. Ltd. $7 £4

Late 19th century Thatcher milk protector. $525 £300

Early 20th century 1 pint Special Milk. $7 £4

Walnut Tree Hill Farm, J. Surin & Co. $7 £4

(Mark Hudson)

255

MINIATURE BOOKS

Some of the earliest examples are miniature Bibles, made perhaps to aid concealment in times and places where there was religious persecution. All Shakespeare's works have been produced in miniature, and the Victorians reproduced works of prose and poetry in this form. Miniature magazines and newspapers were made either as a novelty or as part of children's toy sets. Often of high quality, they are usually authentic reproductions of the original, and if genuinely old, can be quite valuable.

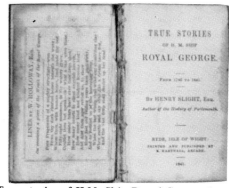

True stories of H.M. Ship Royal George, by Henry Slight, 1841. $45 £25

M.A.P. edited by T. P. O'Connor, September 19th, 1908. $5 £3

Pretty Pets Weekly Magazine, Golden Locks and the Three Bears.
$3.50 £2

Pearson's Magazine, 1908, 3in. high. $9 £5

Tales for Tiny People, Cinderella and the Magic Slipper. $3.50 £2

Home Notes, October 15th, 1908, Featuring Handkerchief Toys. $7 £4

The Wooden Post, miniature magazine. $2 £1

MINIATURE PLATES

These were made by most of the major manufacturers such as Doulton, Wedgwood etc. Some were made for dolls' tea sets, others were made as tiny replicas of large plates and designed to be worn as jewellery, mounted on pin brooches (Limoges). They can be transfer printed or hand painted and range in value from £1 to over £100.

Look out for early plates, and good examples of Blue and White. Those with registration marks are scarce.

Mid Victorian embossed miniature meat plate. $14 £8

Wedgwood 'Chaffinch' plate, Windsor Great Park, 1980. $9 £5

Coalport bone china plate with transfer printed pattern, 3in. diam. $14 £8

K. & E. Krautheum Bavarian Porcelain flower design plate, 3¼in. diam. $9 £5

Mavons Ironstone china floral plate, 3in. diam. $45 £25

Staffordshire plate depicting 'the Olde Coach House, Bristol'. $10 £6

Late 19th century Japanese lotus flower miniature plate. $3.50 £2

Limoges transfer printed plate, showing a gallant and his lady, 2in. diam. $20 £12

Green lead glazed plate, circa 1870, 3in. diam. $25 £14

Late 19th century blue and white miniature plate, 3in. diam. $18 £10

Crown Staffordshire bone china plate decorated with a floral spray. $7 £4

19th century pottery plate with blue florally bordered edge, 3¼in. diam. $20 £12

An early 19th century blue and white plate with beaded border, 3¼in. diam. $50 £30

1930's Italian transfer printed plate with gilt border. $5 £3

MINIATURES

The best known miniatures are pieces of dolls' house furniture which are eagerly collected. The best date from Victorian times when dolls' houses were furnished down to the last mat, picture on the wall and leg of mutton on the kitchen table. Some of these tiny pieces were marvels of exactitude and excellent examples of painstaking craftsmanship. It is possible to find tiny lamps with glass globes, baby's prams with wheels that go round, parlour maids in full costume and miniature washing sets complete with potty for beneath the bed. Other miniatures are the apprentice's pieces which every young cabinet maker in the 19th century had to produce before he became a journeyman. They made chests of drawers with inlaid locks or little chairs which were only just big enough for a child to sit in. High prices are also paid for miniature pieces of china which were produced by almost all the major potteries. They were too big for a doll's house and are more like craftsman's miniatures in scale. There are also working scale models of machines in miniature which fetch very high prices.

A miniature upright piano in burr walnut with central inlay, brass candlestick holders and ivory keyboard, 15½in. high. (Christie's) $1,975 £1,045

A William and Mary walnut oyster veneer and cross-banded chest of small size. (Phillips) $3,280 £2,000

A tin-plated miniature fire surround and grate with moulded uprights and lintel with pierced slightly bowed basket, 12in. wide. (Christie's) $411 £220

A 19th century miniature wallpapered bandbox, American, 4½in. high. (Robt. W. Skinner Inc.) $325 £196

An Empire mahogany miniature sofa, American, circa 1840, 19in. wide. (Christie's) $1,430 £986

Miniature Victorian wash boiler and dolly in brass. $35 £20

258

MINIATURES

A burr-yew wood miniature chest inlaid with lines, on bracket feet, 11in. wide. (Christie's) $4,633 £2,860

Early 19th century miniature Federal mahogany tilt-top tea table, American, 9in. high. (Christie's) $990 £653

A 19th century miniature green painted pine blanket chest, American, 9½in. high. (Christie's) $330 £217

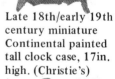

A 19th century miniature Federal mahogany picture mirror, American, 9½in. high. (Christie's) $1,210 £798

A 17th century miniature oak coffer of panelled construction, probably French, 35 x 21 x 23cm. (Phillips) $1,008 £700

Late 18th/early 19th century miniature Continental painted tall clock case, 17in. high. (Christie's) $550 £362

A miniature Chippendale mahogany desk and bookcase, Rhode Island, 1760-80, 16in. high. (Christie's) $2,090 £1,378

Two 19th century miniature painted side chairs, American, 9¾in. and 8¼in. high. (Christie's) $528 £348

A Dutch mahogany and oak miniature clothes press, 21in. wide, 33in. high. (Christie's) $3,168 £1,980

259

MINIATURES

An American, 19th century, miniature painted bannister-back armchair, 9½in. high. (Christie's) $495 £326

A 19th century miniature grain painted bowfront chest-of-drawers, American or English, 12in. high. (Christie's) $1,210 £798

A 19th century, American, miniature classical maple fiddleback chair, 10¾in. high, 8¼in. wide. (Christie's) $550 £362

Mid 18th century miniature Chippendale cherrywood chest-of-drawers, 7¾in. high. (Christie's)
                    $1,540 £1,016

An American, 18th century, miniature Queen Anne maple and pine slant-front desk, with a cherrywood mirror, the desk 11in. high. (Christie's) $3,520 £2,322

Late 19th century miniature Chippendale walnut slant-front desk, American, 7¼in. high. (Christie's) $1,650 £1,088

Late 18th century miniature George III mahogany side table, English, 6in. high. (Christie's) $330 £217

A mid Georgian walnut miniature chest, the base with one long drawer on bracket feet, 13½in. wide. (Christie's)
                    $2,141 £1,210

An American, 19th century, miniature Federal mahogany four-post bedstead with canopy, 15½in. high. (Christie's) $330 £217

MODEL BUSES

Many of the finest tin plate toys represented means of transport – trains, ships, cars and buses. They were first powered by clockwork but as the use of it declined, they were driven by friction motors or battery operated electric motors. Both single and double decker buses were made and they often had interesting advertising along their sides. One Bing model made about 1910 of a vehicle belonging to the United Bus Company Ltd carried a large placard advertising the appearance of Harry Lauder at the Tivoli Theatre. American 'Greyhound' buses were produced by Japanese manufacturers in the 1960's and '70's and trolley buses were made by Brimtoy and Betal. Brimtoy's products are particularly good and rival the German equivalents. When the last Paris trolley bus was taken off the road, a clockwork replica model was made by Joustra and sold well. Model buses range in size from one inch to eight feet in length and prices vary according to condition.

F. G. Taylor – UK – Diecast Trolleybus, Post War Example. $70 £40

Wells – UK – Tinplate London Bus, circa 1960's. $110 £65

Modern Toys – Japan 1960, Battery Operated Old Fashioned Tinplate Bus. $125 £70

Russian Novelty Clockwork Bus Track, circa 1960's. $25 £15

Tootsietoy Greyhound Bus (USA), diecast, circa 1940. $85 £50

Joustra – France – 1950's Clockwork Greyhound Tinplate Coach. $110 £65

(Geoff & Linda Price)

French Dinky — 29f Chausson Coach, circa
1956. $130 £75
29d Somua Panhard, circa
1951. $140 £80

Joustra — France — 1950's Ile de France
Tinplate Coach. $165 £95

Maks — Hong Kong — 1960, Copy in Plastic
of the Dinky Coach. $14 £8

TN — Japan 1960's Tinplate Greyhound
Lines Coach. $80 £45

Gamda — Israel, Leyland Worldmaster Diecast
Coach, circa 1950's. $155 £90

Chad Valley — UK — Tinplate Double Deck
Bus — circa 1949. $120 £70

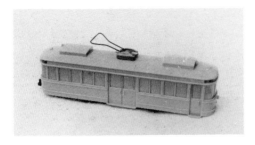

Wiking — Germany — Early Plastic Tramcar —
1950's. $50 £30

Well's Brimtoy — UK — No. 516 Tinplate
Trolleybus, 1950's, Clockwork. $95 £55

(Geoff & Linda Price)

Jye — Spain — 1½ Deck Tinplate Coach, 1950's, Very Rare Model. $110 £65

C.I.J. — France — 1950's Tinplate Coach. $40 £65

Guntermann — West Germany — 1930's Tinplate Tram. $260 £150

Japanese 1960's Tinplate Double Deck Bus. $80 £45

Tipp & Co — Germany — Circa 1950's Tinplate Bonnetted Coach. $110 £65

Wells Brimtoy Greenline Tinplate Coach, 1950's. $105 £60

Dinky Toys — UK, 1963 Continental Touring Coach, 1961 School Bus. $140 £80

HJC — Japan — Tinplate 1950's Greyhound. $105 £60

(Geoff & Linda Price)

MODEL PLANES

The first toy planes made by the Dinky Toy Company were launched on the market in 1934 and given the identification Number 60. The scale used was roughly 1/200. Planes were issued in boxes of six to be sold boxed or singly. Production continued until 1939 when it slowed down and by 1941 came to a standstill because of the lack of raw materials which were needed for the war effort. The original models were made of lead alloy but before 1939 this was replaced by a substitute called Mazak which was an alloy containing aluminium, copper, zinc and some magnesium. Sometimes trace elements that were present made the alloy brittle and cracks appeared. Examine any Dinky toys well because cracks will only get worse. Always store in a cool, dry place out of direct sunlight. The most common model plane produced was the Percival Gull which was produced in many colours but after 1940 the planes were always camouflaged and Spitfires, Hurricanes, Blenheims, Fairey Battles, Armstrong Whitworth Whitleys, Ensigns, Leopard Moths and Vickers Jockys joined the range. Because they were only produced for a short time they are rare and valuable. Boxed sets which are available are The R.A.F. Presentation Set, The Camouflaged Set and The Presentation Set. After the war, Dinky planes were back in production and new ranges were produced in 1946 and in the 50's. Probably the most sought after model to any Dinky collector is number 992 Avro Vulcan. This model of the most famous of the R.A.F. V-Bombers, was produced between 1955 and 1956. The model is quite large and finished in silver. Although it was given the number 992 it carried the number 749.

An original mint and boxed Dinky Vulcan could reasonably be expected to fetch between £1,000 and £1,400 at auction. The original box is extremely rare and adds a great deal to its value.

Lockheed Constellation No. 60C, produced by Meccano France, 1957-63, boxed.

$245 £140

Avro Vulcan No. 992, issued 1955, (not issued in U.K., unknown number released in Canada). $1,800 £1,200

British 40-seat Air Liner No. 62X, 1939-41, boxed. $260 £150

Frobisher Class Air Liner
No. 62, 1939-41, boxed.
$315 £180

Armstrong Whitworth Ensign
Air Liner No. 62P, 1938-41,
boxed. $175 £100

A pre-war Empire Flying Boat
No. 60R, 1937, boxed. $300 £170

Mayo Composite Aircraft
No. 63, 1939-41, boxed.
$525 £300

The first Dinky boxed set,
No. 60, issued in 1934 to
1940. $1,750 £1,000

Armstrong Whitworth
Whitley No. 62T, Silver,
1937-41, boxed. $260 £150

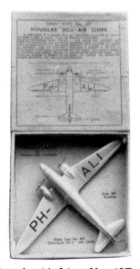

Douglas Air Liner No. 60T,
(supposed to be a DC3 by
many, but is probably a DC2)
boxed. $280 £160

Flying Fortress No. 62G,
1939-41, boxed. $260 £150

Kings Aeroplane (Envoy)
No. 62K, 1938-41, boxed.
$315 £180

MODEL PLANES

Bristol Britannia No. 998, 1959-65, boxed. $315 £180

JU89 Heavy Bomber, 67A, 1940-41, German markings, boxed. $350 £200

Nimrod Dinky Comet (Conversion). $210 £120

A post-war Giant High Speed Monoplane No. 62Y, R/H Gree. $260 £150

Dinky F-4 U.S.A.F. Phantom, U.S. Market only. $175 £100

Shetland Flying Boat No. 701, 1947-49, boxed. $1,000 £600

Atlantic Flying Boat, boxed. $525 £300

Camouflaged Whitworth Ensign Liner No. 68A, 1940-41. $350 £200

Dinky Hurricane, ME109. $70 £40

Camouflaged Frobisher Air Liner. $385 £220

Dinky Diamond Jubilee Spitfire, boxed. $175 £100

Pre-war Frog Penguin, unmade in kits. $35 £20

MODEL TRAINS

The first steam locomotive toys were not made in any number until the 1860's although 'Railway Mania' had the world in its grip for twenty years before that. The earliest type of model trains are called 'floor runners' because there were no tracks, which came later. The first great name in toy trains is Theodore Marklin who was attracted to the idea of making clockwork steam trains. He died in 1866 but his widow and sons carried on the business and made it a huge success. In 1891 they exhibited a full railway system at the Leipzig Trade Fair. Other famous trains were made by the Bing company which was founded in Nuremberg in 1863 by two brothers, Adolf and Ignaz Bing. By 1908 it was described as 'the greatest toy factory in the world' and had a pay roll of 3,000 people. Basset-Lowke in Britain and the famous Hornby company also made toy trains which are collectors' pieces today.

A very rare Hornby gauge 0 clockwork model of the Great Indian Peninsula 4-4-2 No. 2 special tank locomotive No. 2711, circa 1937. (Christie's)
$864   £462

A rare Bassett-Lowke gauge 0 (3-rail) electric model of the GWR 2-6-2 'Prairie' tank locomotive No. 6105, in original green and black livery, circa 1937. (Christie's)
$1,748   £935

A rake of three Darsted gauge 0 CIWL Bogie coaches (39cm), including a sleeping car, a dining car and a baggage, all in fine original paintwork, circa 1965. (Christie's)
$1,440   £770

A rare Marklin gauge 0 clockwork model of the 0-4-0 electric locomotive No. RS1020, in original dark green paintwork, with red and black chassis, circa 1927. (Christie's)
$617   £330

A rake of three very rare gauge 1 Central London Railway four wheel passenger coaches, inscribed 'Smoking', by Marklin circa 1903 (one coupling broken). (Christie's)
$11,313   £6,050

A well restored gauge 0 (3-rail) electric model of the SR 2-6-0 'Mogul' locomotive and six wheel tender No. 897, in original green livery, by Marklin for Bassett-Lowke, circa 1927. (Christie's) $1,440   £770

267

A rare Hornby gauge 0 clockwork model
of the DSB 4-4-2 No. 2 special tank locomotive No. 3596, in original maroon livery,
circa 1934. (Christie's)
$720   £385

A rare Bing gauge 1 live steam, spirit fired
model of a German 4-6-2 Pacific Class locomotive and twin-bogie, finished in original
black livery, circa 1927. (Christie's)
$3,497   £1,870

A Lionel No. 700E gauge 0 (3-rail) electric
model of the New York Central Railway
4-6-4 'Hudson' locomotive and tender No.
5344, in original black livery. (Christie's)
$1,748   £935

A Hornby (3-rail) electric (20v) model of
the LMS4-6-2 locomotive and tender No.
6201 "Princess Elizabeth", in original paintwork, circa 1938. (Christie's)
$1,439   £770

An early and rare gauge 1 hand enamelled
tinplate mainline railway station, by Bing,
circa 1908, 25½ x 9¼in. (Christie's)
$3,086   £1,650

A rake of three Bing gauge 1 MR four wheel
coaches, including two 1st/3rd coaches and
a brake van, circa 1912. (Christie's)
$206   £110

A Bassett-Lowke gauge 0 (3-rail) electric
model of the SR 2-6-0 'Mogul' locomotive
and tender No. 866, in fine original paintwork, circa 1927. (Christie's)
$1,337   £715

A Hornby gauge 0 (3-rail) electric model
of the SR 4-4-0 No. E420 locomotive and
tender No. 900 'Eton', in original green
paintwork, circa 1937. (Christie's)
$1,131   £605

MONEY BANKS

Amazingly high prices are paid by collectors for toy money banks. Most of the 19th century ones available are made of tin and were manufactured in America. Some of them are mechanical and seem to make money disappear. There were magician's hats, which, when money was placed beneath them, it disappeared. A Trick Dog money bank worked by a lever. The coin was placed in the dog's mouth and it jumped through a hoop and put the coin into a barrel. A money bank in the form of a girl with a skipping rope, made in the late 19th century, sold at auction recently for nearly £9000. Money banks took a lot of battering from their owners and finding them in good condition is difficult. Some of them were made of pottery or porcelain and nearly all were smashed in an effort to get at the coins inside but those that do survive are very desirable. They were in the shape of hens, dogs, beehives, fir cones, pillar boxes, chests of drawers, figures and particularly pigs.

A tinplate monkey mechanical bank, German, circa 1930, 6½in. high.
$525 £300

A cast iron novelty bank, by J. & E. Stevens Co., the building with front door opening to reveal a cashier, American, late 19th century.
$435 £250

A 20th century English cast-iron 'Dinah' mechanical bank, by John Harper & Co. Ltd., 6½in. high.
$185 £105

A cast iron money bank of a golly, 15.5cm. high.
(Phillips) $180 £100

'Trick Dog', a mechanical cast-iron moneybox, by J. & E. Stevens, circa 1888, 8¾ x 3in. (Christie's) $575 £330

Late 19th century cast iron owl money bank.
$220 £125

Late 19th century American cast-iron 'Santa Claus' mechanical bank, 6in. high. $875 £500

Late 19th century American cast-iron 'Punch & Judy' mechanical bank, by Shepard Hardware Co., 7½in. high. $805 £465

A mechanical cast iron money box, as a football player with articulated right leg, causing the player to shoot a coin into a goal and ring a bell, circa 1890, 10½in. long. (Christie's) $960 £550

'Bull Dog Bank', a cast-iron mechanical moneybox, by J. & E. Stevens, circa 1880, 7¾in. high. (Christie's) $350 £200

A cast iron 'Always Did 'Spise a Mule' money bank, American, circa 1897, by J. Stevens & Co., 10in. long. $1,225 £700

Late 19th century American 'Uncle Sam' mechanical bank, by Shepard Hardware Co., 11½in. high. $385 £220

A late 19th century cast iron Girl Skipping Rope mechanical bank, 20cm. wide. $15,000 £8,250

Lion and Monkeys cast iron mechanical bank, Kyser & Rex Co., Pat. 1883, 10in. long. (Robt. W. Skinner Inc.) $490 £280

A cast iron mechanical bank, 'Trick Pony', by Shepard Hardware Co., American, circa 1890, 7in. long. (Christie's) $525 £300

NAPKIN RINGS

Napkin rings are made in many materials from plastic to solid silver, and the value varies accordingly. Numbered sets are more valuable than single rings, and a good bone engraved Georgian numbered set of 12 would easily fetch over £100. Silver examples can be accurately dated from hallmarks and priced accordingly. Personalised rings with monogram or inscription are also desirable. Look out too for ornate rings and those made of ebony inlaid with ivory or mother-of-pearl.

A set of four crocus pattern napkin rings by Clarice Cliff, circa 1930. $260 £150

Pair of late 19th century plated napkin rings with embossed decoration. $18 £10

Pair of early 19th century silver napkin rings with beaded borders. $35 £20

Pair of pewter napkin rings in the Art Nouveau style. $18 £10

Doulton napkin rings issued 1935-39, featuring Sam Weller, Sairey Gamp, Tony Weller, Mr Micawber, Mr Pickwick and Fat Boy. $260 £150 each.

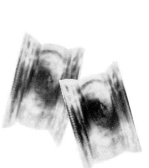

Pair of Victorian silver napkin rings. $35 £20

Pair of 1950's plastic chicken napkin rings. $9 £5

Pair of treen napkin rings with Tunbridgeware decoration. $18 £10

NEWSPAPERS

When it is considered what most of us do with our old newspapers — from wrapping up fish and chips to lighting bonfires — it is a wonder that any have survived from the past at all but those that have are usually kept because they contain accounts of special events. Royal events are favourites and the Prince Charles and Princess Diana wedding supplements will be the collectables of the future. Newspapers relating to historical events like the end of the First World War are kept and they can be valuable for historical research. Newspaper offices usually had bound files of their old newspapers but today most of these are being transferred onto microfiche and bound copies often turn up for sale. Ephemera dealers usually have copies of old newspapers on offer and the price is generally small. In the 1926 General Strike for example emergency editions of most newspapers were produced and mimeographed sheets of the *Graphic* or the *Daily Mirror* sell for around £3 each.

The Carlisle Journal, February
25th, 1915. $35 £19

Cobbetts Weekly Register, June
5th, 1824. $27 £15

The Edinburgh Evening Courant, February 26th, 1824.
$20 £12

Munchner Illustrierte Dreffe, 26th May 1929.
$5 £3

Das Reich, 16th May 1943. $15 £9

(Yesterday's News)

272

The New York Times, January 4th, 1945.
$27 £15

The Commercial Chronicle, February 14th, 1815. $35 £20

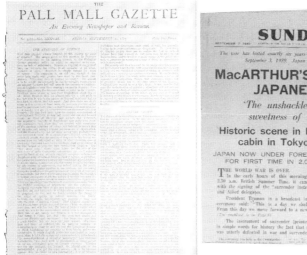

The Pall Mall Gazette, An Evening Newspaper and Review, September 21st, 1883.
$15 £9

Sunday Express, September 2nd, 1945, 'The
World War is Over'. $12 £7

The Morning Chronicle, June 1st, 1820.
$27 £15 The Times, December 4th, 1817. $35 £20

(Yesterday's News)

The Times, June 19th, 1862. $12 £7

The London Chronicle or Universal Evening Post, November 21st, 1761. $85 £50

The English Chronicle and Whitehall Evening Post, March 5th, 1822. $35 £19

The Sussex Weekly Advertiser, February 1st, 1819. $45 £25

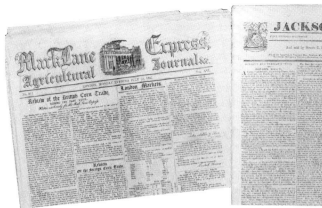

Mark Lane Express, Agricultural Journal, July 19th, 1847. $45 £25

Jackson's Oxford Journal, April 29th, 1826. $45 £25

(Yesterday's News)

The Cambrian, February 12th, 1831, or General Weekly Advertiser for the Principality of Wales. $15 £9

The Edinburgh Gazette, Published by Authority, march 8th, 1844. $20 £12

The English Chronicle, January 12th, 1799. $18 £10

The Edinburgh Evening Courant, March 25th, 1793. $50 £30

Wartime Channel Islands edition of The Star, January 31st, 1945, with German propaganda. $12 £7

Yorkshire Gazette, April 13th, 1850. $35 £19

(Yesterday's News)

The Daily Express, October 29th, 1943. $27 £15

The York Courant and Original Advertiser, May 1st, 1832. $45 £25

Monthly Mercury for June 1691. $245 £140

East Sussex News, July 29th, 1864, with handwritten contemporary advertisement departments. $20 $12

Volkischer Beobachter, 21st May 1944, the official Nazi Party daily. $27 £15

The Guardian, April 6th, 1864, complete with used penny stamp. $130 £75

NUTCRACKERS

Victorian dinner parties ended with fruit and nuts being handed round the table and for the purpose of breaking the nuts elegant nut crackers were provided. They were often given as wedding presents and could be made of Sheffield plate, silver gilt or silver and designed to match the table cutlery. Some had filigree handles and curving grips. Because of the strain to which they were put however, few of these light and elegant nut crackers have survived intact. The most serviceable ones were made of heavier metal and had ivory or bone handles. A few were fitted with a scalpel-like pick for extracting difficult nuts from their shells and they can still be found by collectors.

A pair of cast brass 19th century nutcrackers, the top in the form of a cockerel's head, circa 1800, 5¾in. long.
$105 £60

A 17th/18th century boxwood nut cracker of hinged form, 6in. long. $600 £350

A late 18th century wood figure of a sailor his mouth operating as a nutcracker, 9½in. high. $175 £100

An 18th century French fruitwood nutcracker of lever form, 8in. long.
$875 £500

An 18th/19th century walnut nut cracker in the form of an old woman seated, 7¾in.
$350 £200

A 19th century walnut nutcracker of screw type, 8½in.
$260 £150

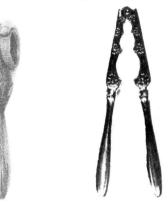

Finely engraved steel nutcrackers, circa 1850, 6½in. long.
$85 £50

An 18th/19th century yewwood nutcracker carved in the form of a man's head, 6in. long.
$525 £300

OCCULT BOOKS

The Occult has always held a sometimes fatal fascination for some people and, for better or worse, there seems to be a surge of interest in this field at the present time. Occult books have abounded in all cultures and ages, from learned mediaeval treatises on witchcraft, through the writings of Aleister Crowley, to modern fiction by writers such as Dennis Wheatley. In valuing these, as for any books, much depends on age, quality and rarity.

Combe (William): The English Dance of Death, 2 vol.s, hand-col. front. and vig. title, 72 hand-col. plates by Rowlandson, 1 cover detached. (Phillips) $1,337 £700

Sun, Moon and Stars, 'a book for beginners' by A. Giberne. $12 £7

Symbolism and Astrology, by Alan Leo, 1914. $15 £9

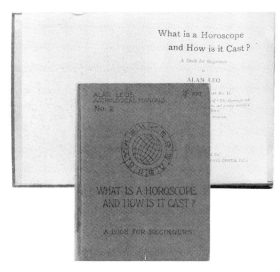

What is a Horoscope and How is it Cast? by Alan Leo, 1914. $12 £7

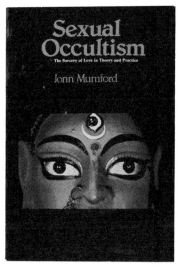

Sexual Occultism, John Mumford, 'The sorcery of love in theory and practice'. $9 £5

OILIANA

The awkward sounding name of "Oiliana" has been coined to describe anything connected with the oil business from oil cans to advertising signs. From the beginning of the century when motoring first began, the oil companies were extremely astute at self advertisement and missed no opportunity of pushing their name into the public eye. Collectors can find, in particular, oil cans which were used on every service station before the invention of self pouring cans, bearing the names of Shell, Castrol and Mobiloil as well as B.P. and the lesser known Pratts. Most sought after are the ones made for Shell and Castrol, especially the High Performance Oil containers and Aeroshell and Castrol R. Another pourer used for Oil Power is also collectable. Some cans were just the old style re-painted and a subsequent style, which persisted till the 1950's, can be seen in the quarter and half pint pourers. The old enamel signs used by the Shell Oil Company on their service stations are very highly regarded by collectors.

R.O.P. Russian Oil Products oil can and grease tin. $70 £40

Shell Oil half pint pourer.
$25 £15

Gamage's Motor Oil, one gallon tin. $175 £100

Lobitos High Quality Motor Oil bottle, Ireland.
$20 £12

Red Lion Glico Motor Oil pourer. $12 £7

Shell Lubricating Oil tin, late 40's. $25 £15

(Mike Smith's Motoring Past)

Castrol Motor Oil guides.
$10 £6 each

Set of three Castrol Motor Oil pourers, half pint, pint, one gallon, 1966. $55 £30

BP 'Buy from the Pump' enamel sign, 18 x 12in. $90 £50

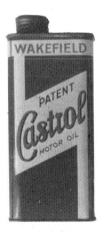

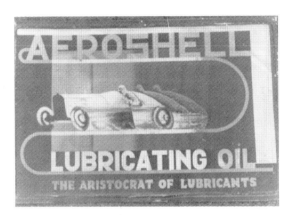

Castrol Motorcycle Oil tin.
$25 £15

Aeroshell Lubricant Oil tin sign. $600 £350

Redex Upper Cylinder Lubricant dispenser. $175 £100

Shell Motor Oil cans, 1930's.
Small $50 £30
Large $40 £25

Castrol Motor Oil tin cut out display sign. $175 £100

Cross Country Motor Oil pourer, USA. $50 £30

(Mike Smith's Motoring Past)

Esso 'Put a Tiger in Your Tank', sign. $80 £45

Pratt's Motor Oil tin sign, 'Do You Need Oil?' $55 £30

Castrol Motor Oil cut out counter display card. $55 £30

Coolie Motor Oil tin from Lagos, Nigeria. $60 £35

Carburol Additive dispenser. $40 £25

Shell Lubricating Oils enamel sign. $350 £200

National Benzole open/closed sign. $150 £85

Glico oil can, one gallon. $55 £30

Fina Oil bottles. $18 £10 each

(Mike Smith's Motoring Past)

PACKAGING

In collecting terms, the word "ephemera" covers things that are thrown away every day and perhaps the biggest dustbin fillers in Britain are pieces of unwanted packaging but passionate collectors see even these are worth saving. There is of course a pecking order in packaging. Old items ranging from Victorian starch packets to the covers on modern bars of soap or packets of custard powder can be valuable and packages for items that are no longer in production change hands at surprising prices. For example £2 will be paid for the little red cardboard cube that used to be put around Oxo cubes. A particular favourite with collectors are the paper packets used for pins and needles which often have not changed their basic design since Victorian times and therefore have a great period appeal. It is best to specialise − in such as the boxes or covers of photographic films for example.

Box of Royalty cigarettes complete with 50 contents. $130 £75

H.P. Sauce box with pictorial list depicting Jack Spratt, 1930's. $14 £8

An original box for Violettes de Parme by Jn. Giraud Fils of Paris, 1920's. $25 £15

Tubelette of Menthol & Wintergreen Cream, with contents. $9 £5

Double A.A. cigarette paper wrap around folder, 1940's, London. $3.50 £2

Packet of Clown cigarettes complete with contents. $9 £5

Pocket of Cooltipt, filter king size cigarettes and contents. $3.50 £2

Glyco Thymoline eye bath complete with box. $8 £5

PACKAGING

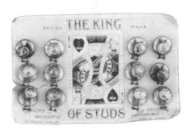

Rytol Universal Developer by Burroughs Wellcome & Co. $9 £5

Twelve Collar Studs made by 'The King' of Studs. $10 £6

Cope's No.1 Shagg, Superfine quality, 1oz. net, complete with contents. $9 £5

A. Lund

Diamond Snap Fasterners, guaranteed rustless. $2 £1

Zant Germicide by Evans Sons Lescher & Webb Ltd. $7 £4

A packet of tea from A. Lund of York. $9 £5

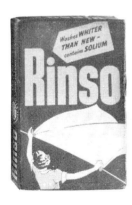

Excelsior Gold Enamel', The only substitute for real Gold Leaf', complete with contents. $28 £16

A packet of Rinso complete with contents. $5 £3

Elastic Thread, for all types of smocking, shirring, knitting. $2 £1

PACKAGING

Eventide tobacco in an airtight tin. $9 £5

Heughan Gripe Cordial, prepared and guaranteed by G. Heughan. $2 £1

Sloan's Ink Eradicator by Waterman Pen Co. Ltd. $3.50 £2

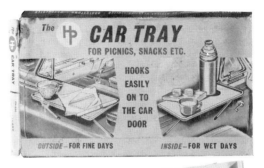

A fine pictorial Royal Baking Powder tin. $9 £5

The HP Car Tray, 'For Picnics, Snacks etc. Hooks easily onto the car door'. $18 £10

A colourful box for Guerlain, 1920's. $18 £10

Sharpes 'Kreemy Toffee' tin. $18 £10

Spencer's Planters Brand mild Indian cigars, complete with contents. $35 £20

Meltonian Neutral Suede Cleaner Liquid for light coloured suede shoes. $2 £1

(Border Bygones)

PAPERBACKS

Paperback books first appeared on the Continent and French yellow back novels were regarded as very daring because they were more explicit in their subjects than English books of the period. The publishing house Tauchnitz brought out paperbacks as long ago as 1837 but it was not for another hundred years that the idea was taken up in Britain in 1935 when the first Penguin books appeared. They started with Andre Maurois' novel 'Ariel' a copy of which, in good condition, will cost a collector around £50 today, and went on to be a huge success. Books came within the reach of people with very little money.

There are cult paperbacks as there are cult everything else and the blue covered early Penguins, which tended to specialise in weighty subjects, are particularly popular. However other collectors specialise in less exalted subjects and seek out the gang and drugs novels written for teenagers in the 1950's and '60's and which only appeared in paperback or some detective and science fiction stories which were never published in hardback either. The novels of Mills and Boon and the huge output of Barbara Cartland who is the author of over 300 novels can all be collected in paperback.

One of the things that collectors look out for in paperbacks are attractive covers which were often the work of well known artists. American Signet and Bantam books often employed an artist called Avati; McKnight Kauffer did many paperback covers and another artist called Heade created covers with lovely ladies on them. Collectors may also look for all the paperbacks by a particular author.

The Carmelites by Georges Bernanos, Fontana Books.
$3.50 £2

Edgar Cayce on ESP, Paperback Library, New York. $7 £4

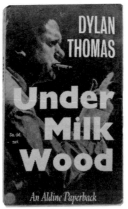

Under Milk Wood, by Dylan Thomas, an Aldine Paperback.
$2 £1

Up the Junction by Nell Dunn, Pan Books.
$5 £3

The Ides of Mad by William M. Gaines, New American Library.
$5 £3

LSD The Problem-Solving Psychedelic, a Tandem book.
$10 £6

(Border Bygones)

PAPERBACKS

Book on Swimming by Professor W. C. Pearson of York. $9 £5

Five Years of Liberal Mis-Rule, printed and published by Jordison & Co. $14 £8

The Gipsy King by J. Bosworth, Dick's Standard Plays. $2.50 £1.50

Tam by Edgar Wallace. $9 £5

Penny Book of Fun. $5 £3

The Governor of Chi-Foo by Edgar Wallace. $9 £5

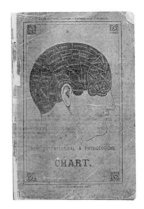

Bus Stop, the Story of the 20th Century-Fox Film, starring Marilyn Monroe. $21 £12

A Diary of the Gladstone Government, Blackwood and Sons. $14 £8

New Phrenological and Physiological Chart, pre 1940. $6 £3.50

Yesterday's Paper

DETECTIVE

The Curse of the Bronze Lamp by Carter Dickson, Pan Books. $4 £2.50

The High Window by Raymond Chandler, Pocket Books Inc. $4 £2.50

The Bandaged Nude by Robert Finnegan, Boardman Books. $5 £3

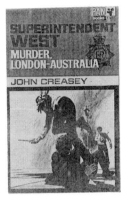

Situation Grave by Hank Janson. $7 £4

Superintendent West, Murder, London-Australia by John Creasey, Pan Books. $4 £2.50

Halo for Nobody by Henry Kane, Boardman Books. $5 £3

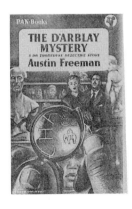

The D'Arblay Mystery by Austin Freeman, Pan Books. $3.50 £2.50

The Square Emerald by Edgar Wallace, Pan Books. $4 £2.50

Inspector West Makes Haste by John Creasey, Pan Books. $4 £2.50

Yesterday's Paper

TEENAGE GANG

Cut and Run by Bill McGhee, Corgi Books. $5 £3

The Little Caesars by Edward De Roo, Ace Books. $13 £7.50

Cosh Boy by Bruce Walker, Ace Books. $9 £5

Savage Delinquents by Alan Bennett. $6 £3.50

Run Tough, Run Hard by Carson Bingham. $6 £3.50

The Wasted Years by Jess Stearn, Macfadden Books. $6 £3.50

Marijuana Girl by N. R. De-Mexico, Soft Cover Library. $14.50 £8.50

Rock 'n Roll Gal by Ernie Weatherall. $10 £6

The Gang Girls by Carson Bingham, Monarch Books. $10 £6

Yesterday's Paper

SENSATIONAL

Redhead Rhapsody by Bart Carson. $6 £3.50

The White Slaves of London by W. N. Willis $8 £4.50

The Streets of Paris by Edwin Laforge, translated from the French. $6 £3.50

Sin Street by Paul Reville, An Archer Book. $6 £3.50

The Troubled Night by Ricky Drayton, Make sure its a Milestone. $6 £3.50

Gertie Vesser by George Ryley Scott, 'Secrets of the Oldest Profession revealed'. $6 £3.50

So Long — Sucker by Max Clinten, a 'Red' Miller story. $6 £3.50

Passion's Plaything by Roland Vane. $6 £3.50

She Who Hesitates by Paul Renin. $6 £3.50

Yesterday's Paper

PAPIER MACHE

Papier mâché was invented by the French and was popular from the early 19th century to the High Victorian period. It was usually coated in lacquer, which was decorated with painting or even mother of pearl inlay, and the greatest craftsmen in the medium were probably Jennens and Bettridge, whose work is now very sought after. Many items were made, from trinket boxes to decorative pieces of furniture.

A Russian papier mache box realistically painted with a scene of two fishermen on a riverbank, signed and dated, 19 x 17.5cm. (Phillips) $423 £260

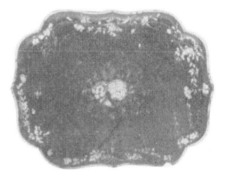

A Regency scarlet and gilt japanned papier-mache tray, with impressed mark 'Clay King St/Covt. Garden', 20¼in. wide. (Christie's)
$8,995 £6,380

A Victorian papier-mache baluster vase with flared rim painted with two oval panels, 13½in. high. (Lawrence Fine Art)
$210 £125

A 19th century papier-mache tray with shaped edge and a design of flowers by Evans. (Lots Road Galleries)
$417 £290

One of a pair of mid Victorian black, gold japanned papier-mache spill vases, 8in. wide. (Christie's) $471 £308

A mid Victorian black, gilt and mother-of-pearl japanned papier-mache table-bureau, 14¾in. wide. (Christie's)
$1,258 £880

An early Victorian black and gilt japanned papier-mache card box with lifting lid, 11¼in. wide. (Christie's)
$550 £385

PETROL PUMP GLOBES

Petrol pumps were first used in America for about ten years before they came to Britain where the first pump was introduced by the A.A. Their pumps were topped with bright yellow globes to show they were associated with the organisation. Very soon retailers took up the idea and the globes on top of the pumps were used as a form of advertising. The first bore the names of Shell, Pratts, Dominion, Redline, B.O.P. and Cleveland. Most companies sold only one grade of spirit at first but soon a variety of types were on offer and the names Perfection Spirit, Ethyl Petrol and High Test were displayed on the globes. Globe shapes changed over the years — Shell's first was round but before long it was transformed into a shell shape. In Ireland the Shamrock brand used a globe in the shape of the plant. Scotland's favourite petrol was called Thistle and its globe had the shape of a thistle top. Vandalism has meant that globes had to be removed from the pumps but a few can still be found if a collector searches around.

Esso High Test Pump
suspended light box. $130 £75

'Not for Resale' globe. $60 £35

Sealed Shell Pump Globe.
$500 £280

Regent TT Pump globe.
$260 £150

National Benzole Mixture,
with Mercury head. $260 £150

Petrol pump globe in
restored condition.
$525 £300

Cleveland Premium Pump
globe. $175 £100

291

PEWTER

Pewter is an alloy based on tin with the addition of other metals which may be lead, brass or copper. It is thought to have been made by the Romans but was most popular in Britain during Elizabethen times when it was employed for church vessels, domestic purposes and civic functions. Pewter began to be used for church vessels in the early Middle Ages when it replaced wood for the chalices. Until the 15th century it was customary to bury a pewter chalice with the priest. Pewter chalices, flagons, alms dishes and collecting plates can still be found in many church vaults. Generally speaking pewter was a makeshift substitute for silver and it was worked in the same patterns and styles as the more precious metal. Some pewter, particularly from Germany, was intricately decorated and cast in relief but such items are rare and pewter is generally spare and workmanlike in design. Artists continue to work in pewter and it appears very successfully in Liberty's Tudric and Clutha designs for serving flagons.

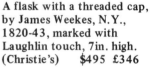

A lighthouse coffee pot, by G. Richardson, Boston, 1818-28, 10½in. high. (Christie's) $330 £230

A WMF electroplated pewter drinking set with shaped rectangular tray, circa 1900, tray 48 x 34cm. (Christie's) $946 £648

A flask with a threaded cap, by James Weekes, N.Y., 1820-43, marked with Laughlin touch, 7in. high. (Christie's) $495 £346

A 19th century pewter leech jar, the pierced lid with carrying handle, 7in. high. (Christie's) $382 £260

A WMF rectangular shaped pewter mirror, 14in. high, stamped marks. (Christie's) $691 £480

A tapering cylindrical mug, by Frederick Bassett, N.Y., 1761-80, marked with Montgomery touch, 4½in. high. (Christie's) $935 £654

A Liberty pewter and Clutha glass bowl on stand, designed by Archibald Knox, stamped Tudric 0276, circa 1900, 16.3cm. high. (Christie's) $656 £453

A rectangular pewter-rimmed kobako, unsigned, circa 1800, 9.3 x 8.3cm. (Christie's) $1,320 £825

Late 18th century porringer, New England, 4½in. diam. (Christie's) $264 £184

A pewter circular plate, marked on base with 'Love' touch, Laughlin 868, Phila., circa 1750-1800, 8½in. diam. (Christie's) $286 £200

A Jugendstil polished pewter triptych mirror in the style of P. Huber, 32.2 x 53.4cm. (Christie's) $626 £432

A Kayersinn pewter jardiniere, stamped Kayersinn 4093, 29.8cm. high. (Christie's) $375 £250

A tankard with S scroll handle, by Parks Boyd, Phila., 1795-1819, marked with Laughlin touch 546, 7½in. high. (Christie's) $2,090 £1,462

A Liberty & Co. 'Tudric' pewter box and cover, designed by Archibald Knox, 11.9cm. high. (Christie's) $380 £264

A covered pitcher of baluster form, by Thos. D. and S. Boardman, 1830-50, marked with Laughlin touch 435, 10in. high. (Christie's) $330 £230

PHOTOGRAPHIC ITEMS

Enlargers, dryers, darkroom lamps, viewers, cutters, tripods are all pieces of photographic equipment that display excellent workmanship and ingenuity of manufacture. In the same field are early stereoscopes of which the Brewster was the most popular in its Victorian hey-day. They were made for viewing daguerrotypes and the ones mounted on pedestals sell for anything between £100 and £1000. Another unusual piece of photographic equipment is the cinematograph and a wealth of both apparatus and film can still be found. However a problem with early films is that they are highly inflammable, so take care. Pathescope, a French firm, pioneered the home movie and their cameras and old films as well as amateur films may provide wonderful documentary material for the years between the wars. Projectors are considered to be not very desirable by collectors because early Bioscopes are very unwieldy, however there are a few projectors that weigh slightly less and they include the Lumiere Brothers Cinematographe camera/projector which sells for around £3000.

Kodak glass and celluloid store sign, 37 x 15in., in black frame, circa 1910, with 'Kodaks' in 8in. gold recessed letter on black background. (Robt. W. Skinner Inc.) $475 £386

A 35mm. Globuscope 360° Panoramic camera No. 1094 with a Globuscope 25mm. f 3.5 - 22 lens with pouch case, film case and film resin all in maker's box. (Christie's) $1,623 £990

A Kodak 27 x 13in enamelled street sign with both sides in white lettering stating 'All "Kodak" Supplies', circa 1920's. (Christie's) $73 £39

An early brass mounted 35mm. hand-cranked cinematograph projector with R.R. lens, 15in. high. (Christie's) $1,755 £1,300

An Arthur Branscombe, 'King Kodak. A topical burlesque in two acts', a play apparently written during 1892. (Christie's) $353 £187

A brass reproduction Petzval-Type daguerreotype camera, signed Voigtlander & Sohn in Wien, no. 084, circa 1956, 12¼in. long. (Christie's) $2,530 £1,765

A metal Kodak store sign, triangular with heavy metal bracket, 'Developing Printing Enlarging'. (Robt. W. Skinner Inc.) $85 £75

PHOTOGRAPHS

One of the most revolutionary inventions was the camera which made it possible to record history at the flick of a switch. After George Eastman invented his Kodak camera in the 1880's, the door was thrown open to ordinary people to take their own photographs — a challenge which they grasped eagerly. There are two schools of photography collecting. Firstly, specialists seek out photographs taken by the famous names of the art — William Henry Fox Talbot, Julia Margaret Cameron, Roger Fenton, Robert Adamson and David Octavius Hill, Matthew Brady and the Rev. Charles Dodgson (Lewis Carroll). Prices paid for their plates are however very high and the more modest collector seeks out the work of less famous people. Views of distant places are well regarded, especially scenes of Indian hill stations during the British Raj or places that have been radically changed by events. Another popular area is photographs of British towns and slum scenes or pictures of ordinary people working at their jobs, particularly agricultural labourers in the days before mechanisation.

Cecil Beaton — H.R.H. Princess Margaret — One of thirty-three gelatin silver prints, 1950's. (Christie's) $685 £385

Bill Brandt — Children of Sheffield — Gelatin silver print, image size 12 x 10½in., 1930's, printed 1980's. (Christie's) $548 £308

Burmese portraits, architecture and topography — thirty-four albumen prints, approx. 8 x 11in., 1880's. (Christie's) $881 £495

Guglielmo Pluschow — Nude studies — Two albumen prints, each approx. 8¾ x 6½in., circa 1900. (Christie's) $391 £220

Count Zichy — A quantity of photographs, majority gelatin silver prints, including advertising and fashion photographs. (Christie's)
$627 £352

F. M. Sutcliffe — A bit of news (at Robin Hoods Bay) — Toned gelatin silver print 8 x 6½in., 1880's. (Christie's)
$685 £385

Bill Brandt — Tic-Tac men at Ascot races — Gelatin silver print, image size 11¼ x 10¼in. 1930's, printed 1980's. (Christie's) $783 £440

Man Ray — R. Rosselini, H. Langlois (Cinematheque Paris), Jean Renoir — Gelatin silver print, 7 x 9½in., titled in pencil and with photographer's ink credit stamp 'Man Ray — Paris', 1940's. (Christie's) $490 £275

Bill Brandt — Cocktails in a Surrey garden — Gelatin silver print, image size 12¼ x 10½in., 1930's, printed 1980's. (Christie's) $744 £418

Herbert G. Ponting — The Potter at his Wheel, Japan — Brown-toned gelatin silver print, 13¼ x 19in., 1902-5. (Christie's) $548 £308

Marville (S...pont) — Reclining nude — Albumen print, 5¾ x 7¾in. mounted on card, 1850's/60's. (Christie's) $489 £275

Baron Wilhelm von Gloeden, attributed to — Three little boys and Young boy seated — Two albumen prints, 1900. (Christie's) $587 £330

Robert Doisneau — Hell — Gelatin silver print, 15¼ x 12 in. pencil signature and number '28961' on reverse, 1950's. (Christie's) $1,273 £715

Anthony Osmond-Evans — Portrait of Mother Theresa — R-type colour print, 20 x 16in., signed by photographer, November 1987. (Christie's) $352 £198

Anon — Russian trader being served tea — Albumen print, 9½ x 7¼in., mounted on card, 1860's. (Christie's) $587 £330

William Henry Fox Talbot — The Fruit Sellers — Calotype, 7¼ x 9in. numbered 'LA 300' in ink on reverse, 1842. (Christie's) $8,330 £4180

Joseph Cundall — Highlanders — Albumen print, 9 x 7¼in. arched top, mounted on card, 1856. (Christie's) $391 £220

Cecil Beaton — Andy Warhol and Candy Darling — Gelatin silver print, 7½ x 8¾in., photographer's credit stamp on reverse, 1969. (Christie's) $392 £220

Anon — Everyday life in London — One of fifty-eight gelatin silver prints, each approx. 15¾ x 19½in., 1950's. (Christie's) $548 £308

Robert Frank — Mother and child — Gelatin silver print, 9 x 13½in., 1950's. (Christie's) $3,133 £1,760

Willy Prager — Girl on beach — Gelatin silver print, 9½ x 7in. photographer's ink credit stamp and number '3223' on reverse, 1920s/30s. (Christie's) $391 £220

M. F. Moresby, J. Robertson and others — Rio de Janeiro, Sydney, Auckland and the Crimea — Part album of approx. eighty-nine photographs and five composite panoramas, 1858. (Christie's) $8,224 £4,620

John Thomson — Street Life in London — Text by Adolphe Smith, with thirty-seven woodburytypes, approx. 4¼ x 3¼in., printed borders and titles, 1878. (Christie's) $3,132 £1,760

Bill Brandt — Coach party, Royal Hunt Cup Day, Ascot — Mammoth gelatin silver print, 24 x 28¼in., mounted on board, printed early 1970's. (Christie's) $352 £198

PIN CUSHIONS

Needlewomen always need a safe place to stick their needles and pins so pin cushions have been available for centuries but it was the Victorians with their passion for prettifying everything that turned them into things of beauty.

Pincushions can be found in many sizes and an enormous variety of shapes, covered with silk, satin, velvet or coarser fabrics, trimmed with lace and ribbon or decorated with embroidery. Some pincushions are inserted like pads inside silver, metal or wooden shoes, boots, birds, hedgehogs, pigs, coaches or dolls. Others are trimmed with intricate beadwork and embroidered with encouraging mottos. They look prettiest when stuck all over with close packed pins, many of them with coloured heads.

Victorian plated pig pin cushion, 4in. long. $35 £20

Late Victorian pin cushion on an ebonised base. $7 £4

Late 19th century plated pin cushion in the form of an elephant. $18 £10

Plated brass pin cushion in the form of a sow, circa 1895. $35 £20

Heart shaped pin cushion inscribed Merry Christmas and Argyll & Sutherland Highlanders. $70 £40

White metal shoe pin cushion, circa 1900. $25 £15

Victorian horse's hoof pin cushion with plated mounts. $25 £15

Bone pin cushion 'Chrystal Palace, London 1851'. $45 £25

Victorian bead work pin cushion. $45 £25

Pin-up magazines are not 'porn' but they are not straight historical magazines either and because they fall between two stools, some book shops are shy of handling them while they are too tame for 'naughty' book shops. They often turn up in bundles of assorted magazines or on market stalls however and there are a few mail order dealers who issue catalogues. A publication called "Yesterday's Paper" lists where they can be bought.

LA VIE PARISIENNE

The period of the pin-up magazine began with "La Vie Parisienne" in the Victorian era when the pictures were drawn and it continues today with the photographed lovelies of "Playboy". Collectors are discriminating about what they look for. Most of them are not interested in anything after 1960 because they do not value full frontal titillation but prefer artistic photography. The hey day of the pin-up magazine was in the 1920's and 1930's when they were published in both Britain and America.

One particularly popular magazine of the period is "London Life" which dealt with all manner of fetishes but in a restrained manner. Copies of magazines dating from that time can be found at prices between 50p and £10 a copy.

Collectors prefer the artwork pin-up and especially look for superb covers like the ones designed for pre-war American magazines by Dryben and Bolles. The lingerie shots found in magazines like 'Spick', 'Span' and 'Silky' are also very popular, One of the most sought after artists is Pett, the man who created Jane of the "Daily Mirror" and examples of his work turn up from time to time.

Esquire — the Magazine for Men, 'World Automobile Supplement', June 1954. $5 £3

Mayfair — Entertainment for Men, 'Winter Wonderbirds'. $2 £1

La Vie Parisienne, 29th May, 1926. $18 £10

Penthouse — the Magazine for Men, Volume 4, No.2. $2.50 £1.50

Solo, No. 44 by Harrison Marks, presenting Ann Wilson. $5 £3

Existentialist, a Capital Publication. $3.50 £2

Leslie Carol, photographed by Roye for the Camera Studios Club. $2 £1

Mentor, 'Pussycat Tina with the Big Game'. $2.50 £1.50

Cavalier, September 1966, cover photograph by Ron Vogel. $3.50 £2

Vue, November 1964, 'Special Book Bonus'. $2 £1

Wink — A Whirl of a Girl, 'Silk Stockings and High Heels'. $6 £3.50

Paris Frou Frou — Magazine Parisien, Froufroutant et Honnete. $3.50 £2

Lovelies, published by Universal Publicity. $3.50 £2

Art and Models Magazine — For Artists and Art Students, No. 1. $10 £6

Yesterday's Paper

Gay Book Magazine, November 1937. $7 £4

Health and Efficiency — The World's Leading Naturist Journal, March 1960. $2 £1

The Naturist — Nudism, Physical Culture, Health, February 1947. $2.50 £1.50

Pamela Green in 3-D, including spectacles. $9 £5

Charm — The Magazine for Students and Photographers. $2.50 £1.50

Continental Keyholes, No. 6, Joyart Photographs. $3.50 £2

Spick, June 1956, 'A New Star is Shining'. $4 £2.50

Fiesta, Volume 6, No. 8, published by Galaxy Publications. $2 £1

Beaute Magazine — A Paris Cocktail, Adele Jergens cover. $2.50 £1.50

Showgirls — The Body Beautiful, 'Burlesk Queens in Action'. $4 £2.50

PIPES

When tobacco was brought to Britain by Sir Walter Raleigh, it was smoked in clay pipes with small bowls and short stems called Cutties. With the passage of time the stems became longer and the pipes were given the name of Churchwardens. During the reign of George I, red wax tips were put on the mouthpieces and thereafter they were called Aldermen. Pipes are no longer made of clay but mainly of brier, the root of the brier shrub. The best pipes of this type are those made by Winchester and Bronseley. However the king among pipes is the Meerschaum — the name means 'sea foam' — which is porous magnesium silicate. Because it is soft it is easily carved and it is white when first carved but slowly turns to a lovely mellow golden colour when stained with nicotine. There are some beautifully carved meerschaum pipes to be found and the best were sold by Gambier of Paris whose pipes were in the shape of animals or caricatures of prominent people.

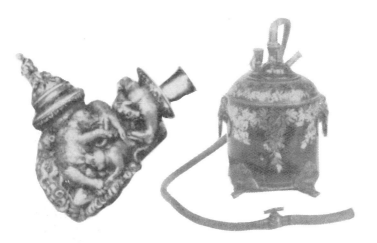

A 17th century Dutch fruitwood pipe, 3.3/8in. long. $3,500 £2,000

A mid Victorian black and gilt japanned tole hubble-bubble, with metal label of Lowe, London, 10½in. high. (Christie's) $346 £242

A Kelsterbach pipe bowl with silver mounts and hinged cover, 1767-68, 7cm. high. (Christie's) $3,142 £2,182

A Staffordshire pottery curled pipe painted with blue and yellow dashes. $525 £300

A Meerschaum trick rider pipe, blossom bowl with lady on ground near running horse, 4.3/8in. long, in leather case. (Robt. W. Skinner Inc.) $375 £260

A carved Meerschaum pipe, the bowl in the form of a head of a bearded king, 29in. long. $525 £300

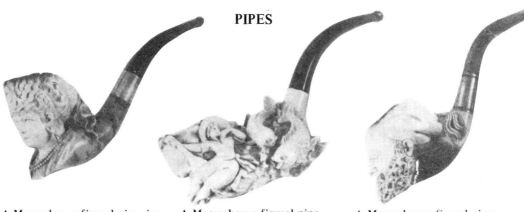

A Meerschaum figural pipe, in the form of a Victorian lady's head, amber stem, bowl 3¼in. long, in leather case. (Robt. W. Skinner Inc.) $400 £277

A Meerschaum figural pipe, conch shell bowl with lady and two dolphins, bowl 4.1/8in. long, and another. (Robt. W. Skinner Inc.) $475 £329

A Meerschaum figural pipe, in the form of Turkish man's head wearing tasseled fez, bowl 3¼in. long. (Robt. W. Skinner Inc.) $350 £243

A pearlware pipe modelled as a man seated astride a green barrel, perhaps Yorkshire, circa 1800, 15.5cm. high. (Christie's)
$1,542 £935

Late 19th century Meerschaum pipe, carved with a lion's head, 7½in. long. (Robt. W. Skinner Inc.) $400 £250

A pearlware pipe modelled as a man, impressed with the name 'Jolly Pickman', circa 1800, 14.5cm. high. (Christie's) $1,542 £935

Carved burl Civil War pipe bowl, American, circa 1862-63. $1,300 £750

Carved Meerschaum pipe with amber stem and silver band, in case. $260 £150

Silver-mounted cast-iron pipe bowl, probably German, circa 1840, 3¾in. high. $875 £500

PLASTER

Plaster, being inexpensive and easily mouldable, is ideally suited to the mass production of the cheap and sometimes nasty seaside souvenir type ornaments. There are, however some very collectable items to be found in the middle range of stylised and colourful Art deco figures of the 30's. The works of notable sculptor Richard Garbe, often depicting women in flowing robes and with streaming hair, are definitely top of the range. Whatever the subject, these pieces are always worked in a gentle and evocative style.

An English plaster panel, in oak frame carved 'Speed with the light-foot winds to run', 42.2 x 37.7cm. (Christie's) $168 £110

A Richard Garbe green-tinted plaster figure of a naked seated maiden, 1928, 104cm. high. (Christie's)
$1,074 £702

A pair of Regency polychrome plaster figures of Chinese figures in court dress with nodding heads, 13¾in. high. (Christie's)
$17,028 £9,900

A Richard Garbe plaster figure of a naked maiden, 1912, 99cm. high. (Christie's) $660 £432

A 19th century tinted plaster bust of a gentleman, after Houdon, 70cm. high. (Christie's)
$827 £440

A James Woolford plaster figure modelled as a diving mermaid with a dolphin, circa 1930, 59cm. high. (Christie's) $315 £216

A 19th century painted plaster wall bracket, in the form of a winged cherub issuing from acanthus leaves, 51cm. (Osmond Tricks)
$86 £48

An early 19th century French plaster bust of a young officer, cast from a model by F. Leclercq, 51cm. high. (Christie's) $1,861 £990

Pair of painted plaster bookends, each modelled as a bowl of fruit, 8¾in. high. (Christie's) $277 £165

A plaster bust of George II, his hair dressed with laurels. (Christie's) $707 £495

A late 19th century English polychrome plaster bust of Florence Nightingale, by T Woolner, 1874, 58.5cm. high. (Christie's) $706 £418

A Richard Garbe plaster figure of a naked kneeling maiden with streaming hair and flowing drapery, 102cm. high. (Christie's) $1,239 £810

A late 19th century French original plaster half length portrait of Mme. La Baronne Cecile Demarcay, signed J. B. Carpeaux, 80cm. high. (Christie's) $29,392 £17,600

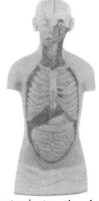

A late 19th century French plaster bust of 'L'Espiegle', signed on the shoulder J. B. Carpeaux, 51cm. high. (Christie's) $2,571 £1,540

A plaster portrait bust of The Hon. Mrs Maryanna Marten by Augustus John, 24in. high. (Woolley & Wallis) $1,353 £1,100

A plaster instructional torso coloured and numbered and arranged so as to dismantle for display purposes, 33in. high. (Christie's) $918 £600

PLASTIC

Plastic arguably came of age as a decorative material in the Art Deco period, when a multitude of different items, often in strikingly geometrical forms and dazzling colours were fashioned from it. Many of these now fetch enormous sums, but items from the 50's too are becoming increasingly popular and are still affordable. 50's plastic jewellery, handbags, radios etc. are recognisable often by their highly stylised design and their softer, pastel colour tones.

Early 1960's silver blue plastic robot with red flashing eyes and three different sonic sounds. $85 £50

1950's green plastic salt and pepper. $5 £2

1950's green plastic perpetual calendar with Venetian scene. $9 £5

Pair of pale blue plastic egg cups, 1950's. $2 £1

1950's green plastic modermistic powder bowl, 5in. diam. $10 £6

1950's pink plastic swan ornament. $9 £5

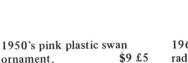

1960's Vidor portable plastic radio. $38 £22

(Border Bygones)

306

PLATES

There are as many different kinds of plates as there are different potteries and porcelain factories. Plates can make a fascinating collection an look well displayed on walls or in glass fronted cupboards. Some collectors stick to the same or matching colours or similar themes in decoration. Before embarking on a serious search for plates, it is essential to buy a good book on china marks and one of the best for English porcelain is Geoffrey Godden's "Encyclopaedia of English Porcelain Manufacturers". A point to bear in mind is that any plate bearing the mark "Bone China" or "Made in England" suggests the date of manufacture is in the 20th century. The word "England" added to a mark implies that it is post 1891 because in that year the McKinley Tariff Act imposed place of origin on a mark. The words Trade Mark were added after 1862 and a pattern mark or number indicates a date no earlier than 1810. The Royal Arms were incorporated in marks after 1800.

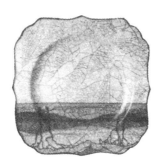

One of a pair of pearlware plates and a creamware plate, one 9¾in. diam., 1810-30. (Christie's) $286 £161

Doulton crackleglaze plate with shaped edge. $27 £18

A Longton Hall strawberry leaf moulded plate, circa 1755, 23cm. diam. (Christie's) $3,448 £2,090

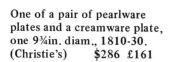

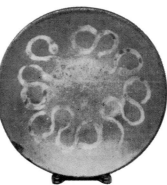

A Castelli small plate, painted with a putto in flight holding a book, 17cm. diam. (Phillips) $802 £420

One of two 19th century slip-decorated Redware plates, American, 11¼in. and 12in. diam. (Christie's) $385 £217

Doulton 'Make Me Laugh' rack plate, Behind the Painted Masque Limited Edition Series, 9in. diam., 1982. (Abridge Auctions) $18 £12

A Rouen shaped circular plate painted in a famille verte palette, circa 1740, 25cm. diam. (Christie's)
$1,948 £1,210

One of a pair of pearlware plates, each octagonal painted with swags of lemons with brown leaves, 1810-20, 7¾in. diam. (Christie's) $198 £111

A Coalport cabinet plate, signed by F.H. Chivers, with ripened fruit on an earthy ground, 10½in. across. (Christie's) $529 £286

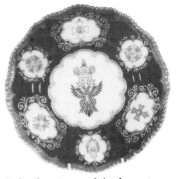

A Bow circular plate painted in famille rose with a Chinese lady, probably Lan Ts'ai Ho, 22.5cm. diam. (Phillips)
$1,586 £950

Doulton 'Short Headed Salmon' rack plate, signed by J. Birbeck, 9½in. diam., circa 1913. (Abridge Auctions) $105 £70

A Coalport porcelain dessert plate from the service presented by Queen Victoria to the Emperor of Russia in 1845, 10in. wide.   (Dacre, Son & Hartley)
$2,557 £1,550

A Barr, Flight & Barr plate, decorated probably in London and in the manner of the Baxter workshop, 23.5cm. diam. (Phillips)
$501 £300

A Maw & Co. circular pottery charger painted in a ruby red lustre with winged mythical beast, 13½in. diam. (Christie's)
$382 £209

A London delft blue and white Royalist portrait plate, circa 1690, 22cm. diam. (Christie's)
$2,541 £1,540

One of a pair of pierced Imari plates, 8in. diam.. (R. K. Lucas & Son) $159 £95

Doulton octagonal plate painted with white pate-sur-pate flowers on a brown ground, by Eliza Simmance, 1878, 10in. diameter. (Abridge Auctions) $195 £130

A Russian Imperial porcelain dinner plate, 23.5cm. diam., cypher mark of Nicholas I in blue. (Phillips) $668 £400

One of a pair of Caughley plates from the Donegal Service, painted at Chamberlain's factory, circa 1793, 21cm. diam. (Christie's) $1,724 £1,045

Doulton 'At the Cheshire Cheese' Dr Johnson Series rack plaque, 13in. diam., circa 1909. (Abridge Auctions) $57 £38

Late 17th century Arita blue and white charger. (Christie's) $2,805 £1,650

Doulton 'Gibson Girl' rack plate, by Charles Dana Gibson, circa 1901. (Abridge Auctions) $60 £40

A Chinese famille verte plate, Kangxi, circa 1725, 9¼in. diam. (Woolley & Wallis) $672 £420

A Castelli armorial plate from the Grue workshop, 25cm. diam. (Phillips) $9,168 £4,800

POISON BOTTLES

Because of the danger of dosing oneself from a poison bottle by mistake, manufacturers made their bottles as recognisable as possible and did this by turning them out in eye catching colours – cobalt blue, viridian green or glowing amber. They also manufactured them in various distinctive shapes.

The first English poison bottle was patented in 1859 and was made of cobalt glass which was the most popular colour for the thousands of bottles that followed until the 1950's when cobalt glass was replaced by plastic. It is the shapes of poison bottles that make them interesting to collectors for they turn up with wasp waists, shaped as binoculars and submarines, with U – bends in their necks or with the glass indented, embossed and ridged all over. Some were even coffin shaped – which must have been a pretty dreadful warning – and others had skulls embossed on their sides. A few stoneware poison bottles turn up printed with the names of hospitals and they cost considerably less than the exotic glass varieties.

Very rare 'Wasp Waist' Poison with rows of diamond points embossed on the front and side panels, patented 1894.
$785 £450

Skull Poisons, Patented by Carlton H. Lee, 1894, in America, cobalt blue glass.
$600 £350

Quine's Patent, aqua glass bottle with 'Poison' embossed on the side, patented 1893.
$130 £75

American, 'Quilt Poison', with cross hatching around the sides of the bottle. **$175 £100**

O'Reilly's Patent, known as Binoculars Poison, embossed on the base 'O'Reilly's Patent 1905', only two of these bottles are known. **$1,400 £800**

Wilsons Patent emerald green, triangular bottle with notched edges, patented in 1899.
$130 £75

(Brian Thatcher)

310

POISON BOTTLES

Submarine poison bottle in cobalt blue glass embossed Poison on the side. $175 £100

Tippers poison bottle with tapering body embossed with Poison across the top of the front, 1904. $175 £100

Martin's Patent bottle with U bend in aqua glass, 1902. $175 £100

Ammonia poison bottles in amber glass embossed Poisonous down the front. $18 £10

Six sided Admiralty poison bottle in green glass. $35 £20

Six sided poison bottle in green, embossed Birmingham Workhouse. $25 £15

Stoneware poison bottle stamped Poison and Royal Infirmary Manchester. $25 £15

Taylors Liverpool Patent, emerald green bottle with a curved back embossed Caution and 'Not to be taken' on the front. $70 £40

Square bodied Admiralty poison bottle with vertical ribbing. $50 £30

(Brian Thatcher)

311

POP ALBUMS

Most people have a few old LPs lying around, and it's surprising how much good condition copies of early albums can now fetch. Most sought-after are Rock 'n' Roll, in particular mint copies of, for example, Gene Vincent, Buddy Holly, the Ventures, the Shadows and Eddie Cochran. 60's releases by artists like Roy Orbison, Gene Pitney and the Hollies, as well as, of course, original Beatles albums are also steadily increasing in value. Much depends on condition, and autographed copies are generally worth double. Look out for good mono LP's in original covers and the rarer, often very valuable, 10″ LPs issued in the 50's. Limited edition or promotional copies of well-known artists are also worth looking for. Note, too, artists who changed their name in mid-career, eg Shane Fenton, who became Alvin Stardust!

Eddie Cochran, Singin' to my baby, Liberty 1158, 1959.
$70 £40

Sidney Bechet with Muggsy Spanier, Ember F.A.2009, 1965.
$55 £30

Bob Dylan, Highway 61 Revisited, CBS 62572, 1965.
$20 £12

Benny Goodman, Let's Hear the Melody, Phillips BBR8064.
$28 £15

Cliff Richard, Cliff and the Drifters, Columbia 33SX 1147, 1959.
$175 £100

The Beatles, Help! Parlophone 1255, 1965.
$45 £25

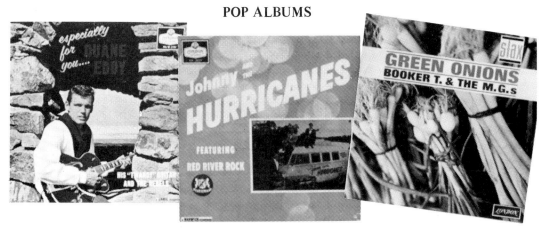

Duane Eddy, Especially for you, London HA-W-2191. $55 £30

Johnny and the Hurricanes, London Records HA2227. $60 £35

Booker T & the M.G.'s, Green Onions, Stax—London, HAK 8182, 1962. $100 £60

The Monkees, RCA Victor RD7844, 1967. $20 £12

Elvis Presley, Elvis is Back ! RCA SF5060. $55 £30

Great Stars of Broadway, Summit ATL4180, 1965. $45 £25

Elvis Presley, Blue Hawaii, RCA RD27238. $60 £35

Eddie Cochran, Cherished Memories, Liberty LB 1109, 1962. $70 £40

Pink Floyd, The Piper at the Gates of Dawn, EMI SCX6157, 1967. $45 £25

Winston Churchill, I Can Hear
It Now, CBS BLD7047, 1955.
$55 £30

The Doors, Elektra, K42012,
1967. $45 £25

Bonzo Dog Band, The Dough-
nut in Granny's Greenhouse,
Sunset SLS50210, 1968.$16 £9

Buddy Holly's Greatest Hits,
Ace of Hearts, AH148, 1967.
$35 £20

Gene Vincent, Capitol T1059,
A Record Date, 1958. $45 £25

Ella Fitzgerald & Billie Holliday
at Newport, Verve 80146, 1957.
$30 £16

Rufus Thomas, Do the Funky
Chicken, Stax 1033, 1970.
$14 £8

Bonanza, Ponderosa Party Time,
RCA Victor RD7520, 1962.
$50 £28

Noel Coward at Las Vegas, CBS
B.L.D.7010. $20 £12

Harry Belafonte and the Islanders, Caribbean! World Records, 1950. $15 £8

The Rolling Stones, Decca LK4605, 1964. $60 £35

Idle Race, Time Is, EMI SLRZ 1017, 1971. $45 £25

Elvis Presley, A Date with Elvis, RCA RD27128, 1960. $55 £30

Bill Haley and his Comets, Rock the Joint! London HA-F2037. $125 £70

Spotlight on the Ink Spots, Pickwick PR110, 1962. $35 £20

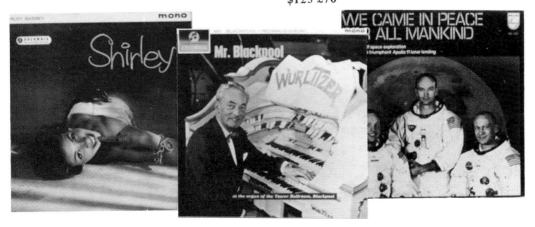

Shirley Bassey, Shirley, Columbia 335X 1286, 1961. $35 £20

Mr Blackpool, Reginald Dixon at the Organ, Columbia 335X, 1964. $45 £25

We Came in Peace for all Mankind, Phillips S.G.L.4321, 1969. $60 £35

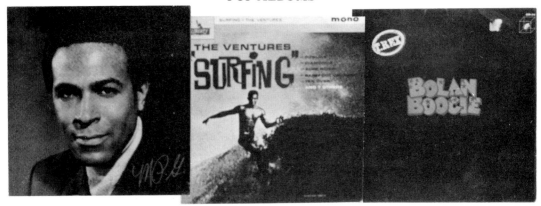

Marvin Gaye, Tamla 292, 1969. The Ventures, Surfing, Liberty T. Rex, Bolan Boogie, Fly 2326
$35 £20   LB1150, 1963. $55 £30   012, 1972. $25 £15

Dance Annette, Walt Disney,   The Searchers, Meet the Sear-   Tommy Steele, Stage Show,
Vista B.V.3305, 1950. $55 £30   chers, Pye NPL18086.   Decca L.P.1287, 1957. $55 £30
                                          $80 £45

Dr Murray Banks, How to Live   Jimi Hendrix, Electric Lady-
with Yourself, Pty. Johannes-   The Raiders, Indian Reservation,   land, Double Album, Polydor,
burg B.C.12475. $30 £16   CBS CQ30768, 1971. $18 £10   1968. $45 £25

POP SINGLES

Record collecting is becoming more and more popular with record fairs and specialist shops springing up all over the country.

As with many other collectables, condition is of paramount importance, and records should be in mint or near-mint condition.

Early 45's in good condition are worth looking for, and records with a misprint on the label will attract a healthy premium. Picture covers and coloured vinyl are also popular with collectors.

Some to look out for are: early Chuck Berry (£25-£35), Bowie singles on Pye (£45-£50), Marc Bolan "Hippy Gumbo" (£100), Fats Domino "Love Me" (£75), Bob Marley "Judge Not" and "One Cup of Coffee" (£50-£100), Mothers of Invention on the Verve label (£25).

The Rolling Stones, 'Little red rooster', Decca 12014 (1964). $7 £4

Elvis Presley, 'Follow that Dream', RCA 211, mono E.P. (1962). $20 £12

The Lemon Pipers, 'Green Tambourine', Pye 25444 (1967). $7 £4

Elvis Presley, 'I got stung', RCA 1100. $18 £10

The Kinks, 'Lola', Pye 17961, (1970). $5 £3

John Lennon, 'Mind Games', Apple R5994 (1973). $14 £8

Traffic, 'Here we go round the mulberry bush', Island WIP6025 (1967). $18 £10

Elvis Presley, 'Return to sender', RCA 1320 (1958). $15 £9

Buddy Holly, 'Raining in my heart', Coral 72360 (1958). $12 £7

Procul Harum, 'A whiter shade of pale', Deram, DM126 (1967). $5 £3

The Shirelles, 'Will you love me tomorrow', Top Rank Jar 540 (1960). $9 £5

Johnny Kidd, 'Shakin all over', HMV8628, mono E.P. (1960). $35 £20

Tired of Living, 'Kiss a lotta frogs', IRC 003 (1981). $18 £10

The Beatles, 'Twist and Shout', Parlophone 8882 (1963), mono E.P. $10 £6

Rufus Thomas, 'Do the funky chicken', Stax 144 (1969). $5 £3

The Shadows, 'Apache', Columbia 4484 (1960). $9 £5

Roxy Music, 'More than this', Polydor Roxy 3 (1982). $3.50 £2

Chris Farlow, 'Out of time', Immediate IM031 (1966). $9 £5

Cliff Richard and the Drifters, 'Living Doll', Columbia 4306 (1959). $12 £7

The Platters, 'Volume 3' E.P., Mercury, MEP9524, mono. $18 £10

John Rowles, 'If I only had time', MCA MU1000 (1968). $5 £3

David Bowie, 'Space Oddity',
Philips, BF1801 (1969).
$20 £12

Four Tops, 'Four Top Hits',
Tamla Motown 2018 (1964).
$18 £10

The Troggs, 'Love is all around',
Page One, POF046 (1967).
$7 £4

The Rockin Berries, 'He's in
town', Piccadilly 7N35203
(1964). $5 £3

Manfred Mann, 'No living
without loving', Mono E.P.
EMI 8922 (1965). $12 £7

Chicken Shack, 'I'd rather go
blind', Blue Horizon 3153
(1969). $14 £8

T. Rex, 'Light of love', EMI
Marc B. (1974). $5 £3

Len Barry, '1-2-3', Brunswick
05942 (1965). $10 £6

Richard Chamberlain's 'Hits',
mono E.P., MGM776. $9 £5

New Vaudeville Band,
'Winchester Cathedral',
Fontana, TF741 (1966). $7 £4

The Beatles, 'I'm happy just
to dance', Capitol 5234 (USA).
$12 £7

The Beatles, 'Please Please Me',
(red) Parlophone 4983 (1963).
$45 £25

Tommy Tucker, 'Hi heel sneakers', Pye 25238 (1964). $9 £5

The Searchers, 'Sweets for my sweet', PYE 24183, mono E.P. (1963). $14 £8

The Rolling Stones, 'Five by five', Decca DFE8590, mono E.P., (1964). $12 £7

Bill Wyman, 'White Lightnin/ Pussy', R.S.19115 (1974). $9 £5

Connie Francis, 'Don't break my heart', MGM K13059 (USA). $5 £3

Billy Fury, 'Halfway to Paradise', Decca 11349 (1961). $9 £5

Judge Dread, 'Big Six', Bigshot BI 608 (1972). $7 £4

The Everly Brothers, 'Bird Dog', London 8685 (1958). $10 £5

Jimi Hendrix, 'Purple Haze', Track 604001, (1967). $14 £8

The Springfields, 'Kinda Folksy', No. 3, Phillips 433624 (1962), E.P. $7 £4

Marc Bolan, 'Jasper C. Debussy', Track 2094013 (1972). $7 £4

Bill Haley, 'Rock 'n Roll stage show', Brunswick OE9279, mono E.P. $25 £15

POSTAL SCALES

The earliest postal scales were made by the manufacturers of scientific instruments such as S. Morden and Co. who had a tradition of using fine wood and brass. As a result many of the early scales are true works of art with mahogany and ebony bases and fine fret cut brass work. Later models are often made of cast iron and are purely functional items with little aesthetic appeal.

Apart from the weight most scales also display the actual postal charges, enabling the collector to date them fairly accurately for there were frequent changes by the Post Office.

Painted metal scales by Precision Eng. Co. (Reading) Ltd., 1961, 8in. high. $26 £15

Brass and mahogany scales by S. Morden & Co., 1906-15, 15in. wide. $525 £300

19th century painted tin scales, 9in. high. $70 £40

Brass and painted metal scales, 1906-15, 11in. high. $45 £25

Set of brass postage scales and full set of weights. $455 £260

Painted metal and brass scales by Triner Scale Co., Chicago, made for the U.K. market, 1935-40, 8in. high. $70 £40

Cartology is the name given to the collecting of postcards and it is a vast field because since postcards first appeared in Austria in 1869, people have been sending them to each other across the entire world in their millions.

The postcard boom began in Britain in 1870 and early ones were designed to take the address on one side and the message and illustration on the other. These cards came complete with a half penny stamp and were seized on as the ideal way of keeping in touch with friends at a low cost. It was not till 1894 that cards were produced for use with an adhesive stamp and in 1902 the vogue for pretty postcards really took off when an Act of Parliament was passed allowing the message and address to be written on the same side. Collectors usually pick a special theme for their collections – and the world is their oyster because there are postcards on every possible subject. Some people collect views of their home towns; others like pin-up pictures of favourite stars; many specialise in cards depicting transport; others in naughty seaside cards like the ones drawn by Donald McGill. Among the most valuable cards are those with moving parts which sell for between £5 and £10 each and cards by manufacturers C. W. Faulkner and Tucks Record Cards are always popular. Shell Aviation cards can go as high as £35 each but the majority sell for lower prices unless they are signed by a celebrity like the card that had the extra bonus of a little sketch by Picasso. It sold for £500.

'Three dogs', German Art card, T.S.N. Series No. 1281. $3.50 £2

Art card of a cat by Louis Wain, published by J. Salmon, Sevenoaks. $26 £15

Embossed chrome lithographic art postcard of a cat, by P. F. Series 7072, France. $5 £3

'I've quite come out of my shell here', a mechanical novelty card by E.T.W. Dennis. $14 £8

Boots Cash Chemists 'English Birds', Series 29 'Pigeons'. $5 £3

Art study of two horses by R. Trache, German A.H. Series 464. $5 £3

CHILDREN

Children playing on a hobby horse, real photograph post-card. $1 50p

Portrait of a pretty young girl, real photograph postcard by C. W. Greaves, Halifax. $2 £1

'Two Young Students' from the Sunshine School of Dancing, Chatham, 28th November 1931. $3.50 £2

Little girl holding a 9mm. rifle, real photograph postcard. $2 £1

Mr and Mrs Caspar's new baby, in Wood Green, London. $1 50p

Little boy in his chain driven pedal car. $5 £3

'Ready for the big fight', study of a boy, unknown photographer. $1 50p

'Fun at the seaside', by Jacksons Faces Ltd., Weston-Super-Mare (Cycling Interest postcard). $2 £1

'Baby on a swing', family study, circa 1907. $1 50p

HUMOROUS

'I saw you first' , German embossed chromo lithograph, 1905. $5 £3

'I didn't want to do it', Valentines Series, 1914. $2 £1

'Patriots', from Raphael Tuck's 'Some' Clothes Series. $3.50 £2

'How can we play 'Husbands and wives' when we're both girls? Women are doing all the men's jobs nowadays!', Donald McGill card published by Inter-Art Comique Series No. 2703. $5 £3

'Summer girls and some are not' by J. L. Biggar, published by E.T.W. Dennis & Sons Ltd. $2 £1

'The voyage was glorious but..' (the spasms!!! - pencilled in), 'Write away' card by Bamforths, 1912. $3.50 £2

'We'se out Sportin', Raphael Tuck's Oilette Card No. 9092. $5 £3

'Oh! You silly girl!' (Police interest). $3.50 £2

'For tampering with His Majesty's Males', from the 'Witty' Series by Bamforth. $20 £12

HUMOROUS

'Things aren't what they used to be' by G. E. Studdy, 'Bonzo' Series card by Valentines. $7 £4

Leslie Lester Ltd., 1950's comic card, 'now all Henry wants to do is stay home every night and play with my pussy'. $1 50p

'A trifle bald perhaps but Oh! Boy! I'm strong with the hens' Alpha Series, 'Smile Messengers'. $2 £1

'Another puzzle for the Post Office. Bill: But I dunno the bloke's address. 'Arry: Can't yer write and arsk him for it?' The Humor of Life as seen by Phil May Series 6075. $7 £4

'I'm frightened of nothing — but this put the wind up me at Wembley!!' 'Felix' the film cat comic card No. 4889. $9 £5

Unusual comic card with Transvestite interest, 'It must be nice to be a girl, my heart it beats like mad, the feeling I've got through wearing these, is the nicest I ever had'. $12 £7

'I'm the new housemaid, won't the Master be pleased!', comic card printed in Saxony. $2 £1

'Everybody's doing it! This is what a sailor did!' comic card circa 1905. $3.50 £2

'Oh, lor! Fancy 'avin' a pain in that!' 'Early' Donald McGill card (1907), published by E. S. card No. 2085. $7 £4

'Greetings from the Territorial Camp, Barrow in Furness'. $10 £6

'Lights Out', Camp Silhouette No. 10, photochrom. $18 £10

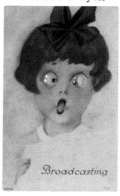

Cut-out postcard, put string through white dots at corner of eyes. $35 £20

'Heroes All', Titanic memorial postcard, April 14th, 1912. $55 £30

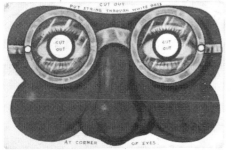

The Alpha postcard 'Broadcasting', produced in Saxony. $7 £4

Chamomile (Anthemis Nobilis), Tucks gramophone record postcard, 'Many Happy Returns of the Day'. $10 £6

'Chin Chin Chinaman, Strikee Matchee on him Patchee'. $10 £6

Wreck of the G.E.R. Cromer to London Express at Colchester, July 12th, 1913. $90 £50

'Herzliche Gruesse aus Nurnberg', model postcard, 1918. $90 £50

POSTERS

Posters were meant to go on walls and they had to put their message across at the blink of an eye. The best of them display a high standard of artwork and printing and many famous artists have been connected with the poster since they first became massively popular at the end of the 19th century. Prices paid for old posters today range from a few pounds to many thousands and rarity, style, content and artist all play a part in determining the cost. Toulouse Lautrec is perhaps the most famous of the poster artists and the ones he drew for the Moulin Rouge have been so often reproduced and copied that they have become almost cliches. Another much copied poster artist is Alphonse Mucha who designed the publicity material for Sarah Bernhardt for six years. Cassandre was a highly regarded poster artist in the first half of the 20th century and it was he who designed the magnificent poster for the liner Normandie looking at it bow on. One of Cassandre's contemporaries was Pierre Fix-Masseau who did wonderful posters for French State Railways. The creation and collection of posters goes on today and anyone who had the presence of mind to collect one Andy Warhol did for the RCA Colour Scanner in 1968 has a valuable property on their hands. Posters have been produced promoting everything from cigarettes to circuses, from films to motor cars and most valuable are lithographs printed on silk which have kept their richness of colour for unfortunately many old posters fade with time. There is a monthly magazine called "The Poster" for aficionados.

La Revue Des Folies Bergere, by Jules Alexandre Grun, lithograph in colours, 1905, printed by Ch. Verneau, Paris, 1246 x 880mm. (Christie's) $225 £150

Chemin De Fer, Martigny-Orsieres, by Albert Muret, lithograph in colours, 1913, on wove paper, printed by Sonor, 1000 x 700mm. (Christie's) $525 £350

Summer; Spring; Autumn; Winter, by Alphonse Mucha, lithograph in colours, 1896, on wove paper, 1040 x 530mm. (Christie's) $10,200 £6,800

Pierre Stephen, lithograph in colours, on wove paper, printed by Bauduin, Paris, 1538 x 1175mm. (Christie's) $630 £420

Ein Rausch In Rot, Maskenball Wilder Mann, by C.M.I., lithograph in colours, 1928, on wove paper, 920 x 612mm. (Christie's) $225 £150

Camp Romain, Vin Rouge, Rose, Blanc, by L. Gadoud, lithograph in colours, on wove paper, 1600 x 1200mm. (Christie's) $240 £160

Laren, Tentoonstelling 1916, Hotel Hamdorff, Zunki Joska, by Willy Sluiter, lithograph in colours, printed by Senefelder, Amsterdam, 1086 x 778mm. (Christie's) $420 £280

For Real Comfort, New Statendam, Holland-America Line, by Adolphe Mouron Cassandre, lithograph in colours, 1928, 1050 x 806mm. (Christie's) $1,500 £1,000

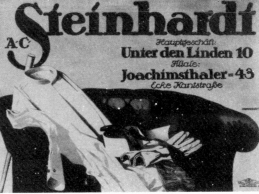

Rhum Charleston, by Leon D'Ylem, lithograph in colours, published by Vercassou, Paris, 1982 x 1275mm. (Christie's) $112 £75

Steinhardt, Unter Den Linden, by Hans Lindenstaedt, lithograph in colours, 1912, on wove paper, 710 x 945mm. (Christie's) $450 £300

Bruxelles, Exposition Universelle, 1935, by Marfurt, lithograph in colours, printed by Les Creations, Publicitaires, Bruxelles, 1000 x 620mm. (Christie's) $105 £70

Etoile Du Nord, by Adolphe Mouron Cassandre, lithograph in colours, on wove paper, 1048 x 752mm. (Christie's) $1,275 £850

Alcazar Royal, by Adolphe Crespin and Edouard Duych, lithograph in colours, 1894, 1010 x 775mm. (Christie's) $420 £280

David Hockney at the Tate Gallery, lithograph in colour, 1980, on wove paper, signed in pencil, 760 x 505mm. (Christie's) $67 £45

Pousset Spatenbrau, by Jean Carlu, lithograph in colours, on wove paper, printed by J. E. Goosens, Lille, 795 x 508mm. (Christie's)
$330 £220

S. V. U. Manes, 150 Vystava, Clenska, lithograph in colours, 1929, printed by Melantrich Praha, Smichov, 1250 x 950mm. (Christie's) $180 £120

'Lenin's Push Into The Business Generation', by K. Poliarkova and R. Mozchaeva, lithograph in colours, 965 x 650mm. (Christie's) $142 £95

L'Oiseau Bleu, by Adolphe Mouron Cassandre, lithograph in colours, 1929, on wove paper, 996 x 616mm. (Christie's) $1,170 £780

Peugeot, by Rene Vincent, lithograph in colours, printed by Draeger, 1170 x 1540mm. (Christie's) $1,200 £800

Poster, 'Dolomiten Ski-Schu Val Gardena (Grodental) m.1300-2200'. (Onslows)
$110 £75

Opera, Bal Des Petits Lits Blancs, L'Intran, by Marie Laurencin, lithograph in colours, 1931, 1600 x 1196mm. (Christie's)
$1,500 £1,000

G. Marconi, Le Maitre De La Radio, by Paul Colin, lithograph in colours, printed by Bedos & Cie, Paris, 1578 x 1130mm. (Christie's)
$330 £220

Soiree De Paris, Spectacles, Choregraphiques et Drama- tiques, by Marie Laurencin, lithograph in colours, signed in pencil and dated 1924, 796 x 578mm. (Christie's)
$255 £170

Jane Renouardt, by Pierre Stephen, lithograph in colours, printed by M. Picard, Paris, 1538 x 1175mm. (Christie's) $150 £100

Raden Van Arbeid, by R. N. Roland Holst, lithograph in colours, on wove paper, 1084 x 794mm. (Christie's) $600 £400

Job, by Alphonse Mucha, lithograph in colours, 1898, on wove paper, printed by F. Champenoise, Paris, 1500 x 1010mm. (Christie's) $5,250 £3,500

Wilhelm Mozer Munchen-Nord Adalbertstr, by Ludwig Hohlwein, lithograph in colours, 1909, on wove paper, 1250 x 911mm. (Christie's) $270 £180

XXVI Ausstellung Secession, by Ferdinand Andri, lithograph in colours, circa 1904, on wove paper, 920 x 602mm. (Christie's) $13,050 £8,700

Raphael Tuck, Celebrated Posters No. 1501, Ogden's Guinea Gold Cigarettes and another. (Christie's) $47 £35

Exposition Des Peintres Lithographes, by Fernand Louis Gottlob, lithograph in colours, 1899, printed by Lemercier, Paris, 1195 x 790mm. (Christie's) $450 £300

G. B. Borsalino Fu Lazzaro & C, by Marcello Dudovich, lithograph in colours, 1932, printed by R. Questura, Milano, 1390 x 1000mm. (Christie's) $375 £250

Nord Express, by Adolphe Mouron Cassandre, lithograph in colours, 1927, on wove paper, 1048 x 752mm. (Christie's) $1,950 £1,300

PRINTING BLOCKS

Old printing blocks come in all shapes, sizes and materials such as woodcuts, lino cuts, zinc etchings, Krishnas, stone, lead and alloys. The bonus of collecting them is that many will still print superb copies of their design, while the late Art Deco Krishnas, for example, are often works of art in their own right. Mounted and framed, they reflect the light and image almost like a modern hologram.

Look out for early stone types and those depicting items of local or historical interest.

A large Armorial, steel die. $35 £20

Late Victorian Pig, 4½in. wide. $14 £8

The Ploughman, brass block. $28 £16

Antimony, tin and lead block of Father Christmas. $10 £6

Plated lead hand, block for posters. $35 £20

Halftone block of an old car, 5½in. wide. $26 £15

Metal printing block of a fireman, 5in. wide. $14 £8

QUACK MEDICINE BOTTLES

Victorians, it would seem, would swallow just about anything, literally and metaphorically, if it came in a recognised medicine bottle and the claims were extravagant enough! Patent cures for everything from corns to coughs (often in the same bottle) were readily obtainable, and the collecting of these containers makes a fascinating and often quite hilarious hobby.

Bottles are mainly of two types, the pre 1850 'pontilled' bottles usually made of lead or flint glass, and very rare, and the post – 1850 quack bottles in various shades of coloured glass. Those having claims embossed on them, especially if they claim to have been endorsed by Royalty are highly prized, as are those which contained exotic substances no longer available, such as Elixir of Opium or Mouse Ear Syrup.

Dr. Solomon's Cordial Balm of Gilead, in moulded aqua glass bottle. $260 £150

J. Cropper's 'Never Failing Gout Mixture', in aqua coloured glass bottle, circa 1850. $35 £20

Miss Pikes Powders for Fits and Nervous Complaints, in a lead glass bottle, circa 1800. $175 £100

George Handyside's small 'Blood Food' in black glass full of attractive yellow bubbles, rare. $85 £50

Dr. Hasting's Naphtha Syrup in rectangular shaped aqua glass pontilled bottle. $140 £80

Edgar's Group Lotion, 'The Children's Life Preserver', in octagonal aqua glass bottle. $50 £30

QUILTS

The tradition of quilting thrived in the homesteads of America at the time of the first settlers when women used to meet together and hold quilting parties. The reason for their industry was to provide warm bedding for their families but some of the quilts they made were very beautiful and traditional patterns were handed down from mother to daughter through the generations. They were made from two thicknesses of cloth with a layer of padding between. The padding was often teased out sheep's wool taken from the scraps that were found sticking to trees or hedges. Quilts were stitched by hand with minute stitches using scraps of any materials that were available, favourite old dresses or cast off clothes. Each piece was stiffened at the back with paper. The women often used old letters or pages from household account books for this purpose and so it is often possible to date old quilts which can be extremely valuable. Some are so precious and fragile that the owners have them framed and glazed.

Early 19th century red and blue patchwork Calamanco coverlet, America, 108 x 100in. (Robt. W. Skinner Inc.) $1,200 £833

Mid 19th century crib quilt, the red, yellow and green calico patches arranged in the 'Star of Bethlehem' pattern, 28in. square. (Robt. W. Skinner Inc.) $400 £250

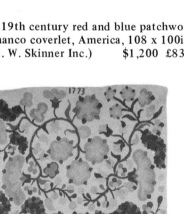

A wool bed rug, worked with a darning stitch in a tree-of-life pattern on a natural wool foundation, dated 1773, 84 x 85in. (Christie's) $11,000 £7,586

An appliqued album quilt, cross stitch name in corner 'Miss Lydia Emeline Keller, 1867', American, 84 x 86in. (Robt. W. Skinner Inc.) $2,100 £1,250

A cotton and wool Jacquard coverlet, New York State, 1816, the field of double rose and flower medallions. (Robt. W. Skinner Inc.)
$425   £241

An Amish patchwork quilt, Pennsylvania, early 20th century, in shades of red, green, blue, purple and black arranged in "Sunshine and Shadow" pattern, 83 x 85in. (Robt. W. Skinner Inc.) $1,400   £795

A patchwork cover of log cabin design worked with brightly coloured pieces of mainly floral printed cottons and worsted, 2.1m. x 2.04m. (Phillips) $299   £160

A pieced and quilted cotton coverlet, American, late 19th century, worked in Triple Irish Chain pattern, 82 x 84in. (Christie's)
$880   £519

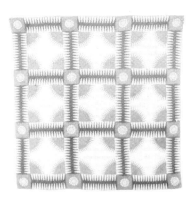

Patchwork quilt, America, 19th century, the red, green and yellow cotton patches arranged in the 'New York Beauty' pattern, 90 x 90in. (Robt. W. Skinner Inc.)
$1,500 £852

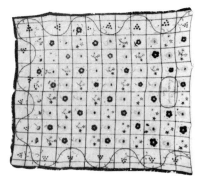

An embroidered blanket, probably New York, 'Lucretia Brush(?) Busti, 1831', large blue and white check, 6ft.4in. x 7ft.4in. (Robt. W. Skinner Inc.) $5,800 £3,918

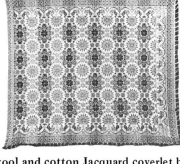

An appliqued and stuffed cotton coverlet, American, late 19th century, worked in Basket of Flowers pattern, 80 x 86in. (Christie's) $2,860 £1,689

A wool and cotton Jacquard coverlet by S. B. Musselman, Milford, Bucks County, Pennsylvania, 1840, fringed on three sides (minor staining), 102 x 82in. (Christie's) $2,640 £1,559

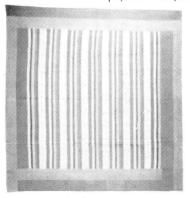

A patchwork quilt, Penn., signed and dated in ink on the back, 'Phebeann H. Salem's(?) Presented by her Mother 1848', 8ft.11in. x 9ft. (Robt. W. Skinner Inc.) $1,900 £1,319

An Amish pieced and quilted cotton coverlet, probably Pennsylvania, early 20th century, of Joseph's Coat of Many Colours pattern, 89 x 89in. (Christie's) $1,210 £714

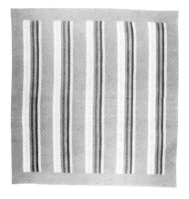

An appliqued and quilted cotton coverlet, Pennsylvania, late 19th/early 20th century, with four spreadwing eagles centering a sunburst design, 67 x 72in. (Christie's) $286 £168

A Mennonite pierced cotton quilt, Lancaster County, Pennsylvania, late 19th/early 20th century, a variant of the "Rainbow" pattern, 84 x 88in. (Robt. W. Skinner Inc.) $1,600 £909

RADIOS

Most collectors of radios tend to specialise in the unusually shaped sets of the 1930's like the circular black Pifco that came out in 1938 and is still a model of superb design. Many were cased in boxes of fine woods and in an enormous variety of styles — some even look like miniature temples or cinemas. Others were made of bakelite which had the disadvantage that it was easily cracked so examine any set carefully. Enthusiasts say that there is no sound to equal the sound of a period radio for it has a mellow tone which has never been matched by modern transistors. Many of the old sets are still in working order so that's a bonus. A more specialised market concentrates on early types of radio sets like a 1922 Marconiphone that looks like an electrical circuit box and the Marconi 1923 long range wireless set encased in a walnut box. Particularly valued are field radio sets, especially those from the First World War.

'Fellophone' Super 3 Bright Emitter battery set, 1922-24.
$350 £200

'Gecophone' 3 Valve All Battery Set 1928. $175 £100

A Marconiphone V-2 two-valve receiver with BBC transfer, two wavelength plates and regenerator unit.
(Christie's) $547 £380

1950's Vidor Lady Anne portable battery/mains radio.
$35 £20

A Walmore crystal set in oak case with BBC transfer, glazed cover and two pairs of headphones. (Christie's)
$79 £55

'Celestion' Speaker, wood cabinet, 1928. $85 £50

'Freed Eiseman' Junior Bedside AC-DC USA Line Cord Set, 1935. $85 £50

Crystal Set with Earphones, 1922. $85 £50

'Bestone' Clock Radio, USA, oak cabinet 1934. $150 £90

'Marconi', 1923, V2 Long range wireless set in a walnut case, 10in. high. $785 £450

'Phillips' Mains AC 'Super Inductance' model 830A, 1932. $260 £150

'Ultra' AC Mains '3', wood cabinet, 1932. $130 £75

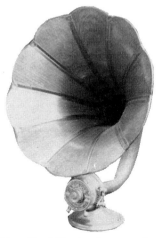

'Amplion' Moving iron speaker, wood petal horn, brass base, 1927. $130 £75

'Ekco' AC Mains model AC74 bakelite, 1939.
                    $130 £75

'Kolster Brandes' Straight 3 1928. $85 £50

RAILWAY TICKETS

The term "ephemera" covers the sort of collectables that most people throw away. Railway tickets are an excellent example and fortunately there have been some canny minded people who haven't chucked their tickets but put them away in a safe place. The reason they did so must have been that the trip was significant to them personally or because they recognised that it was an unusual journey — perhaps the last trip on a certain line before closure.

The railway tickets that are most prized by collectors are the ones which were issued for unusual journeys — hop pickers' tickets from London's East End to the Kent countryside; group tickets for Anglers' Clubs outings or for a day visit to the Woolwich Dockyards. Tickets issued by individual railway companies before nationalisation in 1948 are valuable to collectors and some people try to build up a collection of tickets issued by a particular company or for a specific line. Others specialise in tickets to unusual places or even platform tickets.

Platform Ticket for Ludgate Hill, closed in 1929. $600 £340

Newington Road to Dalston Junction, second class, 1867. (Onslow's) $487 £290

Southern Railway, Coffin Ticket, Waterloo to Brookwood. $45 £25

O. & N. & L.1. & N.R. Montgomery to Cemmes Road, first class 1876. (Onslow's) $218 £130

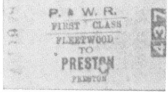

P. & W. R. Fleetwood to Preston, first class 1878. (Onslow's) $117 £70

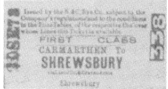

S. & C. R. Carmarthen to Shrewsbury, first class 1878. (Onslow's) $100 £60

A Season Ticket from the pioneering Stockton and Darlington Railway, issued in 1853. $125 £70

New Cross to Blackfriars, second class 1866, overprinted with the letter B. (Onslow's) $168 £100

A Staff Season Ticket, printed on thick card. $17 £10

St Austell to Bodmin Road, Express Train, second class, reverse overprinted C.R. Express. (Onslow's) $218 £130

Booth's Trip, July 14th, 1856, Kidderminster to Birmingham Cov' Carriage. (Onslow's) $58 £35

M. R. Blackwell to Barnt Green, second class 1874. (Onslow's) $117 £70

RAILWAYANA

There is a positive passion for collecting anything connected with trains and railways from cups and saucers that saw service in dining cars to station signs and even whole trains. This is a manifestation of the enthusiasm that the public has shown toward the train ever since the first public railway was opened between Stockton and Darlington in 1825. By 1900 there were over two hundred railway companies operating in Britain so there is a wealth of items to be collected over the length and breadth of the land. People seek out tickets, timetables, train number plates, maps, clocks, lamp standards and even the brass locks from train lavatory doors.

Train nameplates is an especially thriving area and some collectors will go so far as steal them so the ones displayed on trains today are usually replicas. Most of the railway companies produced beautiful posters and photographed views of the countryside which were displayed in railway carriages and these too are eagerly collected. Another popular area is the postcards which were issued by the large companies and can now cost between 50p and £100 a piece depending on rarity. Official view cards are the most common, followed by locomotive cards and map cards. Local publishers also often issued cards with pictures of railway disasters which are rare and pricey today. Poster type cards can fetch as much as £100 and many of them are now being reproduced. Look out for cards issued by lesser known lines like the Barry, Caledonia, Callander & Oban, Cambrian and Cheshire Lines as well as the London, Chatham & Dover, London & South Western and the Midland & Great Northern.

J. C. Bourne — History & Description of the Great Western Railway — from drawings taken specially for this work by David Bogue, London 1846 fifty plates, 12 x 17in. (Onslow's)
$4,725 £2,500

L.M.S. Hotels plated oval dishes, various sizes, vegetable dish with division and cover, muffin dish with liner and sauceboat. (Onslow's) $75 £40

M.R., L.M.S., L. & Y.R., L.N.W. and some other companies, a fascinating official library of photographs, comprising almost one thousand glass negatives, each 8½ x 6½in., covering the period 1900-1939. (Onslow's)
$3,000 £1,600

G.W.R. Stationmaster cap inscribed Kingswear, size 6¾in. (Onslow's) $160 £85

Five L.M.S. harness brasses. (Onslow's) $190 £100

One of a set of six G.W.R. plated grapefruit dishes. (Onslow's) $56 £30

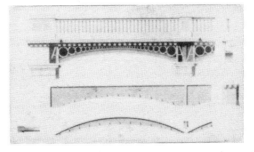

Late 19th century brass acetylene lamp with carrying handle. $70 £40

Contract drawing for Hampstead Road Bridge and detail of ironwork. (Onslow's) $640 £340

A black painted guards oil lamp with colour filters. (Onslow's) $34 £18

The L. & N.R. Railway from 1830 to the Present Time, 1908. $70 £40

L.S.W.R. original panel 15½ x 9in. (Onslow's) $200 £110

Eastern Counties Railway 1st Class season ticket, 1857. (Onslow's) $150 £80

Festiniog Railway, leather backed 1st Class free pass issued to A. G. Edwards esq. (Onslow's) $65 £35

Two Southern Railway
harness brasses. (Onslow's)
$100 £55

L.N.E.R. plated tea pot, milk
jug, sugar basin and whisky
tot. (Onslow's) $80 £45

Two G.W.R. harness brasses.
(Onslow's) $130 £70

Great Northern Railway,
Ireland garter. (Onslow's)
$25 £15

Great Western Railway enamel
sign for the Cornish Riviera.
$260 £150

Cork, Blackrock and Passage
Railway Company garter.
(Onslow's) $180 £100

Great Northern Railway, blue
and white enamel sign,
5 x 8in. (Onslow's) $110 £65

G.N.R. painted wood panel
from carriage interior
advertising the company's
hotels. (Onslow's) $60 £35

Whitland & Cardigan 2nd Class
free pass paper, 1881.
(Onslow's) $95 £50

York Station, from the south,
showing locomotives,
overpainted photograph,
10 x 14½in. (Onslow's)
$350 £190

Ornate platform lamp with
original glass names, 27in. high.
(Onslow's) $260 £140

RECORDS – 78's

It's a pity that many people dismiss old 78's simply because of the difficulty in playing them on modern equipment, for 78's are real nostalgia, and much of the material to be found on them is unavailable on any other format. Reproduction on early discs *is* often poor, but later ones can be of excellent quality and inexpensive equalizers can easily be obtained to cut out hiss. Much classical, music hall, and operatic material is not worth much, but there is a specialist market for some pre-war 78's. Rock 'n' Roll from the 50's is the most popular, however, and some later ones are even produced on early vinyl – the forerunners of the 45's of today. The most valuable are of popular artistes such as Frank Sinatra, Frankie Lane etc., especially when they contain certain songs never released on 45's or LP's. Look out for Elvis Presley on the Sun label (£200 +), Buddy Holly, etc. but remember they *must* be in mint condition.

His Masters Voice 'In the Mood' Glen Miller and His Orchestra. $5 £3

Decca Jazz, 'Rock Island Line', Lonnie Donegan. $10 £6

London American Recordings, 'She's Got It', Little Richard. $10 £6

Parlophone, 'The Shifting Whispering Sands', Eamonn Andrews. $5 £3

Decca, 'Good Companions', Billy Cotton and his band. $5 £3

Columbia Records, 'Lollipop', The Mudlarks. $7 £5

Brunswick, 'Shake Rattle and Roll', Bill Haley and his Comets. $35 £20

Eclipse Records, 8in., 'The Man on the Flying Trapeze', Donald Peers. $2 £1

Pye Nixa, 'The Battle of New Orleans', Lonnie Donegan. $7 £4

Capitol Records Inc., 'Be-bop-a-Lula', Gene Vincent and his Blue Caps. $28 £16

Sun, 'Good Rockin' Tonight', Elvis Presley. $435 £250

Parlophone, 'One o'clock jump', Count Basie and his orchestra. $7 £4

Decca Record Co., 'Singing the Blues', Tommy Steele and the Steelmen. $7 £4

Vogue Coral, 'That'll be the Day', The Crickets. $26 £15

The British Zonophone Co. Ltd., 'I a'int nobody's darling', Jack Hyltons Jazz Band. $5 £3

Parlophone Co., 'A mug of ale', Joe Venuti's Blue Four. $5 £3

His Master's Voice, 'Whistle while you work', from the soundtrack of Snow White and the Seven Dwarfs (Walt Disney). $12 £7

Phillips Records, 'Your cheatin' heart', Frankie Laine. $3.50 £2

His Master's Voice, 'Playin' for keeps', Elvis Presley. $45 £25

Zonophone Records, 'Cuckoo - Waltz', International Novelty Quartet. $2 £1

Columbia, 'Crazy Feet', Fred Astaire. $5 £3

The Gramophone Co. Ltd., Silver Jubilee Message to the Empire, broadcast on May 6th, 1935, by H.M. King George V. $435 £250

Brunswick, 'It's almost tomorrow', The Dream Weavers. $9 £5

Columbia Records, 'Oh Sinner Man', Nina and Fredrik. $7 £4

ROBOTS

The last country to enter the toy making market was Japan. In the pre-war period their toys were regarded as cheap rubbish but today they dominate the market and ninety per cent of the output is theirs. They began making tin plate toys in the 1950's but the big break through came in the 1960's when they began producing battery operated, or occasionally clockwork powered, space men and moving models of robots. Very few of the robots to be found did not originate in Japan. They were based on Robby the Robot from the 1950's film "Forbidden Planet" and they can walk, shoot, talk, give off flashes of light and whirl round. It was robots in particular that caught the public imagination and collecting them has grown into an art form. A pure robot must not have a human face behind its plastic dome. Originally of tin plate, they have been replaced by plastic and these are not quite so highly regarded or valuable.

Attacking Martian, battery operated, moveable legs, chest opens to reveal flashing guns, with box, by Horikawa (mk. 6), Japanese, 1960's, 23cm. high. (Christie's)$1,009 £540

Sparky Robot, clockwork mechanism, moveable legs and sparking eyes, with box, by Yoshiya, Japanese, 1950's, 19.5cm. high. (Christie's) $562 £301

Answer-Game, battery operated immobile, executes simple mathematics, flashing eyes, by Ichida (mk. 3), Japanese, 1960's, 35.5cm. high. (Christie's) $2,494 £1,334

Gear Robot, battery operated, moveable legs with coloured wheel rotating chest and flashing head, possibly by Horikawa, Japanese, 1960's, 22.5cm. high. (Christie's) $622 £333

Busy Cart Robot, battery operated, pushing and lifting a wheelbarrow, with box, by Horikawa (mk. 6), Japanese, 1960's/1970's, 30cm. high. (Christie's) $1,187 £635

Ultraman, clockwork mechanism, moveable arms and legs, with box, by Bullmark (mk. 5), Japanese, 1960's, 23cm. high. (Christie's) $355 £190

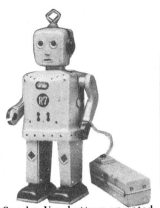

Sparky Jim, battery operated with remote control, moveable legs and flashing eyes, Japanese, 1950's, 19.5cm. high. (Christie's)$1,247 £667

Nando, the mechanism activated by air pressure through remote control, moveable legs and head, with box, by Opset, Italian, circa 1948, 13cm. high. (Christie's)$2,197 £1,175

Astoman, clockwork mechanism, moveable arms and legs, by Nomura (mk. 1), Japanese, 1960's, 23.5cm. high. (Christie's)$1,067 £571

Space Explorer, battery operated box transforms into Robot, revealing '3-D' television screen, with box, by Yonezawa (mk. 2), Japanese, 1960's, 29.5cm. high. (Christie's) $2,434 £1,302

Mr. Robot, clockwork mechanism and battery activated, with box, by Alps, Japanese, 1950's, 20cm. high. (Christie's) $1,602 £857

Dyno Robot, battery operated, moveable legs, opening mask to reveal a flashing red dinosaur's head, with box, by Horikawa, Japanese, 1960's, 28.5cm. high. (Christie's) $770   £412

Confectionary Dispenser, battery operated, with coinslot, transparent chest showing sweets, Italian, late 1960's, 139cm. high. (Christie's) $2,257 £1,207

Giant Robot, battery operated, moveable legs, chest opening to reveal flashing gun, possibly by Horikawa, Japanese, 1960's, 41cm. high. (Christie's) $1,187 £635

Talking Robot, battery powered, mobile, speaks four different messages, with box, by Yonezawa (mk. 2), Japanese, 1950's, 28cm. high. (Christie's) $1,542 £825

ROCK 'N' ROLL & POP MEMORABILIA

One of the most booming areas of the collecting world is rock 'n roll memorabilia which ranges from anything connected with the Beatles to the platform stage boots of Elton John. No rock 'n roll star worth his or her salt will throw anything away ever again now that fans are prepared to pay huge prices for an old jacket worn by Jimi Hendrix and a hat that touched the head of Paul McCartney. Anything connected with the early stars, no matter how tenuous the connection, is worth money. Fan photographs sell well, so do promotional dresses issued to usherettes at Beatles concerts but if the photographs are signed by the stars themselves and if the usherette managed to persuade the Beatles to scrawl their signatures on her skirt, then you are talking real money. Musical instruments played on by the Beatles, an early record by Elvis Presley before he hit the big time, even plastic musical boxes with statuettes of Elvis on them sell for large sums and show no signs of losing their value.

A receipt from 'Mannys Musical Instruments Store' in New York, signed on the reverse 'Love Jimi Hendrix' in black ballpoint pen, c.1969. (Phillips)
$588   £340

An R.I.A.A. presentation gold disc presented to Tito Jackson for the Jacksons LP 'Triumph', c.1980. (Phillips)
$1,384   £800

A good set of all four Beatles autographs in blue ballpoint pen, individually mounted beneath a colour photo from the 'Sgt. Pepper' session, 37cm. x 36.5cm., c.1967. (Phillips) $1,124   £650

Rolling Stones - A set of autographs (incl. Brian Jones) on a sheet of headed notepaper from the 'West-bridge House Hotel' in Pontefract Yorkshire, 30cm. x 21cm. (Phillips)
$692   £400

A good 9 x 8in. black and white photograph of the 'Blues Brothers' signed on the front by John Belushi and Dan Aykroyd, 33cm. x 31cm. (Phillips)
$484   £280

A handwritten letter from John Lennon to a fan, the letter written in blue/black ink pen on white notepaper, 10in. x 8in. (Phillips)
$1,124   £650

Cher - A leather and simulated 'leopard-skin' pillbox hat made by 'Carlotta by Carlos Roncancio' signed 'Cher'. (Phillips)
$726   £420

Two unused Apple mirrors, incorporating the Apple logo surrounded by a black border. (Phillips) $484   £280

'Bad' twelve inch single signed on the front cover 'Michael Jackson' in black felt-tip pen. (Phillips) $294   £170

An R.I.A.A. presentation platinum disc presented to Sting for the LP 'Nothing But the Sun', c.1987. (Phillips) $1,730   £1,000

Elvis Presley's outstanding white one piece stage suit decorated with gilt studs in a 'shooting star' design all over the costume, with letter of authenticity from the suit's designer Bill Belew. (Phillips) $44,980   £26,000

E.L.O. - A rare Australian double platinum award for the LPs 'A New World Record' and 'Out of the Blue'. c. February 1978, 67cm. x 49cm. (Phillips) $380   £220

A copy of a single page of sheet music for the song 'I Am the Walrus' signed 'Love John Lennon' in black ink, c.1979. (Phillips) $1,297   £750

E.L.O. - A red satin promotional jacket for the 1979 LP 'Discovery'. The E.L.O. logo and the word 'Discovery' colourfully embroidered on the back. (Phillips) $121   £70

B.P.I. presentation silver disc for the LP 'Hollies Live Hits' presented to 'Polydor Ltd.' c.1977. (Phillips) $415   £240

A telegram from Ringo Starr to a Dutch newspaper dated 4 June 1964 explaining 'Very sorry I couldn't come to Holland hope to see all my Dutch fans on the next trip - Ringo Starr'. (Phillips) $3,114   £1,800

Sex Pistols - A set of six original streamers used to promote the LP 'Great Rock and Roll Swindle', designed by Jamie Reid, each 15cm. x 71cm. (Phillips) $86   £50

John Lennon - One page of handwritten lyrics 'Instant Karma' c.1970, the last two verses and chorus of the song in black felt-tip pen on card. (Phillips) $7,958   £4,600

Elvis Presley - An American in house platinum disc for the 1977 LP 'Moody Blue'. The award mounted above a plaque. (Phillips) $1,903   £1,100

A Yamaha FG-110 acoustic guitar with nylon strings, once the property of Paul McCartney, circa late 1960s, sold with a letter confirming authenticity from the vendor. (Phillips) $4,152   £2,400

A large print of an oil painting by June Kelly of Elvis signed and dedicated on the front by Elvis 'Billy beautiful pal Elvis Presley', 58cm. x 48cm. (Phillips) $1,211   £700

The Beatles - 'Yesterday and Today' 'butcher sleeve' peeled, (Capitol T2553 mono) with record enclosed, very good condition. (Phillips) $553   £320

Elvis Presley's 'Russian Double Eagle' gold coloured metal belt, intricately meshed with two eagle head fasteners. (Phillips) $4,498   £2,600

Sex Pistols - A promotional poster depicting the withdrawn artwork for the single 'Holidays in the Sun', 81cm. x 82cm., c.1977. (Phillips) $224   £130

Old England 'Flower Power' wristwatch. The watch face coloured gold and bright pink in a 'Flower Power' design, by Richard Loftus. (Phillips) $432   £250

Al Jackson/Booker T and the MGs - A mounted bronze trophy award presented by Memphis Music Awards, 1972, 17cm. high. (Phillips) $484   £280

A cheque from 'Lennon Productions Ltd.' to the 'Freedom Fund' for the sum of 1000 Pounds, signed by Lennon in blue ballpoint pen and dated August 10th, 1971. (Phillips) $2,595   £1,500

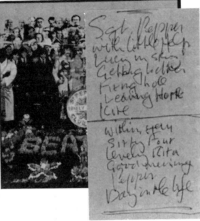

An original sketch by John Lennon executed in black felt-tip pen headed 'Love from John and Yoko' above a self portrait of John Lennon and Yoko Ono signed and dated 'John Lennon 1969'. 22cm. x 17cm. (Phillips) $2,076   £1,200

A handwritten song order in Lennon's hand for the track listing for the album 'Sgt. Peppers Lonely Hearts Club Band' in black ballpoint pen, 20cm. x 25cm. (Phillips) $1,384   £800

John Lennon and George Harrison - A black and white photographic print taken during the lecture given by the Maharishi in August 1967, 68cm. x 58cm. (Phillips) $121   £70

'The Beatles' (white album) PCS7067/8 No.0532377 signed by all four Beatles in full on the rear inside cover in blue felt-tip pen. (Phillips) $1,384   £800

An 8 x10in. black and white photograph of The Who performing on 'Ready, Steady, Go' signed by all four members with doodles by Keith Moon. (Phillips) $328   £190

Bruce Springsteen - One page of handwritten lyrics for the song 'I Got the Fever', with 'Idea 4' written at the top of the page, in ballpoint pen, c.1972. (Phillips) $3,460   £2,000

RUGS

Oriental rugs performed a dual role — they were spread on floors or divans but also hung on the walls like pictures. They were highly prized and looked on as family securities, only to be sold when times were hard. Some of the ones that turn up are very ancient indeed and all were hand knotted so the larger ones represent years of painstaking work which is reflected in the high prices paid for them by collectors. Other well regarded rugs are those designed for Morris & Co at the end of the 19th century. They were woven with the interlacing foliate designs popularised by William Morris and many of them were designed by Morris himself or by John Henry Dearle. Earlier in the century there was a vogue for needlework rugs, many of which only lasted if hung on walls. Those which have survived fetch extremely good prices. Another interesting type of rug are those made during the Art Deco period with angular lines and angles in the design. They were revolutionary in their time and are still eye catching today.

Mid 19th century Bordjalou Kazak rug, 5ft. x 6ft.7in. (Robt. W. Skinner Inc.) $5,100 £3,541

A hand-knotted woollen rug, the design possibly by A. Knox, with Celtic motif in pink and blue on a white ground, 153.5 x 86cm. (Christie's) $527 £345

Marion Dorn, an abstract small carpet woven in khaki and pale blue green, 8ft. x 4ft. 2in. (Lawrence Fine Art) $783 £440

Late 19th century Kazak prayer rug, Southwest Caucasus, 5ft.10in. x 3ft. 4in. (Robt. W. Skinner Inc.) $1,300 £902

A Kazak Karatchoph rug, the tomato red field woven with a cream octagon within diced spandrels, dated 1862, 4ft.5in. x 4ft.9in. (Lawrence Fine Art) $12,139 £6,820

An antique East Anatolian part cotton and metal thread Prayer Kilim, 7ft. 2in. x 4ft.7in. (Christie's) $1,633 £990

351

SCENT BOTTLES

Before the 20th century scent was not sold in individual bottles but purchasers used their own bottles as containers and some of them were very beautiful, made of gold or silver, glass or porcelain and decorated with painting, filigree or enamel. In Victorian times the lady of fashion carried a double ended, overlay scent bottle in her reticule but it was the glass masters of the early 20th century who sold the idea of individually designed bottles to perfume manufacturers and Rene Lalique made a profitable speciality of designing bottles for Coty and Nina Ricci among others. His elegant bottles helped sell the scent inside and other manufacturers eagerly followed his lead, employing artists like Daum, Galle and Webb to design scent bottles which have survived as pieces of beauty in their own right. When early bottles by these makers turn up for sale, they fetch considerable sums and even today it is worthwhile seeking out modern scent bottles which can be very beautiful and distinctively designed. They will be among the collectables of the future.

One of a pair of Lalique glass perfume bottles, moulded as sea urchins, 9.5cm. high, 1930's. $195   £150

A Chelsea double scent bottle modelled as a parrot and a rooster, circa 1755, 7cm. high. (Christie's) $2,692 £1,870

An Apsley Pellatt sulphide and cut glass scent bottle and a stopper, 9.5cm. high. (Christie's) $486 £324

A Baccarat enamelled cut glass scent bottle with gilt metal screw cover, 9.5cm. long. (Christie's)
          $1,296 £864

A glass scent bottle and stopper, inscribed 'Cigalia, Roger et Gallet, Paris', 13cm. high, in original box. (Phillips) $378 £280

An Orrefors perfume bottle and stopper, designed by E. Hald, engraved H 193 24 B9, 15cm. high. (Christie's)
          $633 £440

Jade glass ovoid perfume
flask and stopper, the moulded
body decorated with fish, 7in.
high. (Peter Wilson) $331 £210

Antique cased set of three
'scent bottles with ormolu
mounts and painted porce-
lain stoppers. (Worsfolds)
$230 £160

A Lalique scent bottle and
stopper, the clear glass
impressed and moulded
with stylised marguerites,
13.2cm. high. (Christie's)
$324 £198

Galle cameo glass perfume
bottle and mushroom stopper,
4½in. wide, 3¾in. high.
(Capes, Dunn & Co.)
$739 £440

Lalique perfume bottle
decorated with stylised
flowers, 11.75cm. high,
circa 1925. $345 £300

A Lalique glass perfume
bottle, flattened, square body
with central oval depression,
1930's, 12.75cm. high.
$387 £300

A large Victorian porcelain
scent bottle of circular shape,
by Sampson Mordan, 1885,
5.8cm. diam. (Phillips)
$256 £170

19th century cameo glass
salts bottle with silver
screw top, in case, 4in. long.
(Capes, Dunn & Co.)
$280 £195

An Apsley Pellatt cut-glass
sulphide scent bottle and
stopper, 5.3/8in. high.
(Christie's) $1,100 £628

SCIENCE FICTION MAGAZINES

'Amazing Stories' the first all science fiction magazine was published in April 1926, the brainchild of one Hugo Gernsbach who could, with some reason, lay claim to being the guru of science fiction.

He had been publishing such stories as 'The Scientific Adventues of Baron Munchhausen' since 1911 in the magazine Modern Electrics of which he was the editor. Strand Magazine and Pearsons Magazine also carried a few sci fi stories but Gernsbach was the first to see the full market potential.

Also worthy of note is the British magazine 'New Worlds' published from 1947 and edited by John Carnel. Michael Moorcock, editor from 1967, adopted a policy of making sci fi respectable in a literary sense and did much to advance its popularity.

Thrilling Wonder Stories, 'When Time Went Mad', by Dirk Wylie, a Thrilling Publication. $6 £3.50

Venture Science Fiction Monthly, Zenna Henderson, Alfred Bester, 1960's. $3.50 £2

Astounding Stories, November 1936, 'The Eternal Wanderer', by Nat Schachner. $13 £7.50

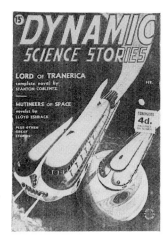

Science Fiction Quarterly, No. 1 – A Double Action Magazine. $7 £4

Amazing Stories, Volume 1, No. 1, April 1926, Hugo Gernsback, Editor. $130 £75

Dynamic Science Stories, 'Lord of Tranerica', a complete novel by Stanton Coblentz. $9 £5

Yesterday's Paper

The 7th Dimension by Victor La Salle. $5 £3

Astounding Science Fiction, 'The Big Front Yard', by Clifford Simak. $6 £3.50

'Before the Beginning', by Marx Reisen, Tit Bits Science Fiction Library. $5 £3

'Cee-Tee Man' by Dan Morgan, Panther Books. $5 £3

Amazing Stories Annual, featuring the new 'Master Mind of Mars' by Edgar Rice-burroughs. $78 £45

Tales of Tomorrow by Randall Conway. $6 £3.50

Fantasy and Science Fiction, including Isaac Asimov, 1960's. $3.50 £2

Science Fantasy, No. 30, Volume 10, 'Destiny Incorporated', by John Kippax. $3.50 £2

Dark Andromeda by A. J. Merak, Panther Books. $5 £3

Yesterday's Paper

SCISSORS

Scissors at first took the form of sheep shears with no central pivot, the cutting action being performed by compressing together the naturally sprung open arms.

Examples found in mediaeval graves are pivoted, but have finger loops set centrally on the arms. It wasn't until the 18th century that the finger loops generally became set on the outside edge of the arms much in the style of modern scissors.

As with many tools, scissors have been adapted for the specific tasks demanded from an individual trade or need and a fascinating collection can be built up of just grape scissors or those for surgeons, hairdressers or dressmakers.

Most 19th century examples found today were made in Sheffield and few made today can compete with them for quality.

An unusual pair of grape squeezing scissors.
$18 £10

Pair of 19th century steel candle snuffing scissors.
$25 £15

Silver scissors with ornate handles, circa 1910.
$70 £40

Pair of George III stork cast ribbon pullers with gilt beak, maker E. Holmes, London, 1801.
$350 £200

Tang silver gilt scissors, 7½in. long.
$14,000 £8,000

A pair of Victorian grape scissors, Sheffield, 1890, 3oz. $350 £200

A pair of grape shears, by Tiffany & Co., circa 1880-85, of shaped scissor-form, 8in. long, 5oz. (Christie's) $4,400 £2,660

A pair of George III extending tongs with ring grips, by Wm. Bateman, 1814, 20cm. overall length. (Lawrence Fine Art)
$508 £407

A snuffer's tray and a pair of snuffers, by G. Cardon, the tray 22cm. wide, Dunkerque, circa 1745, 403gr. $3,150 £1,800

Late 18th century pair of Spanish engraved steel tailor's shears, dated 1791, 14in. long.
$875 £500

SEWING BOXES

Sewing tables, workboxes, bobbin and reel stands are very well worth collecting and some were made in richly polished wood by expert craftsmen, or papier mache, often ornamented with painted flowers and mother of pearl. Sewing chairs and early sewing machines are valuable but the collector with less money can concentrate on the boxes of mixed items that often turn up at auction and contain unexpected treasures like lengths of silk in period wrappers, old cotton reels, ladies' companion sets, wooden mushrooms for darning socks, thimbles, old packets of needles and pins or chatelaines, needle cases, lace bobbins, lacemakers' cushions, embroidery frames, tambour hooks, netting tools and pin cushions. Some of the needle cases were made of Mauchline ware, Tunbridge ware, Fern ware, tortoiseshell, ivory, wood or even gold and silver. All the small things associated with needlework are being avidly collected since the uprise in home crafts and today's needlewomen take pleasure in using the tools that were used by their grandmothers and great grandmothers.

An early 19th century veneered Anglo-Indian Colonial rectangular sarcophagus shape workbox, 14in. wide. (Woolley & Wallis) $2,970 £1,800

Mid 19th century chinoiserie decorated lacquer sewing box, containing ivory implements, China, 14½in. wide. (Robt. W. Skinner Inc.) $550 £384

An Indian fruitwood, ivory and micro-mosaic workbox with mirror-backed interior, 18in. wide. (Christie's) $1,996 £1,210

A Victorian brass and velvet 'perambulator' sewing box, possibly America, circa 1880, 7½in. long. (Robt. W. Skinner Inc.) $400 £258

An early 19th century French satinwood workbox, 12 x 35.5 x 26cm. (Phillips) $2,492 £1,400

A 17th century needlework casket, the front and side panels of raised and stuffed stumpwork, England, 10¾in. wide. (Robt. W. Skinner Inc.) $2,600 £1,818

A 19th century miniature stencilled sewing box, American, 10in. high, 14in. wide. (Christie's) $286 £161

A William & Mary oyster walnut veneered lacemaker's box with brass escutcheon, 21in. long. (Woolley & Wallis) $1,360 £840

Early Victorian Macassar ebony veneered sarcophagus-shaped workbox inlaid with mother-of-pearl, 12in. wide. (Woolley & Wallis) $486 £300

SEWING MACHINES

As early as 1845 an American machinist called Elias Howe invented the first sewing machine and in the years that followed they were produced in an enormous variety of sizes and shapes by different manufacturers but it was the Singer Sewing Machine Company that took the lion's share of the market. By 1890 they turned out ten million machines which were so good that many of them are still useable today. The sewing machines that are valued by collectors are those with immaculate paint and decoration, for many were covered with elegant gilded scrollwork that makes them decorative objects. Early machines to look out for apart from Singer's are the Imperial Sewing Co of Birmingham; the Howe Sewing Machine Co; those imported from Germany by J. Collier and Son of Clapham Road, London; Whight and Mann of Ipswich and the small chain stitch machines sold by James Weir of Soho Square which were pirated copies of earlier machines made in Canada by Charles Raymond.

Late 19th century oak and iron sewing machine. $85 £50

A Grover & Baker hand sewing machine, serial no. 441414, brass disc and gilt lining, on mahogany base, circa 1873. (Phillips) $1,840 £1,150

A Grover & Baker hand-sewing machine, the brass Patent plaque with patents to 1863. (Christie's) $1,584 £1,100

Small chain-stitch machine, made in Germany, imported by Leigh & Crawford, Holborn, London, circa 1888. $140 £80

A European sewing machine by The Coventry Machinists Co. Ltd., with hand wheel for bobbin winding. $1,750 £1,000

'Howe' lock-stitch machine with rubber belt drive and hand-painted floral and gilt decorations, Howe Sewing Machine Co. circa 1876. $260 £150

358

SHEET MUSIC

THE GREAT SONG HIT IN **THE EMPIRE REVUE**

Sheet music need not be old to be worth money for there is a great lack of it from the 1950's and the 1960's still available in good condition. Copies of numbers made popular by singers like Guy Mitchell, Lonnie Donegan, Tommy Steele and the Everly Brothers always find an eager market.

Among earlier items of sheet music those which make the best prices are the ones with elaborate and colourful Victorian lithographed covers from the era of the music hall. The numbers made famous by singers like Marie Lloyd and Florrie Ford were issued in their thousands and they are still very attractive because of the eye catching designs of the sheets and the catchy lyrics and titles of the songs. It was a bright minded song writer who came up with a piece entitled "What's Wrong With Fish?" or "The Scientific Simpleton". During the golden age of musical comedy sheet music poured off the presses and shows like Marie Lloyd's "The Geisha" with its song "Ev'ry little Jappy chappie's gone upon the Geisha, Japanesey, free and easy Tea House girl...." makes the reader want to sing along with it. A good way of tracking down attractive items of sheet music is to search through old music cabinets or in the seats of lift up piano stools where they were always stored. Failing that, there are plenty of dealers who specialise in the subject.

Dreaming Eyes Waltz by Thurley Beale, 1904. $7 £4

He Always Came Home to Tea by F. Burand, 1880s. $32 £18

Are You Sure recorded by the Allisons, 1961. $18 £10

Pinball Wizard by Peter Townshend of the Who, 1969. $5 £3

Bless You for being an Angel by Eddie Lane and Don Baker, 1939. $12 £7

Der Sturmvogel by Carl Faust, 1890. $20 £12

Belgravia Valse by Dan
Godfrey. $18 £10

The Loveliest Night of the Year
by Paul Francis Webster, 1951.
                    $7 £4

I'm Sending a Letter to Santa
Claus by Lanny Rogers and
Spencer Williams, 1939. $3.50 £2

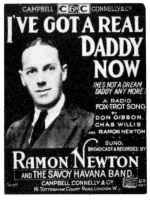

I've Got a Real Daddy Now by
Don Gibson, Chas Willis and
Ramon Newton, 1925. $2 £1

Buttons and Bows by Jay
Livingston and Ray Evans, 1948.
                    $9 £5

Veni-Vidi-Vici by Paul Francis
Webster and Jerry Livingston,
1954. $9 £5

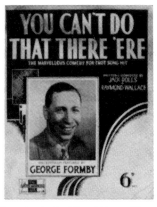

Forty-Seven Ginger Headed
Sailors by Leslie Sarony, 1928.
                    $3.50 £2

You Can't do That There 'Ere
by Jack Rolls and Raymond
Wallace, 1935. $10 £6

South Pacific Song Album by
Rogers and Hammerstein, 1949.
                    $7 £4

Magic Moments by Hal David and Burt Bacharach, 1957. $9 £5

Yes, Tonight, Josephine by Winfield Scott and Dorothy Goodman, 1957. $5 £3

Maybe it's because I'm a Londoner by Hubert Gregg, 1951. $9 £5

There's a Boy Coming Home on Leave by Jimmy Kennedy, 1940. $5 £3

Boomps-a-Daisy! by Annette Mills, 1939. $7 £4

Would You? by Arthur Freed and Nacio-Herb-Brown, 1936. $9 £5

Wings Over the Navy by Johnny Mercer and Harry Warden, 1938. $12 £7

Imagination Valse by Gene Williams, 1920's. $15 £8

The Finger of Suspicion by Paul Mann and Al Lewis, 1954. $7 £4

361

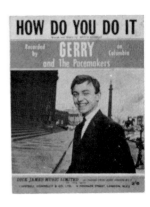

White Christmas by Irving Berlin, 1942. $2   £1

The Girl in the Taxi Waltz by
Jean Gilbert, 1911. $5 £3

How do you do it? by Mitch
Murray, 1962. $12 £7

Two Kinds of Teardrops by
Del Shannon and M. McKenzie,
1963. $10 £6

Oh! My Pa-Pa (O Mein Papa)
by Paul Burkhard, 1953. $5 £3

The Dancing Years by Ivor Novello, 1939. $10 £6

Green Fields by Terry Gilkyson,
Rich Dehr and Frank Miller,
1960. $10 £6

Don't do that to the Poor Pussy
Cat by Leslie Sarony and Frank
Eyton, 1928. $20 £12

My Heart Cries for You by
Carl Sigman and Percy Faith,
1950. $9 £5

SHOES

Very early shoes like the high heeled models worn by men in the 17th century can still occasionally be found but they are the province of museums and fetch large sums of money at auction. Collectors are looking for shoes from the early years of the 20th century, particularly the long toed, strapped shoes of fine leather worn by elegant women of the period. Shoes dating from after 1940 have very little value to collectors – yet. Shoes frequently turn up in second hand clothes shops and are sometimes in superb condition, looking as if they were hardly worn because fashionable women of the time changed their costumes and fashions with a dizzying speed. It is important that they are in good condition because nothing looks sadder than well used shoes. Most desirable are shoes of lizard or crocodile skin, and those made of satin and dating from the Victorian period, also elegant Victorian button boots. Prices of shoes tend to vary between £15 and £25 for a good pair.

A pair of black satin evening shoes by 'Saks, Fifth Avenue', wth stylised platform soles of gold painted wood, from the estate of Gloria Swanson. (Christie's) $160 £88

A pair of mid 19th century boots of brown and white leather, lined with pink kid, and a pair of white kid boots. (Christie's) $1,540 £880

A pair of high heeled evening sandals of 'silver' leather made in Italy by 'Halston', signed on soles 'Elizabeth Taylor' in black felt pen; accompanied by a letter of authenticity. (Christie's) $850 £462

A superb pair of Michael Jackson's purple lace-up dancing shoes, heavily studded with purple glass stones. (Phillips) $7,480 £4,000

A pair of lady's high-heeled shoes of royal blue velvet bound with blue braid, English, circa 1640. (Christie's) $11,520 £8,000

A pair of 19th century tin anniversary skates with adjustable strap at ankle and foot, 9in. long. (Robt. W. Skinner Inc.) $550 £376

SHOP SIGNS

In days gone by shops could be identified from a distance by the signs that hung outside them. During early times when a large proportion of the population could not read, these signs were necessary and they became traditionally associated with certain retailers – the barber's shop had its blood stained bandage wound round a long pole; the chemist its mortar and pestle; the wine merchant its bush; the shoemaker a fine top boot; the pawnbroker his three gilded balls. Today, the signs that have survived are very valuable and there is a strong collecting interest in them. Particular favourites are the wooden blackamoors and Red Indians that used to stand outside tobacconists' shops. Occasionally figures of soldiers were used. There was a shop in Perth that was guarded by a man sized figure of a Highlander in full kilted dress with a huge black busby on his head. When he came up for auction recently he sold for several thousand pounds.

Early 20th century American carved and painted trade sign, 39¼in. high. (Christie's) $550 £401

A carved and painted counter top cigar store Punch figure, by Chas. Henkel, Vermont, 1870, 26in. high. (Christie's) $19,800 £13,655

Late 19th century moulded iron and zinc jeweller's trade sign, America. (Robt. W. Skinner Inc.) $600 £405

An American 19th century painted iron trade sign, 40in. high, 15in. wide. (Christie's) $2,640 £1,619

Late 19th/early 20th century painted and gilded tin and wrought-iron wall mounted trade sign, American or English, 42½in. high, 39in. wide. (Christie's) $4,180 £2,358

A moulded zinc polychrome tobacconist figure, Wm. Demuth, N.Y., circa 1890, 67½in. high without base. (Robt. W. Skinner Inc.) $11,000 £6,875

SIGNED PHOTOGRAPHS

During the boom years of the cinema, fans of particular stars wrote to Hollywood in their millions asking for signed photographs of their idols. The studios did not disappoint them and employed Press Officers to despatch photographs in return but in most cases the signatures were forged by the officers themselves. This means that a signed photograph of Clark Gable may not be so valuable as it seems – the signature is probably not his and because of his huge popularity, there will be thousands of others around. Even signed photographs of famous politicians like Churchill are not necessarily genuine because some employed writing machines to forge their signatures but modern techniques have made it easier to detect these. The most valuable signed photographs are those with a history. If it can be proved that a picture was signed by the person who sat for the photograph, the price escalates. Personal dedications or individual comments added to the signature help in this. It is safest to look for signed photographs of people who would not be products of a studio publicity machine – a signed picture of Picasso or Virginia Woolf is likely to be genuine and could be worth around £150. Even more valuable are portraits of people who were alive in the early years of photographic portraiture – Tchaikovsky and Queen Victoria for example. Signed pictures of them sell for at least £1,000. Collectors especially value signed pictures of Royalty and of the Presidents of the United States (where the writing machine problem does crop up). Certain photographic portraitists can elevate the price of a picture – a Karsh for example will fetch a high price.

'Sincerely', Jean Kent.
$3.50 £2

Edward G. Robinson, Picturegoer Series 658.
$25 £15

George Robey as Falstaff.
$9 £5

'Yours sincerely', Billie Burke.
$3.50 £2

Lauren Bacall, 20th Century Fox.
$25 £15

'Best wishes', Peggy Cummins, Ealing Studios.
$9 £5

A good head and shoulders portrait photograph signed and inscribed 'Sincerely Gary Cooper', 9 x 7in. (Christie's) $225 £121

A half-length portrait photograph signed and inscribed 'To Phyllis from Clark Gable', 9½ x 7¾in. (Christie's) $305 £165

A good half-length publicity photograph, signed and inscribed 'To Betty from Ronald Reagan', 7 x 5in. (Christie's) $445 £242

Rita Hayworth and Maureen O'Hara, two good portrait photographs, each signed and inscribed by subject 'To Teresa', both 14 x 11in. (Christie's) $240 £154

A head and shoulders portrait photograph signed 'Sincerely Boris Karloff', 7 x 5in; with a rare half-length publicity photograph of Lon Chaney in the role of 'The Wolf Man' 1940. (Christie's) $400 £220

A good head and shoulders portrait photograph, with manuscript inscription 'To Hazel Betts Cordially Carole Lombard', 14 x 11in. (Christie's) $284 £154

A good head and shoulders portrait photograph with manuscript inscription 'To Rose Marie Betts with kindest regards Gary Cooper 1938', 14 x 11in. (Christie's) $142 £77

A collection of ten publicity photographs, each signed and inscribed 'To Phyllis . . .' subjects include Grace Kelly, Ingrid Bergman, Mel Ferrer, Ava Gardner, Gene Kelly, Robert Taylor, Lana Turner, Stewart Granger, largest 10 x 8in. (Christie's) $485 £264

A good head and shoulders portrait photograph by Laszlo Willinger, with photographer's ink credit on reverse, and manuscript inscription 'Best wishes always to Hazel Betts, Clark Gable', 13 x 11in. (Christie's) $200 £110

SIGNED PHOTOGRAPHS

A good head and shoulders portrait photograph, signed and inscribed 'Sincerely Spencer Tracy', 7 x 5in. (Christie's) $85 £50

A good head and shoulders portrait photograph signed and inscribed, with a contract comprising a typescript agreement between Hal E. Roach studios and Marjorie Whiteis. (Christie's) $1,830 £990

Two unpublished portrait photographs of Elia Kazan by Bryan Wharton, both taken in London, 1978, each 10 x 7in. (Christie's) $120 £66

A good head and shoulders portrait photograph, signed and inscribed 'To Theresa with sincere good wishes Basil Rathbone', 13¾ x 10¾in. (Christie's) $245 £132

A good head and shoulders portrait photograph of John Garfield in flying jacket, signed and inscribed 'For Victory, Edgar Johnny Garfield', 10 x 8in. (Christie's) $90 £50

Tyrone Power and Robert Taylor, two good head and shoulders portrait photographs each signed and inscribed by subjects 'To Rose Marie Betts . . .', both 14 x 11in. (Christie's) $205 £110

Errol Flynn and Olivia De Havilland, two good head and shoulders portrait photographs, by Elmer Fyer, each with photographer's blindstamp, signed and inscribed by subjects 'To Hazel Betts . . .' both 14 x 11in. (Christie's) $260 £143

A good full-length portrait photograph of Charlie Chaplin in his famous tramp guise, signed and inscribed 'With best wishes, Sincerely Charlie Chaplin', 7 x 5¼in.; and a half-length publicity photograph. (Christie's) Two $570 £308

A good half-length portrait photograph of Susan Hayward signed and inscribed 'To Milton — much love Susan', 12¾ x 9¾in., with portrait photographs of Yvonne De Carlo, and Jayne Mansfield. (Christie's) $650 £352

SILK POSTCARDS

Though some English, Spanish and other examples exist, most hand-embroidered and woven silk postcards are of French origin. These cards were popular with soldiers in France during the First World War, who sent them home to their sweethearts. Few, however were posted *as* postcards, and most were enclosed in envelopes to protect them. Some were made in the form of envelopes, with a scented card, silk handkerchief or printed card insert for a private message. Such inserts usually add about £1 to the value. Most sought after are those of Regimental badges, year dates and scenes. Value can range from £2 for a simple flower to £200 for a T. Stevens 'personality' of the day. Condition is all-important. Being so delicate, silk postcards are very prone to 'foxing' (brown patches caused by damp). Even the most beautiful cards are of little value if damaged or badly foxed.

'Bonne Annee', silk greeting card by La Rosa. $5 £3

Embroidered silk card 'Yours for ever', with enclosed card 'Tell her that I love her', by Fabrication Francaise. $5 £3

'Cartel de Toros', by Alcana, Madrid. $5 £3

'Home Sweet Home', by W. H. Grant, Coventry, postally used in 1915. $35 £20

'United we stand', French envelope type, by Fabrication Francaise, Paris. $7 £4

Woven silk card, 'Flames', Albert, 1914, by E. Deffrene. $25 £15

'To my dear mother from your loving son', by J. S., Paris, 1915. $10 £6

'To my dear wife', envelope type by Visa, Paris. $5 £3

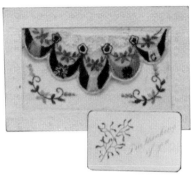

Envelope type with patriotic flags by T.M.T., with insert card 'I'm thinking of you'. $10 £6

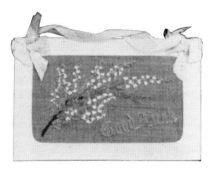

Embroidered silk card 'Good Luck', with silk ribbon. $9 £5

A.S.C. (Army Service Corps) with Regimental badge by J. J. Saint. $14 £8

'From your soldier boy', with woven butterfly, envelope type by M. M., Paris. $9 £5

'Good Luck' card with a felt cat and applied scrap. $3.50 £2

'To my dear sister', envelope type with patriotic flag by H. S. $9 £5

SILVER & PLATE

					Example for 1850
Birmingham	⬡	⬡	B	⬡	
Chester	⬡	⬡	m	⬡	
Dublin	⬡	e	⬡	⬡	
Edinburgh	⬡	⬡	⬡	⬡	
Exeter	⬡	⬡	G	⬡	
Glasgow	⬡	⬡	f	⬡	
London	⬡	⬡	P	⬡	
Newcastle	⬡	⬡	⬡	L	⬡
Sheffield	⬡	⬡	G	⬡	
York	⬡	⬡	⬡	O	⬡

'The family silver' has become quite a cliché, but it is a phrase which accurately reflects the fact that almost every family owns at least one piece of silver, much treasured and perhaps only brought out on special occasions.

The undying popularity of silver is seen, too, in the way it is so often chosen as a present at the major events in our lives such as christenings, weddings etc. Perhaps it is its timelessness, as well as its beauty, that so appeals to us.

Being such a versatile medium, silver has been used for countless purposes, from walking stick tops to gigantic epergnes, and collecting it is also a vast field. Some collectors specialise in one type of item, such as spoons or teapots: others concentrate on one maker, or even a single date. Hallmarks, of course, assist greatly in the dating and valuation of silver items.

Prices vary widely from around £100 for a Victorian Christening mug and spoon, to well into six figures for a presentation piece like a racing chalice. Valuation depends partly on the weight of the silver used, which, of course, fluctuates with the price of bullion, but the quality of craftsmanship and the intrinsic interest of the piece itself is also important. 'The family silver' however has always been and probably always will be worth its pride of place in our homes and in our affections.

A set of three Charles II casters, the smaller casters, 1682, 6in. high, the larger 1683, 7in. high, 22oz. (Christie's) $71,280 £44,000

A Charles II shaving jug, dish and soap box, the jug circa 1677, the dish 1682, the soap box circa 1680, 52oz. (Christie's) $38,005 £24,840

Part of a set of twelve Louis XV silver gilt teaspoons, by Claude-Pierre Deville, Paris, 1769 and 1773, 13oz. (Christie's) $10,450 £7,360

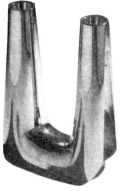

A George III mustard pot, by Samuel Wheatley, 1816, 9.2cm. high. (Lawrence Fine Art) $534 £286

A large silver gilt castletop vinaigrette, the hinged cover chased with a view of Warwick Castle, by Nathaniel Mills, Birmingham, 1839, 1¾in. long. (Christie's) $1,452 £880

A two-branch candelabrum, designed by Soren Georg Jensen, 17.7cm. high, 26oz.10dwt. (Christie's) $2,044 £1,430

An Old Sheffield plate tapering two-handled wine cooler on rococo shell and scroll feet with detachable liner, unmarked circa 1810, 10in. high. (Christie's) $503 £286

Late 19th century Continental silver plated decanting cradle, in the form of a field gun, overall length 15in. (Christie's) $990 £580

A George III partly-fluted pear-shaped tankard, by James Barber, York, 1812, 9in. high, 38oz. (Christie's) $3,564 £2,200

A tea urn, by Eoff & Shepherd for Ball, Black & Co., N.Y., 1839-51, 18in. high, 15in. wide, 112oz.10dwt. (Christie's) $3,520 £2,128

A wine coaster, stamped marks 925.S Georg Jensen & Wendel A/S 289A, 9.5cm. high, 14oz.10dwt. (Christie's) $1,415 £990

A George II Irish tapering cylindrical coffee pot, on moulded circular foot, Dublin, circa 1740. 9in. high, 31ozs. (Christie's) $4,114 £2,200

A Louis XVI silver wine taster, maker's mark TN, cockerel between, Reims, 1781-89, 4in. long, 1oz.15dwt. (Christie's) $1,870 £1,069

A Victorian Provincial escutcheon wine label, possibly by Thomas Wheatley of Newcastle, circa 1850. (Phillips) $113 £65

One of a pair of George III circular decanter stands, by John Roberts & Co., Sheffield, 1806/10. (Woolley & Wallis) $1,152 £720

A William IV silver stirrup cup, cast and chased as a fox mask, by C. G. Gordon, London, 1833, 6½in. long, 12oz. (Christie's) $8,250 £4,836

Pair of late Victorian salt cellars by Hunt & Roskell Ltd., 1901, 6½in. high, 34oz. (Christie's) $9,504 £5,280

A George IV silver wine funnel, by John James Keith, London, 1828, 6¼in. long, 4oz. (Christie's) $1,540 £902

A Ramsden & Carr silver tea-caddy and spoon, London hallmarks for 1931, 10.9cm. high, 13oz.7dwt. gross wt. (Christie's) $2,524 £1,650

Late 19th century silver plated kettle on stand with spirit burner. (Brown & Merry) $582 £320

A George II shaped square salver, by Lewis Pantin I, 1735, 12½in. wide, 52oz. (Christie's) $9,801 £6,050

SOUVENIRS

The coming of the railway opened up the country to people who had never travelled before and John Ruskin said that "every fool in Buxton can be in Bakewell in half an hour, and every fool in Bakewell at Buxton". His jaundiced attitude to the travel enthusiasm of ordinary people overlooked the fact that these new trippers were creating industries in the country including the manufacture of holiday souvenirs. They bought all sorts of things from picture postcards to boxes of sweets and small pieces of china to take home. In the middle of the 19th century the Great Exhibition opened in Hyde Park, London, and it was there that souvenir sellers, particularly W. H. Goss, makers of miniature pieces of china, did a roaring trade. There were many other souvenirs of the Great Exhibition from decorated plates to small items of glassware and they can still be found at reasonable prices.

Seaside souvenir of a Bathing Machine, 65mm. high, by Arcadian China. $18 £10

Jersey fish basket, arms of Saltash, large size, 58mm. (Goss & Crested China Ltd.) $24 £16

Souvenir of Wales teapot by Robert Lewis. $18 £10

Souvenir Album of London, Printed and Published in Scotland. $9 £5

George VI Coronation 1937 Souvenir Periscope. $20 £12

'An O-Fish-Al Souvenir of Douglas, I.O.M.' 1910. $9 £5

A Doulton pin tray made for the Sneyd Collieries & Brickworks Co. Ltd., Staffordshire, circa 1930, c.m.l. & c. $36 £24

Souvenir of the Colonial and Indian Exhibition, with a flip-over booklet depicting Indian scenes. $20 £12

Brass Souvenir of Mannikin Pis, Bruxelles, 3in. high. $3.50 £2

Festival of Britain Souvenir Guide, 1951, Battersea Park. $10 £6

Three folded postcard souvenirs of Woolworth Building, New York. $5 £3

State Opening of Parliament souvenir programme, October 21st, 1947. $7 £4

1937 Coronation Palitoy folding periscope. $21 £12

SPACE TOYS

Space has fired the imaginations of the young and not-so-young for generations, and never more so than now, when it is perhaps regarded as the last Great Unknown. This fascination has been reflected in the continuing and ever increasing popularity of space toys, which, maybe more than any other type, have benefitted from the amazing techniques and capabilities of modern toy production. New space toys, it seems, appear on the market every day. Many will doubtless prove ephemeral, but some, transformer toys, for example, which soared to popularity in the mid-1980's, are worth collecting with an eye to the future, because of the ingenuity and skill of their concept and design. Japanese space toys are very popular too, especially if boxed and in mint or near-mint condition.

A Marx Buck Rogers spaceship, Pat. 1927, lithographed tin, 12in. long. (Robt. W. Skinner Inc.) $175 £134

Marx wind-up 'Buck Rogers' space ship, New York, 1927, 12in. long. (Robt. W. Skinner Inc.) $430 £325

SH-Japanese battery operated Space Station, boxed. (Phillips) $440 £270

Karl Bub, clockwork Atom Rocket Ship, boxed. (Phillips) $181 £110

'Space Explorer', Hong Kong plastic battery operated 1960's robot. $40 £25

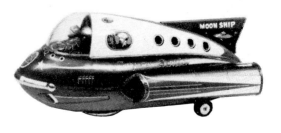

TM, battery operated Supersonic Moon Ship, boxed. (Phillips) $181 £110

SPECTACLES

There is written evidence of people wearing eye-glasses or spectacles in the 13th century and at a museum in Basle, Switzerland, the spectacles worn by the 16th century philosopher Erasmus are on display, looking very similar to those worn today. Early spectacles were only magnifying glasses and most of them perched like pince nez on the bridge of the nose but in 1727 temple glasses with side pieces were introduced by E. Scarlett and bi-focal lenses by Benjamin Franklin in 1785. Surprisingly contact lenses were first introduced in 1887 and about the same time sunglasses were being made. Up till about 1880 the frames of spectacles were made of steel or gold though, if they could afford it, people preferred gold because it was reckoned to have a beneficial effect on the eyes and caused less skin irritation. Until fairly recently oval shaped Victorian glasses with fragile gold frames could be picked up for very little but there is now a growing interest in the different styles of spectacles which has made the price rise.

Late 19th century spectacles with papier-mache case decorated in the Chinese taste. (Christie's) $99 £65

An 18th century pair of steel ring side spectacles with tinted lenses in a leather case, 5in. long. (Christie's) $229 £150

A pair of 18th century burnished steel green tinted protective folding sides spectacles with circular lenses. (Phillips) $434 £280

A pair of silver turn-pin sides 'D' cup blue smoke lenses, together with another three pairs. (Christie's) $382 £250

A pair of 16th century leather nose spectacles, 9cm. wide. (Phillips) $2,480 £1,600

A pair of brass framed Chinese spectacles, with folding sides and quartz lenses. (Christie's) $260 £170

A pair of 19th century brass and tortoiseshell folding-sides spectacles with deep clouded brown quartz lenses, in shagreen case, 6½in. long. (Christie's) $336 £220

A pair of 19th century brass and horn folding-sides spectacles with horn ear pieces and brown quartz lenses, in brown stained sharkskin case, 17.8cm. long. (Christie's) $367 £240

A pair of Chinese brass framed turn-pin sides spectacles with brown tinted quartz lenses, in a brown stained sharkskin case, 6¾in. long. (Christie's) $183 £120

STAFFORDSHIRE FIGURES

Devotees of Arnold Bennett's novels about the Five Towns will be aware of the names Fenton, Longton, Hanley, Burslem, Tunstall and Burmantofts — Bennett left one out — which were the centre of the great pottery industry of the 19th century. It was there that Staffordshire figures were produced in their thousands and bought with eagerness to adorn chest tops and mantlepieces in homes all over the country. At one time there were over 400 factories going full blast in the area around Stoke on Trent to satisfy the demand.

Staffordshire figures were unsophisticated in their modelling and cast in the shape of popular heroes or characters from stories, plays and poetry. There was an especially popular line in politicians and heroes like Wellington and Nelson. They were press moulded and decorated in underglaze blue and black with touches of colour in overglaze enamel and gilding. Early examples have closed bases or a small hole in the base while 20th century pieces are usually slip cast in Plaster of Paris moulds and are open ended.

A group of Napoleon III and Empress Eugenie, the oval base named in gilt moulded capitals, circa 1854, 12in. high. (Christie's) $238 £160

A pair of Staffordshire pugilist figures modelled as the boxers Mollineux and Cribb, circa 1810, 22cm. high. (Christie's) $2,729 £2,052

A figure of The Tichborne Claimant, holding a bird on his left hand, a rifle at his side, 14in. high. (Christie's) $406 £280

A Staffordshire pearlware sailor Toby jug, circa 1800, 29.5cm. high. (Christie's) $1,270 £770

A pair of Staffordshire pearlware figures of Mansion House dwarfs, after the Derby porcelain originals, 15cm. and 17cm. high. (Phillips) $2,254 £1,350

A 19th century Staffordshire pottery portrait figure of the Rev. John Wesley, 7in. high. (Reeds Rains) $116 £75

STAFFORDSHIRE FIGURES

One of a pair of early 19th century Staffordshire pottery figures of putti, 6in. high. (Reeds Rains) $201 £130

A Staffordshire group of a sheep and a lamb standing calmly together on a shaped rectangular base, 10cm. high. (Phillips) $616 £400

A 19th century Staffordshire pottery portrait figure of Wm, Shakespeare, 9in. high. (Reeds Rains) $139 £90

A Staffordshire Phrenology bust by L. N. Fowler, late 19th century, 30cm. high. (Christie's) $1,058 £605

A pair of figures of the Prince of Wales and Prince Alfred, circa 1858, 10¾in. high. (Christie's) $387 £260

A Staffordshire figure of James Blomfield Rush, circa 1850, 10in. high. (Christie's) $1,626 £968

A Staffordshire erotic figure of a barmaid, circa 1820, 19cm. high. (Phillips) $1,369 £820

A pair of Staffordshire figures of a gardener and companion of Ralph Wood type, circa 1780, 19.5cm. high. (Christie's) $4,356 £2,640

A figure of George Parr, holding a cricket ball in his right hand, circa 1865, 14in. high. (Christie's) $819 £550

A Staffordshire group of children, entitled 'Scuffle', 19cm. high. (Phillips) $412 £250

A group modelled as Hercules wrestling with a bull, circa 1810, 5½in. high. (Christie's) $1,266 £850

An Obadiah Sherratt group of Polito's menagerie, circa 1830, 29.5cm. high. (Christie's) $21,546 £16,200

A jardiniere modelled as a rectangular plant holder of wooden slats, impressed Brown, Westhead Moore, 33cm. high. (Christie's) $2,392 £1,650

One of a pair of late 18th century Staffordshire pottery cow creamers, 6¼in. long. (Dacre, Son & Hartley) $2,304 £1,600

Early 19th century Staffordshire bust of John Wesley mounted on a marbleised pedestal base, 11½in. high. (Robt. W. Skinner Inc.) $175 £109

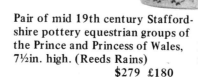

A pair of early Staffordshire figures of Whieldon type, depicting a sailor and a soldier, 15cm. and 15.5cm. high. (Phillips) $7,682 £4,600

Pair of mid 19th century Staffordshire pottery equestrian groups of the Prince and Princess of Wales, 7½in. high. (Reeds Rains) $279 £180

A Staffordshire figure of Napoleon on a floral encrusted rocky plinth, 8½in. high, circa 1825. (Christie's) $154 £100

STEREOSCOPIC CARDS

Stereoscopes were a Victorian invention, and viewers came in various forms, such as 'hand-held' or 'cabinet table'. When the cards are inserted a three-dimensional image appears. Special cameras were produced to take two simultaneous images at different angles and thus create the effect.

Stereoscopic cards were produced in large numbers and could be bought over the counter. 'One-off' rare cards of unusual subjects taken by local photographers can be very valuable indeed.

The 'New Woman' comic stereoscopic photo-print card, circa 1895. $3.50 £2

Rare advertising stereoscopic card, Nestles Swiss Milk Chocolate with 'Indian Rhino-ceros Jim', 1890's. $45 £25

Three hunters - Stereoscopic daguerreotype, hand-tinted, gilt-painted, 1850's. (Christie's) $2,937 £1,650

Rotary Photo Company No. 31450A, real photo stereoscopic card of Mr Oscar Asche. $5 £3

Excelsior stereoscopic tours card, published by Mr E. Wright, Burnley. 'State coach and horses after the explosion at Calle Mayor, Madrid', 1890's. $35 £20

Stereoscopic card No. 12030, published by B. W. Kilburn, 1897. 'Russian torpedo boat with its crew, Moscow, Russia.' $20 £12

Stereoscopic card No. 12188, published by B. W. Kilburn, Littleton, N.H., copyright 1897, 'Russian Homes'. $14 £8

SWEET CIGARETTE PACKETS

The first confectionery cigarettes to be sold in packets were made of chocolate and names to look out for are Fry's who sold a brand called Campaign, Lyons, Maynards and Clarnico. They were popular from the beginning of the 20th century and the packets for them lead the field as far as collectors are concerned. It was not until the 1940's that sugary sweet cigarettes were also packaged for sale and before that they were sold loose.

Some brands to look for are the Coronation series issued in 1953 and the Olympics issue of 1956 but there were also many new and colourful designs issued to attract the juvenile market. Manufacturers appealed to their customers by taking packet themes from favourite television programmes like Wagon Train, The Lone Ranger, Wyatt Earp and Hawk Eye. Science fiction was also well represented with Star Trek sweet cigarettes, as well as Thunderbird and Fireball. Barratt and Co brought out a brand with packets featuring Walt Disney characters, especially Mickey Mouse and Snow White and the Seven Dwarfs which are great favourites with collectors. Packets vary in size because the cigarettes were sold in different number combinations – fives, sixes, sevens, tens, twenties and twenty fives. Occasionally packets of 50 appeared at Christmas time. Today, because of the anti-tobacco legislation and health fears, sweet cigarettes no longer officially exist and are always described as "candy sticks" on their packets.

Cheftain, Boys Scout's Cigarettes, 1958. $7 £4

Rin-Tin-Tin, Cadet Sweets, 1960. $9 £5

Mickey Mouse, Barratt & Co., 1935. $35 £20

Virginia, Liam Devlin, 1955. $9 £5

Campaign Chocolate Cigarettes, J. S. Fry & Sons. $45 £25

Navy Cut, Kane Products, 1958. $5 £3

TEA CADDIES

The word "caddie" comes from the Malay "kati" which means a measure of tea, around one and a quarter pounds. It was imported into the English language when tea began to be brought to this country in ship loads to cater to the new upper class taste for drinking it but it was very expensive, working out at about £10 a pound. For that reason people who bought small amounts of the precious leaf did not want to waste a single shred and they stored their tea in special little chests or boxes with locks to prevent pilfering. The earliest and most pedestrian caddies were made of pottery or porcelain but when it became the fashion for the tea to be carried into the drawing room along with the tea things for the lady of the house to dispense into the tea pot herself, caddies of gold or silver and more commonly fine woods began to appear. Chippendale, Sheraton and all the fashionable cabinet makers of the day produced caddies to match the styles of their furniture and they were ornamented with brass, ormolu, tortoiseshell, coloured straw or paperwork and inlaid with exotic woods. Some of them are very beautiful and the finest examples have moved into the top bracket of collectables. However there are cheaper ones still to be found, especially those made of painted tin with hinged upper lids which Victorian housewives kept on their kitchen shelves.

A Regency shaped tortoiseshell tea caddy, on bun feet. (Hetheringtons Nationwide) $704 £440

An early 19th century blond tortoiseshell tea chest, the hinged lid reveals two lidded compartments with silver plated knobs, 7in. long. (Woolley & Wallis) $429 £260

A George III satinwood, rosewood and fruitwood tea caddy, the crossbanded lid with a silver plaque with initials J. E. R., 12¾in. wide. (Christie's) $1,676 £1,242

A two-compartment Tunbridge-ware tea caddy. (David Lay) $250 £140

A George III satinwood, marquetry and painted octangular tea caddy with hinged top, 6½in. wide. (Christie's) $957 £626

A Regency tortoiseshell tea caddy with gilt metal lion handles, 12½in. wide. (Christie's) $660 £462

A Regency tortoiseshell veneered rectangular tea chest with wire inlay, 7in. long. (Woolley & Wallis) $445 £295

A George III treen (applewood) tea caddy formed as a large apple with hinged cover and ebonised stem, 6in. high. (Christie's) $4,653 £3,300

Early 19th century painted tin tea caddy, America, 5¼in. wide, 5in. high. (Robt. W. Skinner Inc.) $500 £280

Regency mahogany tea caddy of sarcophagus form with brass lion ring handles. (G. A. Key) $264 £160

A Regency burr walnut and mahogany two division tea caddy with glass mixing bowl. (Hobbs Parker) $504 £300

A George III laburnum tea caddy with a divided interior, on bracket feet, 10in. wide. (Christie's) $1,180 £638

CHINA

A Meissen tea caddy with domed shoulder, circa 1755, 10.5cm. high. (Christie's) $623 £385

A Leeds creamware tea canister of octagonal shape, 12.5cm. high, incised no. 25. (Phillips) $2,087 £1,250

A Berlin Reliefzierrat rectangular indented tea caddy and cover, painted in colours with putti playing on clouds, circa 1700, 14.5cm. high. (Christie's) $4,114 £2,200

Late 18th century Whieldon pattern square shaped pottery tea caddy, 4in. high. (Reeds Rains) $259 £180

A pair of South Staffordshire opaque tea caddies for Bohea and Green, circa 1760, about 13.5cm. high. (Christie's) $7,088 £3,960

A Meissen rectangular tea caddy and cover, circa 1735, in fitted case, 11cm. high. (Christie's) $3,456 £2,400

A Meissen rectangular tea caddy and cover painted in Silbermalerei with chinoiserie figures, circa 1740, 13.5cm. high. (Christie's) $4,713 £3,273

A Lowestoft blue and white arched rectangular tea caddy, blue crescent mark, circa 1775, 10cm. high. (Christie's) $243 £183

A Lowestoft blue and white rectangular octagonal tea caddy, circa 1765, 13cm. high. (Christie's) $1,686 £1,188

TEAPOTS

Because the first tea came into Britain from China, the practice of pouring it out of a special china pot accompanied it and the early teapots resemble those used by the Chinese, with the same sort of decorations and swinging handles of cane across the top of the lid. Europe's china manufacturers recognised the opportunity of appealing to customers with well designed and prettily decorated tea pots and some of those which survive are exquisite, especially by Meissen, Wedgwood, Derby, Rockingham and other high class manufacturers. Some stuck to Chinese style decorations but others were a riot of pretty flowers and elegant gilding. In the late 19th century novelty teapots began to appear, some in the shape of animals. Minton produced one like an elephant in the 1870's. Others were in the shape of people with one arm acting as the spout and the other as the handle. Every artistic period has produced its characteristic teapots. Clarice Cliff's angular versions are the epitome of the Jazz Age and more recent teapots often return to Chinese or Japanese styles like the ones made by potter Lucie Rie.

A black basalt tea kettle and cover, circa 1800, 23.5cm. high, (base cracked, rim to cover repaired). (Christie's) $359 £270

A Worcester blue-scale globular teapot and cover, blue square seal mark, circa 1770, 14.5cm. high. (Christie's) $766 £540

A stoneware teapot and cover by Lucie Rie, covered in a matt manganese glaze, circa 1958, 15cm. high. (Christie's) $469 £324

A stoneware teapot by Shoji Hamada, the cut-sided body with short spout and arched handle, 18.7cm. high. (Christie's) $1,496 £935

A Frankfurt Faience teapot and cover, painted in a bright blue with Chinese style figures, 13.5cm. high. (Phillips) $1,670 £1,000

A Bottger rectangular teapot and cover painted in Schwarzlot enriched in gilding by I. Preissler, circa 1720, 15cm. high. (Christie's) $60,214 £37,400

TEAPOTS

A Worcester faceted teapot, cover and stand, circa 1765, 14cm. high. (Christie's) $1,452 £880

A pearlware cylindrical teapot and cover, applied with figures of Lord Rodney and Plenty, circa 1785, 13cm. high. (Christie's) $653 £396

A Staffordshire saltglaze tartan ground Royalist teapot and cover with loop handle, circa 1750, 14cm. high. (Christie's) $15,336 £10,800

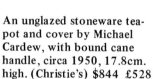

A Linthorpe teapot, the design attributed to Dr. C. Dresser, 21.3cm. high. (Christie's) $172 £118

A Minton majolica-ware teapot and cover in the form of a Chinese actor holding a mask, 14cm. high, impressed Mintons, model no. 1838, date code for 1874. (Phillips) $660 £400

An unglazed stoneware teapot and cover by Michael Cardew, with bound cane handle, circa 1950, 17.8cm. high. (Christie's) $844 £528

A Rockingham Cadogan teapot, of peach shape, 4½in. high, impressed Brameld. (Dreweatt Neate) $103 £55

A Vincennes bleu lapis conical teapot, blue interlaced L marks and painter's mark of Thevenet, circa 1753, 11cm. high. (Christie's) $1,742 £1,210

A Minton majolica-ware teapot and cover in the form of a monkey, 15.5cm. high, impressed Mintons, model no. 1844, date code for 1876. (Phillips) $1,023 £620

A Wedgwood Whieldon pine-
apple teapot and cover,
10cm. high. (Phillips)
$1,386 £900

A Capodimonte oviform
teapot with scroll handle
and spout, blue fleur-de-lys
mark, circa 1750, 14.5cm.
wide. (Christie's)
$1,188 £825

A Wedgwood creamware
globular teapot and cover,
painted in the manner of
David Rhodes, circa 1768,
15cm. high. (Christie's)
$2,913 £2,052

A Staffordshire creamware
oviform 'pebble-dash' teapot and cover of Whieldon
type, circa 1760, 13cm.
high. (Christie's)
$18,150 £11,000

Sir Roger de Coverley Series
teapot, 5in. high, circa 1911,
depicting Sir Roger in the
garden. $100 £60

An 18th century Worcester
porcelain teapot, the domed
lid with flower finial, 6in.
high. (Hobbs & Chambers)
$207 £115

A stoneware teapot with
cane handle by Bernard
Leach, circa 1920, 17.2cm.
high. (Christie's)
$1,080 £750

An 18th/19th century Kakiemon type mokkogata teapot
with shallow domed cover
and arch-shaped handle,
19cm. long. (Christie's)
$1,248 £918

A black glazed terracotta
teapot and cover, printed in
yellow and decorated in
enamels and gilt, 16cm. high.
(Phillips) $80 £50

TEDDY BEARS

Some of the prices paid in auction for Teddy Bears have caused eyebrows to be raised in astonishment. A good Steiff bear can easily command over £1000 and the world record is over £8000. The two words 'good' and 'Steiff' make a great difference. The history of the Teddy bear only goes back to 1902 when keen hunter President Theodore Roosevelt of USA was shown in a political cartoon refusing to shoot a cuddly little baby bear. An American toy maker called Morris Michtom made a cuddly toy bear and asked permission to call it after Theodore so the Teddy bear was born and soon every child except the very poor had one. The most famous Teddy bears were made in Germany by a crippled dressmaker called Margarete Steiff who saw a copy of the Roosevelt cartoon. Her bears were not as endearing as Michtom's because they had humped backs, long arms and long noses but they caught the popular market and Miss Steiff marked them with a distinctive button stapled into one of their ears which give collectors a guideline to the authenticity of their bears.

A pale plush covered teddy bear with brown glass eyes, cut muzzle and reinforced felt feet, 22in. high. (Christie's) $374   £198

An early gold plush tumbling teddy bear, the body of wood and cardboard, containing a key-wind mechanism, 9in. high. (Lawrence Fine Art) $97 £55

A honey plush covered teddy bear with boot button eyes, wide apart ears, 13½in. high, with Steiff button in ear (one pad moth eaten). (Christie's) $831   £440

A golden plush covered teddy bear with pronounced hump, pointed snout and with Steiff button in ear, 29in. high. (Christie's) $4,719 £2,860

German straw-filled teddy bear with hump back, pad feet, long nose and button eyes, 11in. high. (Giles Haywood) $311 £190

A silver plush covered teddy bear with button eyes and felt pads, 14in. high, with Steiff button. (Christie's) $1,039   £550

TEDDY BEARS

A pale golden plush covered teddy bear with embroidered snout and slight hump, 15½in. high, with Steiff button. (Christie's)
$1,337 £935

A plush covered polar bear with button eyes, felt pads and joints at hips, 16in. long, with Steiff button, circa 1913. (Christie's)
$727 £385

A golden plush covered teddy bear in the form of a child's muff, 15in. high. (Christie's)
$290 £176

A musical teddy bear with swivelling head operated via his tail, 43cm. high. (David Lay) $360 £200

A plush covered pull-along bear mounted on a wheeled frame, 23in. long, with raised letters, Steiff button, circa 1920. (Christie's)
$790 £418

A clockwork somersaulting teddy bear dressing in gold felt jacket, blue trouser and white vest, by Bing of Nuremberg, 9in. high. (Christie's) $943 £572

A gold plush teddy bear, with metal Steiff disc in left ear, German, circa 1907, 25in. high. (Hobbs & Chambers)
$3,200 £2,000

A long cinnamon plush cover, teddy bear with large button eyes, central face seam, wide set ears, 21in. high, circa 1905, probably Steiff. (Christie's) $2,910 £1,540

A golden plush covered teddy bear with boot button eyes, cut muzzle, hump and elongated limbs, with Steiff button in left ear, 19in. high. (Christie's) $871 £528

389

TELEPHONES

"Mr Watson, come here, I want you," was the first complete sentence ever spoken over a telephone in June 1875 by Alexander Graham Bell in Boston, USA. Although attempts to invent a speaking machine had been going on for at least twenty years, notably by a German inventor called Professor Philip Reis Friedrichsdorf, Bell was the first to utilise continuous current in his application. His name is in the record books today by a lucky chance for another inventor Professor Elisha Gray, filed his own patent for a similar appliance only a few hours after Bell's. It took prolonged litigation before Bell's claim triumphed. In 1878 the first telephone switchboard for commercial operation was opened at Newhaven, Connecticut, and from that day, the world took to the speaking machine with alacrity.

Many of the oldest telephones that can be found today are of the Ericsson type which was used in Sweden, Denmark, France, Germany and Britain. They look magnificent with polished mahogany or walnut stands and brass fittings. There is also a vogue among collectors for finding old fashioned telephones like the light French ones that have been much copied in reproduction and the ones that were wall mounted with a speaker at face level. Interior decorators and theatrical or television companies are always on the look out for period telephones and a particular favourite is the phone on a stand with a hook at the side for the earpiece which was in common use in British homes before the Second World War. The slightly later heavy black or white phones with weighted bases look well too in modern homes.

Supplied by the G.P.O., year of manufacture 1920's. $175 £100

Manufactured by L. M. Ericsson (England), supplied by National Telephone Co., and later by G.P.O. This is a magneto instrument, years of manufacture 1890-1920. $435 £250

Supplied by Grammont, Paris, year of manufacture 1924. $260 £150

The main part of this telephone was made in Germany, but the handset was made in Britain, supplied by The British Home and Office Telephone Co., London. These telephones were in use in the Ritz Hotel, London, in the 1930's and 40's. $175 £100

Supplied and manufactured by The British L. M. Ericsson Manufacturing Co., Beeston, Notts, these instruments were used in large offices, hotels and houses. This particular phone was part of an 18 station intercom system, year of manufacture 1926. $225 £130

Supplied by Franco-Radio Telephone, Paris, year of manufacture, 1940's. This is a magneto instrument. $175 £100

Supplied by Association des Ouvriers en Instruments de Precision, Paris, this is a magneto instrument. $210 £120

British supplied and manufactured by Gent & Co. Ltd., Leicester, now part of the Chloride Gent Group. This telephone is part of an intercom system, year of manufacture 1920's and 1930's. $175 £100

Supplied and manufactured by G. E. C., Coventry, year of manufacture 1910–mid 1920's. These instruments were used in small hotels, offices and country houses. This telephone was part of a five station intercom system. $175 £100

THEATRE PROGRAMMES

The years between 1890 and the First World War were the heyday of the theatre and the music hall when glittering stars strutted the boards in every city in the land because they all had more than one theatre and it was a common practice for families to go there once a week. If a show was particularly good or if the star particularly admired, programmes were often tucked away in drawers as souvenirs and today they can be worth far more than the original cost of a theatre seat. Because most of them have been stored out of light and never used again, they are usually in excellent condition. Some people tended to save theatre programmes for Gala performances or because stars like Lily Langtry, Sarah Bernhardt, George Robey, Harry Lauder, Noel Coward or Ivor Novello were appearing. The bigger the name, the more collectable the programme. Modern theatre goers should save programmes of special performances for one day they will be the stuff of collections.

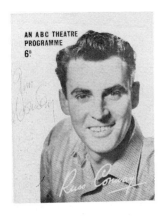

An ABC Theatre Programme, Russ Conway at the Regal Theatre, Gloucester, signed. $9 £5

ABC, Great Yarmouth, Peter Noone with Herman's Hermits, 1969. $3.50 £2

An ABC Theatre Programme, Max Bygraves, 1962. $2 £1

The Palladium Programme, Monday, May 4th, 1931. $14 £8

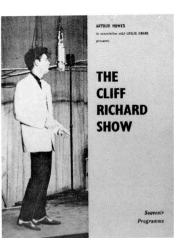

The Cliff Richard Show Souvenir Programme, 1959. $20 £12

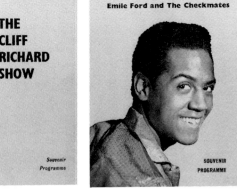

Emile Ford and the Checkmates, Souvenir Programme, 1960. $9 £5

(Border Bygones)

392

Richmond Theatre, 'Before the Party', February 11th, 1980. $2 £1

The Lanchester Marionette Theatre directed by Waldo and Muriel Lanchester. $10 £6

'Gone with the Wind', Palace Theatre, Shaftsbury Avenue, London. $2 £1

Bostock and Wombwell's Royal Menagerie, originally established in 1805. $26 £15

Talk of the Town Theatre Restaurant Souvenir Brochure. $5 £3

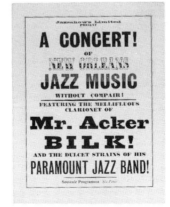

Vic Oliver in Idiot's Delight, Birmingham Theatre Royal. $3.50 £2

Jazz Shows Ltd., present Mr Acker Bilk. $5 £3

'Cavalcade' Programme, Theatre Royal, Birmingham, 1933. $2 £1

(Border Bygones)

Strand Theatre '1066 and All That', 1935. $2 £1

His Majesty's Theatre, 'Nero', Souvenir Programme, 9th March 1906, 50th Performance. $14.50 £8.50

The Mermaid Theatre, 'Hadrian VII', 1968. $2.50 £1.50

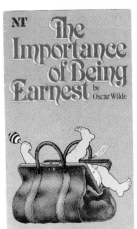

The National Theatre, 'The Importance of Being Earnest', 1982. $1 50p

Victoria Palace, Jack Hilton's 'Crazy Gang' Review, 1959. $3.50 £2

Palace Theatre, Anna Neagle in 'The Glorious Days', 28th February, 1953. $2 £1

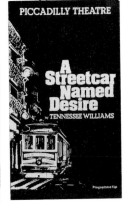

Savoy Theatre, 'Whose Life is it Anyway?' Tom Conti, December 1978. $1 50p

Her Majesty's Theatre, Proprietor and Manager, Mr Herbert Beerbohm Tree, '12th Night' Souvenir Programme, 9th April 1901. $21 £12

Piccadilly Theatre, 'A Streetcar Named Desire', 1974. $1 50p

THERMOMETERS

The first thermometer was invented by Galileo who lived at the end of the 16th and beginning of the 17th centuries. His thermometer was a simple glass tube ending in a bulb and the open end immersed in water. He noticed when the water was heated, it rose up the tube which could be calibrated. The most common thermometer in use for many years after that was a simple tube with red liquid in it and mercury in the bulb. Galileo's invention could not only be used in assessing the degree of fever in sick people or measuring the weather but it helps with jobs like brewing, cooking, hatching chickens, gardening and photography. Today the old fashioned thermometer is gradually going out of use as electronic devices and heat reactive pads are being introduced but there are thousands of old ones around and collectors are snapping them up fast.

Red Indian plastic novelty spirit thermometer. $5 £3

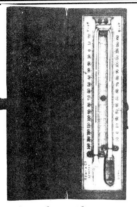

An oak cased thermometer with ivory dial engraved 'Kemp & Co. Ltd., Bombay', 4¾in. long circa 1850. $175 £100

Brass cased incubator mercury thermometer with inbuilt hook. $9 £5

Duckham's Oils enamel sign. $140 £75

An early 19th century mahogany wheel barometer and thermometer signed J. Watkins, London, (Christie's) $1,650 £1,100

Late 19th century brass framed thermometer, 10in. high. $12 £8

A 19th century wheel barometer and thermometer inscribed Zuccani, London. (Parsons, Welch & Cowell) $651 £440

Stephens Inks enamel sign. $130 £85

TINS

Tin is a naturally occurring ore which if found at various places in Britain but most particularly in Cornwall where it has been mined for centuries. When it is beaten out it becomes very white and resembles silver. It is very malleable and gave the name 'tinkers' to wandering families who made a living making and selling domestic utensils of tin. The use of tin boxes for keeping things safe and dry goes back a very long way but it was with the upsurge in Victorian manufactures that tin box making became a mass production industry. Everything from dressmakers' pins to loose tea, tobacco, sweetmeats, food, starch and cleaning materials was sold in tins. They can be found with company names and trademarks, printed decorations and colourful designs. After the use of the original contents many tins were kept as containers. Old biscuit and confectionary tins are particularly good for the variety of their designs and shapes.

Wilkinson's Pontefract cakes tin. $5 £3

Thorne's Premier Toffee 'Simplicity' toffee tin. (Border Bygones) $14 £8

Mackintosh's Sampler chocolate tin. $14 £8

J. & J. Coleman mustard tin with hinged lid, 14cm wide, depicting floral scenes in panels. (Phillips) $85 £50

World Famous Smith's Potato Crisps tin. $18 £10

J. & J. Coleman mustard tin depicting a scene of a farmer, son and donkey, with decorated edges. (Phillips) $85 £50

Mackintosh's Nurseryland toffee tin. $14 £8

Yardley's Old English, Lavender Solidified Brillantine tin, 3in. high. $14 £8

His Masters Voice nickel plated three compartment needle tin. $25 £15

Keen Robinson & Co. Ltd.,
mustard tin decorated with
various Victoria military
scenes with Union Jacks,
15 x 18cm. (Phillips)
$131 £75

J. & J. Coleman mustard tin
decorated with various scenes
by Sir E. Landseer, 14 x 21cm.
(Phillips) $131 £75

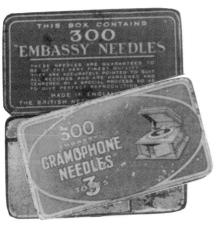

Embassy three compartment
tin in red containing 300
needles. $45 £25

An interesting wax taper
container by W. C. & J.
Field and Bryant & May's.
$45 £25

Taddy — a Myrtle Grove
cigarette tin, depicting a pretty
girl, 8 x 7.5cm. (Phillips)
$219 £130

Cadbury's Dairy Milk
chocolate churn. $25 £15

1950's Oriental style tin tea
container. $7 £4

Victorian money box tin
depicting coins of the Realm.
$20 £12

TITANIC MEMORABILIA

The fate of the 'Titanic' has fired the imagination of each succeeding generation, and interest in what seems likely to become one of the great legendary tragedies of our times continues unabating. The recent seabed pictures of her hulk have only served to increase this fascination, which is reflected in the prices paid for almost any object connected in some way with the great liner.

The fact that each item usually has a romantic story attached to it of course adds to its attraction and value.

A napkin ring belonging to a survivor and carried by her on the voyage recently sold for £500, while letters sent by passengers can still command up to four figures.

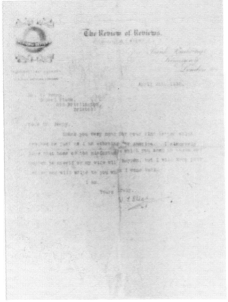

A typed letter to Mr R Penny from W. T. Stead, dated 9 April 1912, on The Review of Reviews writing paper. (Onslow's) $1,467 £900

White Star Royal Mail Steamer Titanic, artist drawn, pre-sinking colour postcard, postmarked 1st August 1912, State Series, Liverpool. (Onslow's) $228 £140

Titanic Leaving Southampton, glossy monochrome postcard, published by Nautical Photo Agency, N.W.7. (Onslow's) $228 £140

'The Iceberg', a contemporary bromide photograph with ink inscription, 'Iceberg taken by Capt. Wood S.S. Etonian 12 April 1912 in 41° 56N 49° 51W S.S. Titanic Struck 14 April and sank in three hours', 200 x 255mm. (Onslow's) $374 £230

White Star Line Olympic and Titanic Smoke Room, a monochrome postcard to Master Tom Richmond, 14 Lennox Road, Crookston, Paisley, Lothian, postmarked Queenstown 3.45pm 11 April. (Onslow's) $2,445 £1,500

A bronze Carpathia medal awarded to R. S. C. Cowan, the captain, in recognition of gallant and heroic services, from the survivors of the S. S. 'Titanic'. (Onslow's) $1,059 £650

Launch of White Star Royal Mail Triple-Screw Steamer Titanic at Belfast, Wednesday, 31 May 1911, at 12.15pm, a printed card admission ticket in two portions, each numbered 1246, overall size 84 x 136mm. (Onslow's) $1,793 £1,100

The new White Star liner 'Titanic', artist drawn pre sinking photographic postcard, Real Photos Series. (Onslow's) $2,600 £1,600

S.S. Titanic, the cast brass nameplate from Lifeboat No. 12, 322mm. long x 39mm. wide. (Onslow's) $9,128 £5,600

White Star Line Triple-Screw R.M.S. Olympic and Titanic 45,000 tons each, The Largest Steamers in the World, a colour postcard from R. Phillips to Mr. Wm. Squires, 4 Northfield Cottages, Ilfracombe, Devonshire, postmarked Queenstown 5.45pm 11 April. (Onslow's) $3,260 £2,000

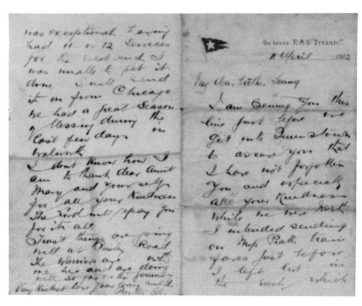

On board R.M.S. 'Titanic', an autographed letter on official writing paper signed by Pastor John Harper, 11th April 1912. (Onslow's) $6,200 £3,800

"My Dear Brother Young, I am penning you this line just before we get in to Queenstown to assure you that I have not forgotten you and especially all your kindness while we were North. I intended sending on Mrs Pratt's train fares just before I left but in the rush which was exceptional having had 11 or 12 services for the week-end I was unable to get it done. I will send it on from Chicago. We had a great season of blessing during the last few days in Walworth. I don't know how I am to thank dear Aunt Mary and yourself for all your kindness the Lord will repay you for it all. Trust things are going well at Paisley Road. The warriors are with me here and are doing well so far on the journey. Very kindest love your loving auld Pastor J.H."

"While on a visit to Paris I met my friend who wishes me to write a few words on *Titanic* disaster, on 14 April 1912 just before midnight came the awful crash. Which was so unexpected officers and crew did not know what to do, boats launched and not nearly filled and terrible to relate not saving one-third of the passengers aboard including the crew and was caused through absolute carelessness. I did not see my husband again after he put me in lifeboat No.11. I saw the *Titanic* gradually disappearing also eight distress markers she sent up heard the explosions and then disappear under the water taking hundreds of souls with her. We had neither lights, water or provisions in our boat, it was intensely cold and scarcely anyone properly clothed in the early dawn we could see the ice field and we were simply in the midst of enormous icebergs we were picked up by S.S. *Carpathia* about 6.00 a.m. I cannot speak too highly of her captain officers crew and passengers. F. Angle a survivor 15 Oct. 1913"

A contemporary account written by Mrs F. Angle of the disaster dated 15 October 1913, on two sheets. (Onslow's) $978 £600

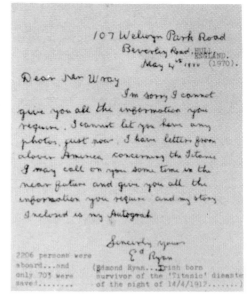

Edward Ryan was a small child on board the *Titanic*, his father Patrick was a victim in the disaster and his grandfather Thomas Ryan with assistance from Thomas Scanlon MP brought a claim against The Oceanic Steam Navigation Company, owners of The White Star Line, of negligence and were awarded a judgement of £100.

A letter from Edward Ryan to Mr W. Ray, 4th May 1920. (Onslow's) $75 £45

TOBACCO TINS

Lingering in old garden sheds, full of nails or faded seed packets, there are still thousands of old tobacco tins, disregarded by their owners but possible treasures for collectors. The collecting of these tins is growing into a craze in Britain as well as America, Australia and New Zealand. Beautifully designed tins in good condition are rising rapidly in price.

The ones most commonly found date from between 1880 and 1930 when tobacco companies vied with each other in the design and attractiveness of their tins. They were printed with pictures of pretty girls, a man about town or a seaman, complete with pipe in his mouth of course. The tins varied in size and some were large enough for a tobacconist to make a feature of in a window display. Every company produced these tins but the more unusual names to look for are Taddy, Lusby or Kriegsfeld.

Ringer's A1 Light tobacco. $3.50 £2

Player's Gold Leaf Navy Cut. $10 £6

J. G. Dill's Best Cut Plug. $14 £8

Afrikander Smoking Mixture tin. $9 £5

Lambert & Butler Log Cabin, circa 1900-20. $20 £12

Sweet Leaf Smoking Mixture, circa 1900. $45 £25

Hignetts Golden Leaf Navy Cut. $14 £8

Benson & Hedges Ltd., Cairo Cigarettes tin. $14 £8

Bishop's Move tobacco. $14 £8

TOBY JUGS

The name 'Toby' has long associations with conviviality. It was used by Shakespeare for his character Toby Belch and by Laurence Stern in Uncle Toby in 'Tristram Shandy'. Today it has come to mean a jug fashioned as a seated male figure in tricorn hat, one corner of which was used as a pourer for the beverage within, and a pipe or mug of beer on his knee.

Popularisation of this image was largely due to the Doulton company, who from their foundation in 1815 manufactured Toby jugs, albeit of the traditional brown salt glazed type. In 1925 however, coloured Toby jugs were introduced by Harry Simeon, and their potential was immediately recognised by Charles Noke, who intensified their colours still further and developed them into one of the company's best sellers. Some later Toby jugs have abandoned the traditional 'period' image, and represent such modern characters as Charlie Chaplin, George Robey and even Winston Churchill.

A Ralph Wood Toby jug of conventional type, circa 1770, 25.5cm. high. (Christie's) $2,692 £1,870

A Third Period, Churchill Toby jug, dated 1927, 164mm. high. (Goss & Crested China Ltd.) $175 £115

A pearlware Toby jug painted in Pratt colours, perhaps Yorkshire, circa 1800, 23.5cm. high. (Christie's) $907 £550

A large Clarice Cliff 'Churchill' Toby Jug, inscribed on base 'Going into Action, May God Defend the Right', 30.5cm. high, signed 'Clarice Cliff' No. 292'. (Phillips) $1,365 £750

'The Best is not Too Good', Doulton Toby jug issued 1939-60, 4½in. high. $70 £40

A Pratt ware Toby jug and cover, the man seated wearing ochre knee-breeches, blue coat and ochre, with caryatid handle, 26cm. high. (Phillips) $1,107 £580

A Pratt type Toby jug modelled as a rotund gentleman seated, entitled 'Tobey', 9¾in. high, circa 1790. (Christie's) $930 £600

A mid 19th century Russian Toby jug from the Korniloff factory, 21.5cm. high. (Phillips) $1,085 £650

A Ralph Wood Toby jug of conventional type, circa 1770, 25cm. high. (Christie's) $888 £626

Sairey Gamp, small seated Toby 4½in. high, issued 1948-60. $110 £65

Charlie Chaplin Toby jug issued by Doulton in 1918, 11in. high. $7,000 £4,000

Jolly Toby designed by H. Fenton, 6½in. high, 1939. $60 £35

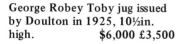

George Robey Toby jug issued by Doulton in 1925, 10½in. high. $6,000 £3,500

Old Charley issued 1939-60, designed by H. Fenton, 5½in. high. $60 £35

Cliff Cornell, blue suit, limited edition of 500 issued in 1956, 9¼in. high. $600 £350

TOKENS

Tokens were issued for short periods during the 17th, 18th and 19th centuries for local use due to shortages of low denomination currency, mostly in penny, halfpenny and farthing values. Look out for workhouse pennies given to paupers by various towns in the early 1800's, also advertisement tokens issued by various trades. Graded and priced like coins, 17th century tokens are the most valuable. Modern tokens, of course, also exist for gaming machines, promotions etc, and these can add to the range of a collection.

A circular, gilt lined love token box, probably French, 2½in. diam. (Christie's) $492 £308

Two penny tokens in brass for Hereford Brewery, late 19th century. $7 £4

'Spade guineas' gaming token made of brass, late 19th century. $5 £3

Comemorative gilded brass token for the opening of the Thames Tunnel in 1843, designed by Brunel. $14 £8

Early 18th century eclesiastical token of hammered copper. $15 £9

Charing Cross six penny token in silver. $18 £10

Late 18th century gaming token made by Rettli, dated 1795. $10 £6

George II token from Parrins & Gotto, Oxford Street, London. $7 £4

Half guinea gaming token, 1788, 'In memory of the good old days'. $3.50 £2

Georgian half guinea gaming token. $3.50 £2

TOOLS

Given the artistry of old time carpenters it is hardly surprising that the tools they used would be objects of beauty. For several years there has been a growing vogue for collecting old woodworking tools and Victorian carpenter's kits with their well worn handles and lovingly preserved blades are among the most desirable. Some of them were the tools of working men but occasionally a set turns up which was used for a hobby like fretwork which was very popular with gentlemen in the 19th century and the tools for it are exquisitely fine. The wood plane is perhaps the most sought after single woodworking tool and there are at least fifty different types available ranging in size from three inches to seventeen inches long. Early examples with makers' names on them can sometimes be worth hundreds of pounds. Another popular item is the brace and bit and there are some very old ones around. Braces fitted with interchangeable bits came into use in the beginning of the 19th century but the tool was in common use for at least four hundred years before that.

An 18th century beechwood router or 'Old Woman's Tooth', 9½in. long. $1,347 £770

An ultimatum brace by Wm. Marples with boxwood infill, handle and head with ebony ring. (David Stanley Auctions) $2,402 £1,550

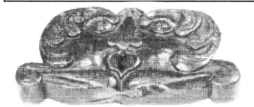

German made steel saw setter. $35 £20

An early 18th century lignum vitae and steel upholsterer's hammer, inscribed J. Sarney and 1716, 9½in. long. $1,059 £605

Early 25½in. try plane with flat iron handle. (David Stanley Auctions) $558 £360

French 'Bouvet a Plat' or coachbuilder's router in cormier wood by Mines de Suede. (David Stanley Auctions) $635 £410

A 19th century crimping machine of Thomas Clark type. (David Lay) $187 £105

Pair of mahogany steel tipped trammels with knurled brass tightening screws, 9in. overall. (David Stanley Auctions) $178 £115

A mahogany sash fillester with boxwood fence and stem wedges. (David Stanley Auctions) $178 £115

A 13½in. panel raising plane, by I. Dogdell, with replaced sole fence and offset handle (spur chipped) round topped iron, by R. Moore. (David Stanley Auctions) $418 £270

A mahogany staircase saw with 7½in. blade. (David Stanley Auctions) $53 £38

A hand-operated diamond cutting machine with copper cutting wafers. (David Stanley Auctions) $93 £60

An early R/H side axe, 11½in. edge, with star decoration, sharply cranked handle. (David Stanley Auctions) $85 £55

A beech plough by Gabriel, with brass thumb screw at the end of the stems. (David Stanley Auctions) $1,085 £700

A 19C two-handled French floor plane. (David Stanley Auctions) $141 £100

A bookbinders plough complete with cutting press. (David Stanley Auctions) $124 £80

A shipwright's large ash brace with 18in. sweep and 2in. fixed centre bit. (David Stanley Auctions) $217 £140

An early goosewing axe with 18½in. blade, two smiths marks and simple decoration. (David Stanley Auctions) $141 £100

A Swiss jewelling and wax lathe lacks tool rest. (David Stanley Auctions) $58 £38

A Stanley No. 196 circular rebate plane. (David Stanley Auctions) $775 £500

TOYS

The Victorian toyshop must have been a wonderful place, like a set for "The Nutcracker Suite", full of toys – dolls' houses, rocking horses, dolls, teddy bears, tin soldiers that marched across the floor banging drums, board games, kites, spinning tops and enormous metal hoops. There is an enormous variety for collectors. Some of the most unusual are optical devices of which Victorian parents greatly approved because they were reckoned to combine amusement with education. Zoetropes, stereoscopes, magic lanterns, phenakistiscopes, thaumatropes and kaleidoscopes were all very popular and a magic lantern with its original slides and or a three dimensional viewer with its pictures, is a very valuable find indeed. Other popular toys which were brought out of the nursery cupboard for amusement on rainy days included all kinds of board games, jig-saw puzzles and model theatres with paper dolls whose limbs were articulated by making them in sections and joining them together with thread.

A model of a butcher's shop, the building consisting of upper floor with four windows label-led 'Bull Butcher', 9in. wide. (Lawrence Fine Arts)
$836   £462

A googlie-eyed doll with watermelon mouth, moulded and painted hair, 15in. high, by Herdel Schwab & Co. (eyes missing, small neck chip). (Christie's)
$4,195   £2,220

A bisque headed Jack-in-the-Box with musical movement, the box 4½in. high. (Christie's)
$540   £286

A fine Schoenau and Hoff-meister Princess Elizabeth bisque head doll with blond mohair wig, weighted blue eyes, 41cm. (Phillips) $3,179 £1,700

A painted wooden Noah's Ark, 19th century, the painted woo-den vessel with brightly pain-ted floral frieze, 18in. long. (Lawrence Fine Arts)
$1,632   £902

A papier mache shoulder headed doll with moulded elaborate hairstyle, the cloth body with kid arms, 15½in. high. (Christie's)
$935   £495

A German painted tinplate clockwork Billiards Player, the moustached gentleman dressed in grey, 28cm. long. (Phillips) $411 £220

An Aston Martin Junior, a hand crafted replica of the V8 Volante. Fitted with a rear mounted Honda 350cc four-stroke 8 h.p. engine, British racing green. Scale 4:7. 8ft.6in. long, 3ft.6in. wide. 40 m.p.h. maximum. (Bearne's) $14,432 £8,200

A Japanese clockwork TV Film Crew open station wagon, finished in orange with red wings, 29cm. (Phillips) $160 £85

A cloth character doll with painted hair and features, the stuffed body wearing leder hosen, 18in. high, by Kathe Kruse. (Christie's) $1,351 £715

A child's wooden toy theatre with orchestra pit and hinged sides, each with two boxes, 28in. wide, Nuremberg. (Christie's) $374 £198

A bisque doll shoulder head with fixed blue eyes, the blonde curls held in place with a blue band, 8in. high, marked 60. (Christie's) $582 £308

A short plush covered nodding Boston terrier with pull growl and lower jaw, on wheels, 18in. long, circa 1910, French. (Christie's) $873 £462

A bisque headed character baby doll with blue lashed sleeping eyes, 10in. high, marked Simon & Halbig. (Christie's) $582 £308

A flock covered papier mache pull-along rabbit with moving wired ears, on green painted platform, 5in. long, with inscription reading C.L. Braithwaite 1843. (Christie's) $187 £99

A child's pedal car, modelled on a Bentley sports, of wood and metal construction, 65in. long, In need of restoration. (Bearne's)
$2,288   £1,300

An automaton modelled as a Scottish terrier with black fur, open mouth and teeth, moving on small wheels, 11in. high, by Descamps. (Christie's) $374   £198

A Bandai battery operated Volkswagen Beetle, finished in metallic red, 37.5cm. long. (Phillips) $150   £80

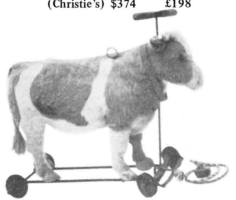

An all-bisque boy doll with painted blue eyes, closed mouth, dressed in regional Greek costume, 7½in. high. (Christie's) $291   £154

A Steiff plush longhorn bull on wheels, Steiff metal button in ear, 14in. (Lawrence Fine Arts) $398   £220

A painted felt character child doll with brown eyes glancing to the left, in original red felt coat, 22in. high, in original box and from the 109 series by Lenci, circa 1927. (Christie's)
$790   £418

A velvet covered rabbit with button eyes set on red velvet with rattle in body, 13in. high, Steiff, circa 1905. (Christie's) $311   £165

A Bing clockwork straw-filled Easter Bunny, GBN mark on ear clip, 15cm. high. (Phillips) $561 £300

A Lehmann 683 Halloh cyclist toy in excellent condition, boxed. (Phillips) $5,049 £2,700

Britains Royal Army Corps ambulance wagon with canvas canopy, together with three nurses, some wear. (Lawrence Fine Arts) $258   £143

A clockwork lion, the papier mache hide covered body with moulded papier mache head and counterweighted moving lower jaw, 29in. long. (Christie's) $727   £385

A white plush covered duck with amber glass eye, felt beak and legs, 14in. long, with swing ticket reading Jemima Puddle Duck. (Christie's) $291   £154

A Lenci fabric doll dressed as a boy with short fair blond mohair wig, painted brown eyes, 41cm. (Phillips) $785 £420

A Victorian doll's house, the front with a balustrade balcony supported by four doric columns, painted in cream with a brick paper ground, 32in. wide. (Lawrence Fine Arts) $756   £418

F. Martin tin plate toy — The Scyther, the moustached gentleman with yellow and red hat, circa 1898, 20cm. (Phillips) $710 £380

A Victorian doll's perambulator, the bodywork black with fine yellow lines, some wear, 33in. high. (Lawrence Fine Arts) $1,035   £572

A fine and rare Armand Marseille bisque head character doll with dark mohair wig, painted blue eyes, 18in. high. (Phillips) $6,171 £3,300

A Victorian rocking horse having a carved and dapple painted wood body, 53in. wide. (Bearne's) $968   £550

TRADE CARDS

Trade cards were given away by travelling salesmen and sometimes presented to customers by storeholders. They advertise all manner of goods from sewing items to musical instruments and 'quack' cures, and reflect the humour and freedom of the advertising of Victorian times.

The quality of artwork on some is surprising, and some well-known artists were probably involved in their design. Technically, too, they reflect the best of the age in terms of chromolithographic printing and pictorial excellence.

Look out for good clean examples with colourful, pictorial fronts and printed details of the product on the back. Unusually shaped cards are also prized. Sometimes these cards turn up in scrap albums and even inside books, and they do represent a worthwhile investment.

Hagan's Magnolia Balm, 'For beautifying the complexion', presented by J. W. Robinson, Druggist and Chemist, Southbridge, Mass. $5 £3

'Now dollies, if you be good we'll have Bromangelon for dessert. Nothing but the addition of hot water required'. $3.50 £2

Kendall Mfg. Co., French Laundry, 'To protect yourself from the evil effect of using soap made from impure materials', Providence, R.I. $5 £3

'Compliments of Fechheimer's Shoe Department, 102 W. Fifth Street. Admiration'. $7 £4

Prize Lincoln Buck Wilton, 'Compliments of the Domestic Sewing Machine Co. $10 £6

J. & P. Coats' Thread, 'I say Sissy! the umbrella that boy has got was certainly not sewed with Coats colored thread'. $7 £4

Hires' Rootbeer, 'An uninvited guest', the Charles E. Hires Co., 11-119 Arch Street, Philadelphia. $9 £5

Brown's Iron Bitters, 'A certain cure for diseases. Beware of imitations'. $5 £3

'A flat Dutch cabbage', E. F. Harmeyer, Walnut Street, Cincinnati, Ohio, Agricultural Implements. $7 £4

'Perfumed with Austen's Forest Flower Cologne', W. J. Austen & Co., Oswego, N.Y. $7 £4

Sailing ship trade card for Vouwie Bros, 'Forest City Baking Powder, absolutely pure'. $20 £12

'Agers Dry Hop Yeast is the best in use', Dole & Merrill Mfrs., Boston, New York. $5 £3

Hoyt's German Cologne, 'Fragrant and lasting', E. W. Hoyt, Lowell, Mass. $9 £5

'The White is the Sewing Machine of the Day', by C.H. Burdick, Boxo, Brookfield, New York. $18 £10

'Balls Health Preserving Corset is the best in the world', Walter H. Tarr, Cincinnati, Ohio. $7 £4

Presented by Household Sewing Machine Co., Providence, R.I., T. S. Arnold, Agent. $14   £8

'King of the Blood', D. Ransom, Son & Co., Proprietors, Buffalo, New York, 'Read the testimonials'. $7   £4

Willimantic Six Cord Thread, 'The best, so good, so smooth, so strong, so free'. $9   £5

Lautz Bros. & Co., Master Soap, Buffalo, New York. $7   £4

The Allenburys' Clock, 'This clock can be used to inform the mother as to the hour for giving baby his next bottle.' $20   £12

'For Tomato Catsup, E. F. Harmeyer, 227 Walnut Street, Cincinnati, Ohio, Agricultural Implements'. $5   £3

Beatty's Organs, Beatty's Piano's, Washington, New Jersey, 'The largest piano and organ establishment on the globe'. $9   £5

'Use Tarrant's Seltzer Aperient, to regulate the stomach, the liver, the bowels'. $7   £4

Warren & Wing, New England Agents, Tremont Street, Boston, Household Sewing Machine Co. $14   £8

TRADE CARDS

Austen's Forest Flower Cologne, 'The most fashionable and lasting perfume of the day'. $5 £3

'A good angels visit, Scovill's Sarsaparilla and Stillingia or Blood and Liver Syrup.' $10 £6

'Dran Pa oo ought to put on one of Carters Backache Plasters', Carter Medicine Co., New York. $3.50 £2

J. G. White, 'Harness, Trunks and Bags, Carriage Trimming', Sign Big Trunk, Cooperstown. $5 £3

A large scrap type trade card by Hoeninghausen's Central Tea Store, Detroit, Michigan. $9 £5

'Dr White's Cough Drops are the best, they are in truth a veritable delicacy'. $7 £4

Industrial Insurance, Metropolitan Life Insurance Co., Central Block, Lewiston, Me. $5 £3

Horsfords Acid Phosphate, 'For mental and physical exhaustion, Dyspepsia'. $5 £3

John English & Co. 'Imperial diamond drilled eyed needles', patent Great Britain, 1863. $5 £3

TRADE CATALOGUES

Apart from the fact that they are excellent examples of the fine quality printing of the Victorians, trade catalogues are prized by collectors of specific items if they deal with the subject in which they are interested. Trade catalogues issued by pottery and porcelain factories for example make it possible to date with accuracy any of their products; similarly with biscuit manufacturers whose catalogues tell a collector in which year certain tins were issued. There were catalogues produced by manufacturers of everything from fishing tackle to furniture. Builders' merchants produced catalogues and so did plumbers' suppliers but they have a limited appeal. The catalogues make interesting reading because they were beautifully produced on good quality paper and often in full colour.

R. A. Harding, Manufacturer of Invalid Carriages and Motors. $15 £9

The 1956 Gadgets Annual compiled by V. M. Lawrence-Swan. $45 £25

Knitted Comforts for Men on Land and Sea, by J. & J. Baldwin, Halifax. $7 £4

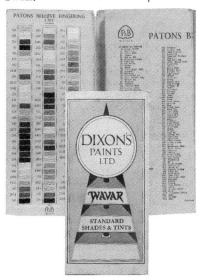

Dixon's Paints, Standard Shades & Tints. $3.50 £2

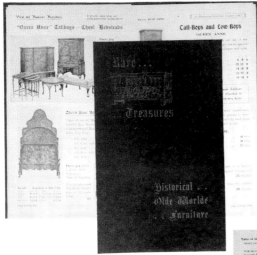

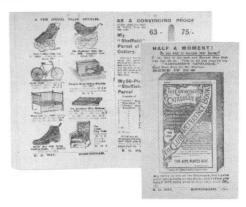

The Canvasser's Catalogue, the Club Reference Book. $9 £5

Olde Worlde Workshops of Adam B. Smith. $7 £4

Handbook of Knitting and Crocheting, Scotch Wool & Hosiery Stores. $5 £3

Books for Presents and Prizes by Wells, Gardner Darton & Co. Ltd. $14 £8

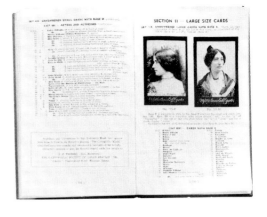

Brushes, Hamilton & Co., Decorators and Grainers brushes, 1904. $5 £3

The Guinea Gold Booklet compiled by the Cartophilic Society. $50 £30

(Border Bygones)

TRAVEL POSTERS

One of the most noticeable developments of recent years is the rise in interest in that old favourite, the Poster.

Travel Posters in particular are fetching very good prices — and rightly so, for they demonstrate in the most colourful and attractive manner a lifestyle long since gone when travel, for the sake of it, was a pleasure indeed.

Poster — To London by Sleeper from Edinburgh (Waverley) To King's Cross by Alexeieff. (Onslow's) $4,960 £3,200

Norfolk Coast, poster by Picking, published by L.M.S. (Onslow's) $692   £400

The Famous Bathing Pool at Hastings and St Leonards, poster by Gerald Spencer Pryse, published by L.M.S. (Onslow's) $1,176   £680

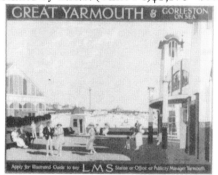

Gt. Yarmouth and Gorleston On Sea, poster by H. G. Gawthorn, L.M.S. Best Way Series No. 35. (Onslow's) $1,003   £580

Clear Road Ahead Monmouth Castle, poster by Terence Cuneo. (Onslow's) $328   £190

Central Wales Spas For Health Recreation and Pleasure, poster by Montague B. Black, L.M.S. Best Way Series No. 28. (Onslow's)$813 £470

Getting Ready On The East Coast, poster by Frank H. Mason, quad royal. (Onslow's)
$553   £320

The Continent via Harwich, poster by Higgins. (Onslow's) $363 £210

The Broads, poster by Gerald Spencer Pryse. (Onslow's) $294 £170

Hunstanton, poster by Higgins. (Onslow's) $121 £70

Plant Your Works On The L.N.E.R., poster by Andrew Johnson. (Onslow's) $95 £55

Tours in Connemara Galway Achill and The West of Ireland, poster by Fhugo D'Alesi, 127 x 92cm. (Onslow's) $190 £110

The Broads, poster by Gerald Spencer Pryse. (Onslow's) $346 £200

Tynemouth, poster by Alfred Lambart. (Onslow's) $588 £340

Discretion in Mixing Cocktails and Serving Crusted Port, published by L.N.E.R. (Onslow's) $622 £360

The Continent via Harwich, poster by Higgins. (Onslow's) $294 £170

Saltburn By The Sea, poster by H. G. Gawthorn. (Onslow's) $276 £160

In Winter to Vienna, published by Waldheim-Eberle, double royal. (Onslow's) $103 £60

L.N.E.R. Camping Coaches In England and Scotland, poster, published by L.N.E.R., 1939. (Onslow's) $138 £80

Skegness Is So Bracing, poster by John Hassall. (Onslow's) $605 £350

The Royal Route Via Sandringham To Broadland, poster, published by Midland & Gt. Northern Joint Railways. (Onslow's) $501 £290

Continent via Harwich, poster by Tom Purvis. (Onslow's) $432 £250

Hunstanton, poster by Wilton Williams. (Onslow's) $397 £230

"Queen of Scots" All Pullman, poster by Fred Taylor. (Onslow's) $1,072 £620

Belgium Harwich via Zeebrugge, poster by Higgins. (Onslow's) $294 £170

TRAVEL STICKERS

Travel stickers have not yet really taken off as collectables, but it should not be long before they do. Logically, mint examples must be scarce, since most would be used at the time of issue or purchase and, after years on a car screen, would be impossible to remove without damage.

Flag shaped stickers were very popular in the 50's and 60's. Soft plain plastic ones are more desirable as they can be re-used, whereas self-adhesive types cannot be removed.

Hot Car Magazine give-away, 1975. $2 £1

Hednesford Raceway, Auto Thrills, 1960's.
$4.50 £2.50

Hungarian Puli, dog show sticker. $2 £1

Service with a Smurf, National.
$2 £1

You're following a Burmah smile. $3.50 £2

Saudi Arabia travel sticker.
$3.50 £2

Herefords Offer You More. $2 £1

Mevagissey, flag type.
$1 50p

Birmingham Motoring Festival, 1975. $2.50 £1.50

Strongbow Cider. $1 50p

TRENCH ART

Trench Art is the name given to the souvenirs that serving soldiers during the two Great Wars turned out in their spare time from the debris and fragments they picked up around them. Particular favourites for their expertise were cigarette lighters which were made from pieces of shrapnel or bullet cases. Another common product was paper knives made from a brass bullet with a blade stuck on top. The most common however were ashtrays which were often carved with messages or initials and the date. Occasionally it is possible to find excellent models of ships, planes, tanks or field guns made by men idling their time away in the war zones. Some of these show great artistic ability and are prized by collectors. A word of caution – some of the bullets used in Trench Art can still be dangerous. It used to be fashionable for them to be displayed on the mantelpiece near roaring fires and it is a miracle that they did not explode.

Brass trench art aeroplane made from bullet and shell cases.   **$50 £30**

Combined lighter and ashtray dated 1944.   **$18 £10**

Pocket cigarette lighter made from scrap brass.   **$10 £6**

Brass bullet case button hook.   **$10 £6**

Bullet case lighter with pen grip.   **$9 £5**

Leather riding crop with two 303 brass bullet cases forming the handle.   **$10 £6**

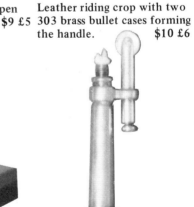

A large brass and aluminium table lighter.   **$25 £15**

Brass table lighter with screw top mounted on a mahogany base.   **$25 £15**

Bullet case pocket lighter. **$9 £5**

TYPEWRITERS

The first attempt to invent a typewriter took place in 1714 when a patent was granted to an Englishman called Henry Mill but it was never manufactured. The next important step was taken by an American, Charles Thurber who patented his idea of a machine working with a platen in 1843 and from then on attempts were more numerous but unsuccessful in producing readable copy. The first practical typewriter was invented by three Americans, Sholes, Glidden and Soule in 1867. It worked on a shift key mechanism which is the same method as modern machines.

Early typewriters demand good prices today and they are numerous because in the decade between 1870 and 1880, there were over 50,000 of them sold by the new companies Remington, Oliver, Smith, Underwood and Yost.

More rare are unusual machines like the German Edelmann, the Lambert which had a circular dial like a telephone dial in the middle of it; the Hammond which had piano type keys and the Hall which was presented in a walnut case.

A Mignon Model 2 typewriter in good working order with all original parts.
$3,000 £1,750

A Hall typewriter, No. 2498, in mahogany case, American, circa 1885, 15¼in. wide.
$600 £350

A Lambert typewriter No. 2908, by the Lambert Typewriter Co., New York.
$435 £250

A Merritt typewriter with rubber typeface and inking pad, American, circa 1900.
$700 £400

Rare Corona special folding typewriter in red lacquer body, circa 1910, 12¼in. wide.
$600 £350

Rare Merritt typewriter, linear index mechanism, with plunger selector, circa 1895, 12¼in. wide.
$1,750 £1,000

Rare Hammond No. 1 typewriter with swinging sector mechanism, circa 1886, 14in. wide.
$1,500 £850

Williams No. 3 typewriter with grasshopper action type bars, circa 1895, length of platen 13in.
$875 £500

American Columbia typewriter No. 2, with circular letter index, 9¾in. wide, circa 1890.
$1,250 £700

An Edelmann typewriter on shaped cast-iron base, German, circa 1897, 10½in. wide.
$700 £400

The society magazine *'Vanity Fair'* was published in London from 1869 till 1914. It did not survive the Great War perhaps because of the decimation of its clientele. It carried news of the society functions, the Royal family, satire, fashion but, most notably, it carried cartoons, not always flattering, of eminent society figures of the day. These cartoons were coloured lithographs and they were also sold to the public as coloured prints made from the original plates. Copies that can be found today are valuable because the plates are no longer available.

The cartoons are of very fine quality, measuring approximately seven inches by twelve in most cases and a short, witty biography of the subject which was always added must be included for the cartoon to have its full value. They were published in a numbered series but those that are most highly regarded are the rarer ones and those in pristine condition. A number of well known artists contributed caricatures to Vanity Fair including Phil May and the famous Spy.

Sir Henry Drummond Wolff, 'Consular Chaplains', September 5th, 1874. $35 £20

Mr Alexander J. Beresford-Hope, M.P., 'Batavian grace', September 10th, 1870. $45 £25

Prince George Frederick Ernest Albert, K.G., 'Our Sailor Prince', May 24th, 1890. $70 £40

Mr Henry Fawcett, M.P., 'A radical leader', 21st December 1872. $45 £25

The Right Honourable Sir William Robert Seymour Vesey Fitzgerald, G.C.S.I., Bombay, May 2nd, 1874. $60 £35

Sir Thomas Salter Pyne, C.S.I., Afghan Engineering, February 15th, 1900. $55 £30

The Duke of Sutherland, 'Simple and unassuming, he is the very Duke of Dukes', July 9th, 1870. $45 £25

Sir Roderick Impey Murchison, 'A faithful friend, an eminent servant, and the best possible of Presidents', November 26th, 1870.
$60 £35

Brigadier-General Sir Evelyn Wood, K.C.B., V.C., 'The Flying Column', November 15th, 1879. $60 £35

Lord Lytton, 'The best specimen now extant of the utterly immovable politician', October 29th, 1870. $35 £20

VIDEOS

Videos feature among the 'new wave' of collectables of the 90's. Mint or near-mint copies are preferable, and beware of poor condition ex-rental or 'pirate' tapes. Like records, good films can be re-issued on budget labels aimed at the 'sell through' market. A good example is Disney material – Disney have released much more in America than here and scarce material can be found. Here, in addition to VHS and Beta, there is the deleted Philips Video 2000 format and the earlier Philips Video 1000, both of which are now collectors' items. Then there is the video disc system, again now obsolete but very sought after. (Note that American formats are not compatible with our systems.) Look out for collectable films such as original copies of the Blues Brothers (£200-£300), adult cartoons such as Fritz the Cat (£50-£150), and some more unusual 'horror films'. Banned films, too, will always be sought after.

Caged Fury, Pyramid
Productions. $35 £20

Elvis Presley, Girls, Girls, Girls,
Videoform, 1983. $100 £60

Bruce Li in Fist of Fury,
Hokushin Audio Visual Ltd.
$260 £150

Sharon Tate in '12 plus 1',
1983 release, Ariel Films.
$175 £100

Cut and Run, Medusa Home
Video, 90 minutes, 1985.
$50 £30

Teen Wolf starring Michael J.
Fox, E.V. Films. $100 £60

(Video Vision)

427

Monty Python's Flying Circus, Series 2, Episodes 1–4, BBC Video, 1985. $90 £50

Warner Bros., Mono Hi-Fi 1986 Nightmare on Elm Street, Part 2, 82 minutes. $130 £75

The Fabulous Fantastic Four, Guild Home Video, 66 minutes. $55 £30

A Passage to India, directed by David Lean, Thorn EMI, 1985. $140 £80

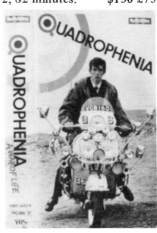

Quadrophenia, Polygram Video, 1979, 113 mins, music by The Who. $122 £70

Convoy, Kris Kristofferson and Ali MacGraw, E.M.I., 1978, 106 minutes. $70 £40

Platoon, RCA Columbia Pictures, Beta, 1986, 115 minutes. $130 £75

Walt Disney's Pinocchio, Rank Home Video, original copy, 84 minutes. $140 £80

Michael Jackson, 'Thriller', Vestron Music Video, International, 60 minutes. $55 £30

(Video Vision)

WALL MASKS

In the 1930's wall plaques were very fashionable. They could be made of glass, brass, wood, pottery, plaster or porcelain but it was the plaster ones that were most common especially the three flying ducks which became a cartoonists' joke when portraying middle class homes. Today the ducks are making a comeback and they are snapped up by collectors. Cheap plaster plaques were given away as prizes by fairground operators and so were carved wooden plaques showing interior scenes. Slightly more exclusive were pressed brass plaques featuring "Olde Worlde" scenes like stage coaches in inn yards and monks roistering around refectory tables. The upper end of the plaque market include Clarice Cliff's hand painted ones which sell for high prices today and some very attractive plaques were produced by Minton, Imari and Wedgwood. Goldscheider and Newport made plaques in the form of stylised masks as did Doulton whose mask of a woman's face in green celadon by Charles Noke is one of the most expensive that can be found today.

A Royal Doulton face mask, 'Jester', probably HN1630, 28.5cm. long, c.m.1. & c., date code for 1937.
(Abridge Auction) $200 £140

A Goldscheider tin-glazed earthenware wall mask, Wien, Made in Austria, inscribed 8874, 36cm. high.
(Christie's) $811 £495

A Royal Doulton 'Grey Friar' wall mask, 7¼in. high. circa 1940-41. (Abridge Auction)
$525 £350

A Goldscheider pottery double face wall plaque, the two females in profile, 12in. high.
(Christie's) $596 £385

Glazed Florence Goss wall vase, with radiating hair and feathers, 120mm. high. (Goss & Crested China Ltd) $435 £250

A Lenci pottery wall plaque in the form of a young woman's head, wearing a colourful scarf, dated 1937, 29.5cm. (Bearne's)
$619   £360

WAR POSTERS

War posters were an essential part of the propaganda of both sides from the First World War onwards. Perhaps the most familiar posters from that time, and certainly the most frequently reproduced, are the recruiting posters. Few will be unfamiliar with the classic 'Kitchener Needs You' or 'Women of Britain say "Go!"' signs which resulted from the decimation of the regular British Expeditionary Force in 1914.

Second World War posters were aimed also at the home-based civilian war effort, with major artists making their contribution. 'Careless talk costs lives' and 'She's not so dumb' reflect the constant preoccupation with security. The US and Germany also issued propagandist and recruiting posters, the German ones dating from World War Two often emphasising, in dark grey tones, the dour, "iron-hard" quality of the German forces.

Strictly Between These Four Walls Careless Talk Costs Lives, poster by Fougasse. (Onslow's)
$147   £85

Come Into The Ranks and Fight For Your King and Country, poster by W. H. Caffyn, double royal. (Onslow's)
$51   £30

Holidays By The Sea Take Care of Minefields, poster by Chan, double crown; and one other. (Onslow's)
Two $77   £45

Join The Regular Air Force A Career With Adventure, poster by Winslade, double royal. (Onslow's) $112   £65

Daddy, What Did You Do In The Great War?, poster by Savile Lumley, double crown. (Onslow's) $536   £310

Women Of Britain Say Go, poster by E. V. Kealey, double crown. (Onslow's)
$294   £170

Take The Road To Victory
Join The W.A.A.F., poster by
Foss, double crown. (Onslow's)
$60   £35

Everyone Should Do His Bit
Enlist Now, poster by Baron
Low, double crown, (Onslow's)
$190   £110

Every Woman Not Doing Vital
Work is Needed Now, poster
by Winslade, double crown.
(Onslow's) $103   £60

To Make the World a Decent Place to Live In,
Third Liberty Loan, 92 x 142cm. (Onslow's)
$80 £45

They Kept the Sea Lanes Open, Invest in
the Victory Liberty Loan, 74 x 100cm.
(Onslow's) $80 £45

Halt the Hun, Buy U.S. Government Bonds, double crown.
(Onslow's) $70 £40

U.S.A. Bonds, Third Liberty
Loan Campaign, Boy Scouts
of America, double crown.
(Onslow's) $225 £130

Teufel Hunden, German
nickname for U.S. Marines,
double crown. (Onslow's)
$42 £24

WEIGHTS

Weights come in many shapes and sizes and were produced for such diverse users as apothecaries, jewellers, greengrocers etc. Complete sets are worth more than single weights. After a weight was cast, a lead insert would be put in and trimmed to the exact weight before official stamping. Weights for commercial purposes had to be periodically checked and impress stamped, and these markings can make a weight much more interesting.

A set of Apothecary Weights in a bakelite box by W. & J. George & Becker Ltd. $35 £20

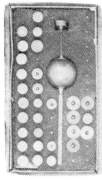

An early hydrometer with float and thirty brass weights, English, 1750-80, 7½in. long.
$525 £300

A pair of W. & T. Avery snuff scales, to weigh 1lb., class B. No. A189 with brass pans, together with a set of 5 weights. (Osmond Tricks)
$210 £120

A cased set of Jacobus Listingh coin weights, Dutch, dated 1659, 3½ x 6¼in., in leather slip case.
$5,250 £3,000

A set of brass Troy Weights from ¼oz. – 2oz. $35 £20

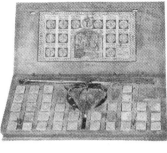

An 18th century Dutch rectangular wooden box containing an iron and brass balance, together with weights, 25cm. long.
$4,800 £2,750

Great Western Railway solid iron balance weight. $18 £10

WHISTLES

Since earliest times man could make whistles from reeds but there were also more elaborate versions like the one carved from the leg bone of a swan that survives from the Middle Ages. The materials they can be made from ranges through bone, ivory, gold, jet, brass, agate, wood, porcelain and silver. They have been used for a variety of functions from summoning dogs to alerting workers and sounding alarms. Collectors look for dog whistles in the shape of a dog and some of them were made in porcelain by the Derby factory. Other desirable whistles include silver military ones and 18th century bosun's whistles which were also made of silver. Whistles used by members of the police and railway officials are very desirable if they carry some crest or insignia. The most interesting whistles are those which double up with, or are disguised as, another object and they can be found incorporated with pen knives, tape measures, spoons, pencils or rattles.

A goldwashed silver and coral rattle whistle, hallmarked Birmingham, 1862, 6in. long. (Robt. W. Skinner Inc.) $290 £235

A Victorian cast whistle formed as the head of a dog, by Samson Mordan, London, 1886, 2½in. long. (Christie's) $739 £462

An 18th/19th century mahogany choir master's pitch pipe, 12½in. long. $300 £175

The Acme Thunderer with plated chain, circa 1950. $5 £3

Rare George II bosun's whistle, London, 1740, 4¼in. long. $3,500 £2,000

Good quality silver military whistle and case with Tudor rose decoration. $525 £300

Victorian silver whistle and penknife, London 1879. $350 £200

Early 19th century Derby whistle, 4.5cm. wide. $430 £250

Silver police whistle, dated 1888. $175 £100

WINE

Collectors of wine usually enjoy drinking it too, but if *they* are one and the same, the bottles they select for the two purposes most usually are not; wine is collected as as an investment, and valuable and rare bottles are seldom, if ever, consumed.

The name and description on an auction catalogue is often enough to carry one in imagination to some sunlit Southern vineyard slope, though the estimated price beneath can amount to many times the actual cost of getting there. Wine buffs judge their bottles not only by the name and vintage, but also by the condition of the label, the neck level in the bottle, and the colour, so even if they are never to be tasted, they still have to be carefully and correctly stored.

Wine is a very lucrative collectable, if you have the necessary patience, and can resist the temptation to taste your treasure.

1 bottle Romanee-Conti—Vintage 1924, Domaine de la Romanee-Conti, excellent level only 1½in. below cork, deep colour maturing at rim. (Christie's) $605 £365

Three magnums of Clos des Lambrays—Vintage 1947, Cote de Nuits, Heritiers Cosson, levels very high, only 1in.-2in. below corks. (Christie's) $682 £412

1 bottle Chateau Mouton-Rothschild—Vintage 1874, Pauillac, 1er cru classe, Chateau-embossed capsule, neck level, deep colour and pristine labels. (Christie's) $1,320 £798

1 bottle Chateau Margaux—Vintage 1888, Margaux, 1er cru classe, Recorked by Whitwham & Co., 1981, with neck level, original cork attached to neck of bottle. (Christie's) $418 £252

Two bottles of Romanee-Conti—Vintage 1934, Domaine de la Romanee-Conti, excellent level on 1in.-2in. below corks, deep colour to rim, labels slightly soiled. (Christie's) $902 £545

1 bottle Les Gaudichots—Vintage 1929, Domaine de la Romanee-Conti, excellent level only 1in. below cork, deep colour, label soiled. (Christie's) $572 £345

1 bottle Chateau Lafite—Vintage 1945, Pauillac, 1er cru classe, neck level. (Christie's) $682 £412

Two bottles of Chateau d'Yquem—Vintage 1940, Sauternes, 1er grand cru classe, excellent honey gold colour, neck level, labels slightly stained. (Christie's) $1,012 £611

1 bottle Chateau Latour—Vintage 1874, Pauillac, 1er cru classe, Recorked by Whitwham & Co., 1982, excellent colour.(Christie's) $1,485   £897

1 jeroboam Chateau Lafite—Vintage 1949, Pauillac, 1er cru classe, with a neck level, deep colour, and pristine label. (Christie's) $2,420 £1,418

1 double magnum Chateau Petrus—Vintage 1953, Pomerol, neck level and pristine label. (Christie's) $3,630 £2,194

1 bottle, with original cork attached, Chateau Mouton-Rothschild—Vintage 1888, Pauillac, 1er cru classe, Recorked by Whitwham & Co., 1980, level in neck. (Christie's) $682 £412

1 bottle Chateau Petrus—Vintage 1945, Pomerol, excellent top-shoulder level, label slightly tattered and soiled. (Christie's) $1,650 £997

Three bottles of Chateau Cheval-Blanc—Vintage 1929, Saint-Emilion, 1er grand cru classe (A), two recorked by Whitwham & Co., 1982. (Christie's) $1,045 £631

1 jeroboam, in original case, Chateau Mouton-Rothschild—Vintage 1929, Pauillac, 1er cru classe, high-shoulder level, garnet colour and pristine label. (Christie's) $8,800 £5,320

435

1 bottle Chateau Haut-Brion—Vintage 1899, Pessac, Graves, 1er cru classe, Recorked by Whitwham & Co., 1979, excellent neck level and deep colour, label soiled. (Christie's)
$902 £545

Two bottles of Chateau Haut-Brion—Vintage 1906, Pessac, Graves, 1er cru classe, one recorked by Whitwham & Co., 1980, top-shoulder level, excellent deep colour and good labels.   (Christie's)
$572 £345

1 bottle Chateau Lafite—Vintage 1858, Pauillac, 1er cru classe, Recorked by Whitwham & Co., 1980, with a neck level and deep colour. (Christie's)
$2,420 £1,463

1 magnum Chateau Mouton-Rothschild—Vintage 1878, Pauillac, 1er cru classe, Recorked by Whitwham & Co., 1980, neck level and deep color, label soiled. (Christie's)
$2,860 £1,729

1 double magnum Chateau Lafite—Vintage 1865, Pauillac, 1er cru classe, with deep colour and level in the neck, with Christie's slip label. (Christie's)
$17,050 £10,308

1 bottle Chateau d'Yquem—Vintage 1921, Sauternes, 1er grand cru classe, top-shoulder level and deep amber gold colour. (Christie's) $902 £545

1 bottle Chateau Mouton-Rothschild—Vintage 1899, Pauillac, 1er cru classe, Chateau-embossed capsule, neck level and deep colour. (Christie's) $902 £545

Six bottles of Barolo Riserva—Vintage 1947, Piedmont, Giacomo Borgogno & Figli. (Christie's) $858 £518

1 bottle Chateau Lafite-Vintage 1888, Pauillac, 1er cru classe, Recorked by Whitwham & Co., 1980, and with neck level. (Christie's) $792 £478

WRISTWATCHES

The first watches were made with only one hand and were carried in the fob pocket of the trouser waistband, moving to the waistcoat in the 19th century. The invention of the wrist watch did not take place till the 20th century.

Early watches had a lever and cylinder escapement and were made by Mudge, Tompion, Graham, Quare, Frodsham, Breguet, Leroux, Barraud and Ellicott. When wrist watches appeared a multitude of makers adopted the idea but the one which is most sought after is the Rolex, especially slim rectangular ones made in the 1930's. The Rolex Prince was produced in stainless steel, gold, silver or striped gold and the case was curved for the wrist. The movement was of nickel silver. The Rolex Oyster first appeared in 1927 and for sheer reliability has become a by-word. Ladies' Rolex Oysters fetch about half the price of those for men which can go for around £1000 for an automatic. Among women's watches the most desirable are Art Deco diamond set models by Patek Philippe and Vacheron & Constantin.

A circular Swiss gold gent's wristwatch with chronograph, by Universal, Geneve, the signed movement jewelled to the centre, 36mm. diam. (Phillips)

$2,618   £1,400

An early platinum and gold Cartier Santos gent's wristwatch, the movement signed Cartier, with roman numerals and blued steel hands, 25mm. long. (Phillips)

$11,220   £6,000

A circular Swiss gold automatic gent's wristwatch, by International Watch Co., with centre seconds and baton numerals, 34mm. diam. (Phillips)

$374   £200

A gentleman's wristwatch in heavy metal circular case, inscribed Audemars Piguet and Co., Geneve, 34mm. diam. (Christie's)

$790   £418

A rectangular 18ct. gold gent's wristwatch, the movement with silvered dial signed for J. W. Benson, London, 1937, 39mm. long. (Phillips)

$524   £280

A Swiss two colour gold circular gent's wristwatch, by Supra, with gilt Roman numerals and subsidiary seconds, 27mm. diam. (Phillips) $304   £180

A hexagonal Swiss gold wrist-watch, by Rolex, the movement with engraved silvered dial and blued hands, 31mm. long.
(Phillips) $524   £280

A Swiss gold hexagonal gent's wristwatch, by Cartier, the signed dial with Roman numerals, 31mm. long.
(Phillips) $2,197   £1,300

A Swiss gold circular gent's wristwatch, by Vacheron and Constantin, the signed sil-vered dial with subsidiary seconds, 28mm. diam.
(Phillips) $2,704   £1,600

An 18ct. gold rectangular wristwatch signed Vacheron & Constantin, Geneve, with monometallic balance, jew-elled to the centre with 17 jewels, 32mm. x 25mm.
(Christie's) $1,443   £825

An 18ct. gold Cartier wrist-watch, the white and grey enamelled dial numbered 1-24, the plated movement signed Bouch-Girod, 33mm. diameter. (Christie's)
$2,887   £1,650

A stylish square gold wrist-watch inscribed Patek Philippe, Geneve, the plated movement adjusted to five positions, 26mm. square.
(Christie's) $2,117   £1,210

A Swiss gold circular gent's wristwatch, by Patek Philippe, the signed dial with baton numerals and subsidiary seconds, 34mm. diam.
(Phillips) $2,281   £1,350

A circular half hunter cased Swiss gold gent's wristwatch, by Rolex, the front with enamel numerals opened by a button at the VI position, 31mm. diam.
(Phillips) $1,496   £800

A fine and rare split second wrist chronograph, signed Patek Philippe & Co., Geneva, the nickel 25-jewel movement with mono-metallic balance.
(Christie's) $93,500 £52,406

A steel oyster perpetual bubble back gent's wristwatch, by Rolex, the signed silvered dial with Arabic numerals, (Phillips) $676   £400

A lady's Swiss gold wristwatch, by Corum, the case in the form of a Rolls-Royce radiator, with 'R.R.' badge and 'Spirit of Ecstasy' mascot, 28mm. long. (Phillips) $1,156   £680

An 18ct. gold circular wristwatch, the movement signed Russells Limited, the signed enamel dial with subsidiary seconds, London 1926, 33mm. diam. (Phillips) $473   £280

A Swiss two colour gold Rolex Prince wristwatch, the signed silvered dial with Arabic numerals and subsidiary seconds below, 42mm. long. (Phillips) $4,394   £2,600

A rare 18ct. gold split-second chronograph wristwatch in circular case, the signed movement with monometallic balance, jewelled to the centre with 20 jewels. (Christie's) $3,657   £2,090

A rectangular Dunhill wristwatch in yellow metal case, the white enamel dial with mottled brown centre, 33mm. x 28mm. (Christie's) $423   £242

A Swiss gold cushion shaped gent's wristwatch, by Longines, the signed dial marked for Alex Scott, Glasgow with subsidiary seconds, 31mm. long. (Phillips) $574   £340

An 18ct. gold Cartier Panta calendar wristwatch, with quartz movement, heavy brick-link gold bracelet and invisible deployant Cartier clasp - 26mm. x 35mm. (Christie's) $8,085   £4,620

A rectangular Swiss white gold lady's wristwatch by Baume & Mercier, Geneve, the bezel set with thirty-six diamonds, 28mm. long. (Phillips) $1,533   £820

ZEPPELIN MEMORABILIA

The Zeppelin was invented by Count von Zeppelin around 1900, and the term strictly applies only to the German airships of the First World War period. Memorabilia is not common but does exist in such forms as bookends made from Zeppelin timber and items jettisoned from, for example, the crippled German L33 as it struggled unsuccessfully to reach Germany after a bombing raid on London in 1916. (It crashed and was scuttled by its crew.)

'Zeppelin' a white metal cigarette and match holder, 22.8cm. long. (Christie's) $267 £187

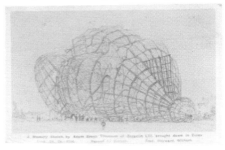

A Memory Sketch by Adam Eruce Thomson of Zeppelin L33, brought down in Essex, September 23rd, 1916. $18 £10

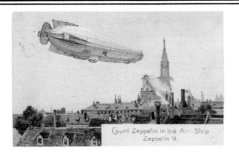

Count Zeppelin in his airship Zeppelin III, postcard by Cook & Sons (Soap) 1908.
                                                    $15 £9

A Tipp R101 tinplate Zeppelin, German, circa 1930, 25½in. long. $1,750 £1,000

"Zepp" Charm, made out of framework of Zeppelin, brought down in Essex, September, 1916. $14 £8

An Imperial German World War I Zeppelin crew badge (Army). (Wallis & Wallis) $470 £285

Commemorative serviette for the R101 Zeppelin, 5th October 1930. $60 £35

Index

INDEX

INDEX

While this series of handy volumes has been specially devised to provide busy dealers and collectors with an extremely comprehensive reference library of antiques and their values, the information will also prove to be of great general interest to those with just a few pieces they wish to sell or appraise.

Each volume is crammed with over 2,000 detailed illustrations highlighting the distinguishing features of a broadly representative selection of specialised antiques and collectibles accompanied by descriptions and prices computed from recent auction figures.

Pocket size with a sturdy binding, perfect for use in shops, flea markets and at auctions, *"The Lyle Antiques and Their Values Identification and Price Guides'* are your keys to smart antique buying or selling.

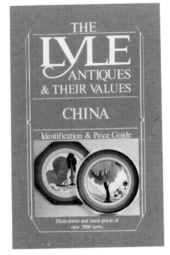

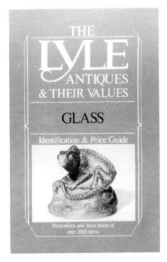

Lyle Publications

JUST £4·95